A HISTORY OF ROME

Moses Hadas, professor of Greek and Latin at Columbia University, is the author of A *History of Greek Literature* (1950) and A *History of Latin Literature* (1952), and the editor of the Modern Library *Tacitus* (1942), *Cicero* (1951), and *The Greek Poets* (1953). He has published many translations of classical literature, among them, *The Stoic Philosophy of Seneca*, A148.

A history of ROME
from its origins to 529 A.D.
as told by the Roman historians

Prepared by Moses Hadas

DOUBLEDAY ANCHOR BOOKS

Doubleday & Company, Inc.
Garden City, New York

COVER BY ANTONIO FRASCONI
TYPOGRAPHY BY JOSEPH P. ASCHERL

Preface

For the modern reader Rome has a twofold claim: it has been a paramount factor in shaping subsequent European history and civilization, and the Roman experience in itself offers instructive paradigms of political behavior and specimens of cultural achievement. To exploit the lessons of the Roman experience the methods of scientific historiography are essential; because they are biased in approach and oblivious to social and economic factors the literary records must be subjected to criticism and supplemented by other data, chiefly inscriptions and coins. But for apprehending the contribution of Rome to subsequent European history the actual experience is less important than the ancients' conception and interpretation of it and the form in which they transmitted it to posterity and in which posterity, until the nineteenth century, accepted it. From the point of view of influence, distortions of fact in the accepted literary tradition are truer than the actual facts as established by scientific antiquarians. It is the literary tradition that this book attempts to summarize. Its design is to present a continuous history of Rome from the legendary beginnings to the age of Justinian as the ancients conceived and transmitted it, so far as possible in their own words.

The main thread of the story is carried by selections from the ancient sources; continuity between disparate passages is provided by transitional interpretive paragraphs, distinguished from the ancient material typographically, which summarize events not dealt with in the selections. The sources of the selections are indicated in footnotes; their general reliability may be gauged from the Table of Sources at the end of the volume, where the dates, scope, and reputation of the ancient authors used is briefly indicated. The Chronology will serve as a corrective for inevitable distortions of scale. It happens that the more attractive of the ancients, Livy and Tacitus in particular, are very full for the periods they cover, and hence move far too slowly for the purpose of this book. They can be used, therefore, only for selected episodes. It is hoped, nevertheless, that all the major historians are sufficiently well represented to give the reader a sense of their quality.

The translations are the editor's own; where technical expertness was involved, as in Claudius' letter or the Theodosian Code, he has leaned heavily on standard versions. For the full history of the period involved the standard works in English are Volumes 7–12 of the *Cambridge Ancient History* and Volumes 1 and 2 of the *Cambridge Medieval History*.

Cordial thanks are due to Mr. Jason Epstein for the welcome opportunity of making this book, and to Mrs. Margaret Davidson for her kindness in typing it.

MOSES HADAS

Columbia University
  25 June 1955

CONTENTS

LIST OF MAPS

A HISTORY OF ROME

1. Kings and Early Republic

"In the beginning Rome was ruled by kings." That is how Tacitus begins his Annals, and that is all that can be said with assurance of the earliest history of Rome. But legend not only specified the date at which Rome was founded—21 April 753 B.C.—but carried the story of the Romans back four centuries further to 1184 B.C., the traditional date of the fall of Troy. Like the Hebrews, the Romans considered themselves an elect, charged with a mission of universal scope, and their early history was therefore a kind of Scripture. The foundation legends are so manifestly contrived that no one can accept them as history, but they are historically important nevertheless because they were universally accepted and so conditioned the actual course of history.

In outline the legend is as follows. After the sack of Troy (whose original founder, Dardanus, had come from Italy) Aeneas, who had been providentially preserved for the mission, was divinely instructed to lead his people, carrying with them their lares and penates, to their promised land. After a difficult journey, during which they are tempted to give up their quest and repeatedly receive divine encouragement and promises of future greatness, they arrive in Italy. They merge with the native Latins, whose name they accept, and under Aeneas' son Ascanius establish a kingdom first at Lavinium and then at Alba Longa. At Alba Longa they are ruled by a lineal succession of kings (who bear transparently mythical names); the thirteenth was Proca.

[1]Proca had two sons, Numitor and Amulius. To Numitor, because he was eldest, he bequeathed the ancient realm of the Silvian line. But force proved stronger than a father's wish or the respect due an elder. Amulius drove his brother out and ruled instead. Adding crime to crime, he destroyed Numitor's male issue, and deprived his daughter Rhea Silvia of the hope of children by the specious honor of appointing her a Vestal, which obliged her to perpetual virginity.

But the establishment of this great city, the inception of this empire next in might to heaven's, was determined, I hold, by the fates. The Vestal was ravished and produced twins; as the father of this doubtful issue she named Mars, whether she believed it was so or whether a god's responsibility gave the fault decency. But neither gods nor men screened mother or children from the king's cruelty. The priestess was manacled and thrown into prison, the boys he ordered flung into the river. Providentially the Tiber had overflowed its banks into stagnant pools, which made the regular channel inaccessible and led the messengers to expect the infants would be drowned even in still water. So, as if discharging the king's orders fully, they set the boys down in the nearest overflow, where the Ruminalis fig tree now stands; formerly, it is said, the name was Romularis. In those days the neighborhood was wild and desolate. The prevalent story is that, when the floating basket which carried the children was left on dry ground by the receding water, a thirsty she-wolf from the nearby hills was attracted by the infants' wail and very tenderly gave them her teats; the keeper of the king's herd—his name is said to have been Faustulus—found her licking the boys with her tongue. Faustulus, the story adds, carried them home to his wife Larentia to rear. Some hold that Larentia was called "She-

[1]Livy, 1.3.

2

wolf" by the shepherds because she was free of her body: hence the origin of the fabulous tale. Such being their birth and rearing, they grew up to be stout farmers and shepherds and ranged over the forests for game. And when they had thus grown stalwart in body and spirit they not only faced wild beasts but attacked robbers loaded with booty and distributed their takings among the shepherds. With these shepherds they shared their pursuits, serious and playful, and their band increased daily. . . .

Once when they were known to be preoccupied with celebrating the Lupercalia they were ambushed by robbers who were incensed at the loss of their plunder. Romulus defended himself, but Remus was taken captive and delivered to King Amulius with the charge that they had raided Numitor's fields; they had collected a band of young fellows, it was alleged, and had pillaged like an invading enemy. Consequently Remus was handed over to Numitor to be punished. Even from the beginning Faustulus had suspected that the children he was bringing up were of the blood royal. He knew that the babes had been exposed at the king's order, and that the time when he had taken them up corresponded exactly; but he had resolved to avoid hasty disclosure unless opportunity offered or necessity compelled. Necessity came first: constrained by fear, he imparted the facts to Romulus.

As it happened, Numitor too, when he had Remus in custody and heard that the brothers were twins, noticed their age and their far from servile character and was struck with the thought of their being his grandchildren. His inquiries led to the same conclusion, so that he was on the point of acknowledging Remus. From all sides, then, a plot was woven against the king. Romulus ordered his shepherds to come to the palace at an appointed time by diverse routes—he was not equal to open violence—and Remus

3

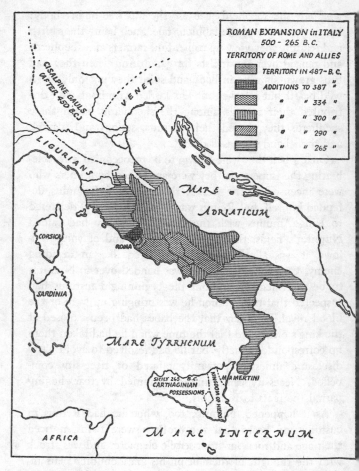

ROMAN EXPANSION in ITALY
500 - 265 B.C.
TERRITORY OF ROME AND ALLIES

TERRITORY IN 487- B.C.
ADDITIONS TO 387 "
"   " 334 "
"   " 300 "
"   " 290 "
"   " 265 "

CISALPINE GAULS
(AFTER 450 B.C.)

VENETI

LIGURIANS

MARE ADRIATICUM

CORSICA

ROMA

SARDINIA

MARE TYRRHENUM

SICILY 265 B.C.
CARTHAGINIAN
POSSESSIONS

MAMERTINI

KINGDOM OF HIERO

AFRICA

MARE INTERNUM

supported him with another party procured in Numitor's
house. And so they attacked and slew the king. At the beginning of the tumult Numitor shouted that an enemy
had invaded the city and attacked the palace, and so had
drawn the Alban youth off to defend the citadel as an

4

armed garrison. When he saw the young men approaching to congratulate him, after they had dispatched the king, he instantly convoked a council and set forth his brother's crimes against himself; the origin, rearing, and discovery of his grandchildren; the death of the usurper, and his own responsibility for the deed. The brothers marched through the crowd with their band and hailed their grandfather king, and the unanimous shout of approval from the entire multitude ratified the new king's title and authority.

When the Alban state was in the hands of Numitor, Romulus and Remus conceived a desire to build a city in the area where they had been exposed and reared. The population of Albans and Latins was excessive, and there were also the shepherds; their combined numbers made it likely that Alba and Lavinium would be eclipsed by the city which they would build. But these plans were interrupted by their hereditary curse, lust for rule, which resulted in a shameful rivalry. The beginning was innocent enough. Since they were twins and consideration of age could give no priority, they agreed that the guardian gods of the place should choose which should give his name to the new city and rule it when it was built. For awaiting the auguries Romulus took the Palatine and Remus the Aventine. Remus is said to have received the first augury—a flight of six vultures. The omen had already been announced when double the number appeared in Romulus' quarter. Each was hailed king by his own followers, the one party claiming kingship on the basis of priority, the other on the number of the birds. The altercation proceeded from angry taunts to blows, and in the broil Remus was struck down. A commoner story is that in derision of his brother Remus jumped over the new walls, whereupon Romulus slew him in a rage, adding the imprecation: "Any other who leaps over my walls shall have the same!" Thus Romulus acquired sole power, and the city thus founded was called by its founder's name.

Romulus attended to certain religious and legislative requirements of the new city, enlarged it, and enhanced its dignity by adopting, from the Etruscans, the use of the curule chair, the purple-bordered toga, and lictors. To increase its strength he invited landless men from outside to settle in it, and chose a hundred leading citizens to be designated Fathers.

[1]Now the Roman state was strong enough to be a match for any neighboring nation in war, but from the scarcity of women its greatness could last for one generation only, for there was neither hope of progeny at home nor marriage rights with neighboring states. Upon the advice of the Senate, therefore, Romulus sent emissaries to the states round about to solicit alliances with the privilege of intermarriage for his new subjects. . . . Nowhere did the embassy receive a favorable hearing. Men despised them and at the same time feared that a power growing great in their midst would endanger themselves and their posterity. Frequently they were dismissed with the query: "Are you welcoming female rabble too? That is the kind of marriage suitable for you." This the Roman youth resented bitterly, and the business pointed to inevitable violence. To provide a time and place appropriate for its exercise Romulus dissembled his resentment and set on foot ritual games to Equestrian Neptune which he called Consualia. Then he gave orders that the show should be advertised among the neighbors, and the Romans made the celebration as sumptuous as their taste and resources allowed so that it should engage attention and raise expectation. A view of the new city was an added attraction, and crowds gathered, especially from the nearest places, Caenina, Crustumium, and Antemnae.

[1]Livy, 1.9.

The Sabines came en masse, with their wives and children. They were hospitably received in different houses, and when they had viewed the layout of the city with its walls and numerous houses they marveled that Roman power had increased so rapidly.

The time came for the show, and when all eyes and minds were centered upon it, a preconcerted tumult arose and young Romans darted this way and that to carry the girls off. . . . The performance broke off in a panic, and the parents of the girls fled in grief, charging that the laws of hospitality had been trampled upon and invoking the god to whose festival they had been lured by the pretense of religion and good faith. Nor were the kidnaped girls any more hopeful or less indignant. But Romulus went about personally and explained that the fault was their fathers' pride in refusing marriage rights to neighbors. "However, you shall be joined in wedlock," he said, "and share your husbands' property, citizenship, and, dearest of all to the human heart, children. So soften your anger, and bestow your affections where chance has bestowed your persons. Often has injury made way for kindness; you will find your husbands the more considerate because each of us will endeavor to be not only a good husband but as far as he can to make up for the parents and country you have lost." This plea was seconded by the cajoling husbands, who excused their act on the ground of passion and love, the most efficacious of all pleas to a woman's heart.

After victories over Caenina, Crustumium, and Antemnae, the Romans are attacked by the Sabines. The Capitoline hill is lost by the treachery of Tarpeia and recovered by the heroism of Mettius Curtius. Romans and Sabines stood poised for battle on the site of the Forum.

[1]At this crisis the Sabine women, whose wrong had given

[1]Livy, 1.13.

rise to the war, with hair disheveled and dresses torn, female shyness crushed by disaster, boldly threw themselves amidst the flying missiles. Charging in from the flank, they parted the hostile lines, parted their fury, implored their fathers on this side and their husbands on that: fathers-in-law and sons-in-law should not stain themselves with impious bloodshed nor brand their children, their fathers' grandsons, their husbands' sons, with the infamy of parricide. "If you disdain the relationship, the kinship of marriage, it is upon us you must direct your fury: we are the cause of wounds and slaughter to husbands and parents. Better we perish than lose either of you and be widowed or orphaned." Men and officers alike were touched; silence fell, there was a sudden hush. The leaders step forward to make terms: they not only conclude peace but combine the two states into one.

After victory over Fidenae and one inconclusive war with Veii, Romulus approaches death and transfiguration (716 B.C.).

[1]Such were Romulus' immortal achievements. While he was conducting a review of the army in the Campus Martius near the marsh of Capra suddenly a storm of crashing thunder arose and enveloped the king in so thick a cloud that he could not be seen by the assemblage. Thereafter Romulus was not on earth. The panic of the Roman soldiery was allayed when the tempest gave way to clear and untroubled sunlight. The empty throne the senators who had stood near it explained by saying that Romulus had been rapt aloft by a blast; the soldiers believed the tale, but kept a gloomy silence, as if struck by fear of orphanhood. But then when a few had taken the initiative all hailed Romulus as god born of a god, king and father of Rome. They implored his favor and prayed he would always pre-

[1]Livy, 1.16.

serve their progeny with gracious benevolence. Even at that
date I believe there were some who secretly maintained that
the king had been dismembered by the senators; such a
rumor has trickled down, but in very veiled terms. Admiration for the hero and active terror have legitimized the other
version. Credit is also said to have been conferred upon it
by the shrewdness of one man. When the city was distressed by the loss of their king and bitter against the senators, Proculus Julius, who is reported to have possessed sufficient prestige to carry any matter, stepped forward in the
assembly and declared: "Fellow citizens, this day at dawn
Romulus, the father of this city, glided down from heaven
and presented himself before me. As I stood before him
awe-struck and abashed and prayed it might be lawful for
me to look directly at him, he said, 'Go proclaim to the
Romans it is heaven's will that my Rome shall be capital
of the world; accordingly they must cherish soldierliness,
and they must be assured, and transmit to posterity the
assurance, that no human power can withstand Roman
arms.' So saying," Proculus concluded, "he departed on
high." It is remarkable how that gentleman's tale was credited and how longing for Romulus on the part of the commons and the army was allayed by the belief in his immor-
tality.

*Romulus was succeeded by Numa Pompilius (715–672
b.c.), who was credited with organizing Rome's religious
institutions, according to Livy for political reasons.*

[1]Numa secured the good will of the neighboring states
by alliances and treaties. Heretofore military discipline and
fear of foreign enemies had kept the people under restraint,
but with the apprehension of foreign danger removed it was
likely that idleness would unbridle their temper; Numa
therefore made it his first business to imbue them with fear

[1]Livy, 1.19.

of gods, a most effective device for an ignorant and as yet uncivilized populace. And because he could not impress them deeply enough without some miraculous fiction, he pretended that he held nocturnal conferences with the goddess Egeria and that it was by her instruction that he instituted rites most acceptable to the gods and appointed appropriate priests for each of them. . . . [In regulating the calendar] he made public business permissible on certain days and forbidden on certain others, for it would sometime be expedient that the people should not be able to act.

The third king was Tullus Hostilius (672–640), under whom, because of its king's treachery, Alba Longa was sacked and its people amalgamated with the Romans.

[1]Horsemen were sent ahead to transfer the population to Rome, and then the legions marched in to demolish the city. When they entered the gates there were not, to be sure, the rioting and panic customary in captured cities, when gates have been smashed, walls leveled with battering rams, citadels stormed, when the yells of the enemy and the rush of armed men through the streets confound everything with steel and flame. A funereal hush, a speechless grief so froze all hearts that they were too dismayed to think what they should leave behind or carry with them. Now they would stand at their stoops asking one another's advice, now they would roam aimlessly through their houses for a last look. But when the shouts of the horsemen bidding them march became insistent, when the crash of razed buildings could be heard from the outskirts of the city and dust rising in a cloud from separate quarters had covered everything, then everyone snatched up what he could and departed, leaving behind his lares and penates and the house in which he had been born and brought up. An unbroken line of refu-

[1]Livy, 1.29.

gees filled the streets, and their mutual commiseration, when they encountered others, brought fresh tears. Pitiful cries could be heard, especially women's, when they passed revered temples beset by armed men and left their gods as it were prisoner. When the Albans evacuated their city the Romans leveled all buildings, public and private, to the ground; a single hour gave over to destruction and desolation the toil of four hundred years during which Alba had stood. The temples of the gods, so the king had decreed, were spared. Rome grew by Alba's ruin; the number of its citizens was doubled.

The next king was Ancus Martius (640–616), who was followed by an Etruscan succession: Tarquin the Elder (616–578), who beautified the city; Servius Tullius (578–534), who organized the population into classes; and Tarquin the Proud (534–510), whose arrogance brought the monarchy to an end.

[1]A certain portent so thoroughly alarmed Tarquin that he resolved to consult Delphi, the most celebrated oracle in the world. Nor would he trust the response to any but his two sons, whom he sent to Greece through lands then strange and seas even stranger. Titus and Arruns took as companion for their journey Lucius Junius Brutus, son of the king's sister Tarquinia and a young man of a far different character than the appearance he put on. When he heard that the leading men in the state, including his own brother, had been killed by his uncle, he resolved to leave nothing in his temper for the king to fear and nothing in his fortune for him to covet; where justice afforded no security he would seek safety in contempt. Accordingly he simulated stupidity and allowed the king to deal as he would with himself and his belongings. Even the name Brutus ("Dullard") he did not resent, so that the spirited

[1]Livy, 1.56.

liberator of his people might await his hour under its concealment. It was this Brutus whom the Tarquins took to Delphi, more as a butt than a comrade. He is said to have carried as a gift to Apollo and an emblem of his own character a staff of gold concealed in one of cornel wood hollowed out to receive it.

When they had come to Delphi and discharged their father's mandate, the young men conceived a desire to ask which of them would be ruler at Rome. From the cavernous depth, it is said, this response was delivered: "His shall be the highest sway at Rome, young men, who shall be the first to kiss your mother." The Tarquins gave strict orders for secrecy, so that Sextus, who had stayed behind at Rome, might remain ignorant of the oracle and hence without a share in rule. They themselves used lots to determine which would kiss his mother when they returned to Rome. Brutus judged that the Pythian utterance had a different meaning, and so as if he had stumbled he fell and touched earth with his lips, reasoning that she was the common mother of all mankind. . . .

[During the siege of Ardea] the young princes passed their idle hours dining and drinking together. Once when they were drinking at the quarters of Sextus Tarquinius where Collatinus Tarquinius too was dining, they fell to talking of their wives. Each praised his own in extravagant terms, and when rivalry grew warm Collatinus declared there was no need for words when a few hours would show them how far his own Lucretia surpassed the others. "Why don't we take horse, if we have energy and enterprise, and inspect our wives' characters in person? The best proof is what a man sees when he comes unexpected." They were all flushed with wine. "Come on, then," they cried, and galloped off to Rome, where they arrived as darkness was beginning to fall. From Rome they went to Collatia, where they found Lucretia very differently employed than the princes' wives. These they had seen whiling their time away in luxurious banqueting with their friends, but Lucretia was sitting in her parlor, late in the evening, busy with her wool, surrounded by maids working by lamplight. The award for womanliness went to Lucretia. She received the Tarquins and her husband graciously, and the victorious husband courteously invited the princes into his home. It was then that Sextus Tarquin conceived a villainous desire to force Lucretia's virtue; not her beauty alone but her proven chastity pricked him on. But for the present they concluded their nocturnal escapade by returning to the camp.

[1]A few days later, unbeknownst to Collatinus, Sextus Tarquin went to Collatia with a single attendant. His design was not suspected, and he was graciously received and after dinner brought to a guest room. When everything seemed safe and everyone asleep, fired with passion and with sword drawn he approached sleeping Lucretia. Holding her down with his left hand on her bosom, he said: "Silence, Lucretia! I am Sextus Tarquin. My sword is in my hand. You will die if you utter a sound." Frightened out of her sleep, the woman saw there was no help but only imminent death. Then Tarquin declared his love, begged, mingled threats with prayers, brought to bear all the arguments that could sway a woman. When he saw she was obdurate, that not even fear of death would move her, he compounded that fear with scandal: by her corpse, he declared, he would place the naked body of a slave he would murder, so that it would be said she had been killed for foul adultery. With this awful prospect victorious lust downed stubborn modesty as if by violence, and Tarquin departed, exulting in his ruthless assault on a woman's honor. Down-

[1]Livy, 1.58.

cast at her disaster, Lucretia sent the same message to her father at Rome and her husband at Ardea: "Come with a single trusted friend; you must do this and do it quickly; a horrible thing has happened."

Lucretius brought Valerius, Volesus' son, and Collatinus brought Junius Brutus, with whom he chanced to be going to Rome when his wife's messenger encountered him. Lucretia they found sitting downcast in her room, and when her husband asked, "Is all well?" she answered, "All ill. What can be well for a woman when she has lost her chastity? The print of a strange man is on your bed, Collatinus. But only my body has been violated. My spirit is guiltless. Death shall be my witness. But pledge your honor with your right hands that the adulterer shall not go unpunished. Sextus Tarquin is the man who last night returned hostility for hospitality and by force of arms won the pleasure that is my bane, and his too if you are men." They took the pledge in due order; they consoled the sick-hearted woman by turning the guilt from the helpless victim to the sinning agent: "It is the mind that sins, not the body; where there is no intention, there is no blame." "What he must pay," said she, "is for you to determine; as for me, though I absolve myself of sin, I do not free myself of punishment. Never shall unchaste woman cite Lucretia's example as a plea for life." She had hidden a razor under her dress; this she plunged into her heart, and fell dying upon her wound. Husband and father raised the death wail.

Brutus shook off his simulated torpor and aroused the people to shut their gates against the Tarquins, who went into exile. Thus kingship ended at Rome (510 b.c.); Brutus and Collatinus became the first pair of consuls. To recover their position at Rome the Tarquins obtained the support of the Etruscan king, Lars Porsinna of Clusium.

14

[1]Porsinna believed it would promote Etruscan security for Rome to be ruled by a king, and Etruscan dignity for that king to be an Etruscan, and so marched to war against Rome. Never before was the senate so terrified; Clusium was very powerful, and Porsinna's reputation formidable. They feared not only the enemy but also their own citizenry; the plebs might receive kings into the city in a panic, and accept servitude as the price of peace. Many concessions were therefore granted to the plebeians by the senate at this time. The food supply received special attention, and agents were dispatched to the Volsci and to Cumae to buy grain. The monopoly of salt, which was very dear, was taken from private individuals and assumed by the government. The plebeians were relieved of imposts and taxes, and the burden shifted to the rich who could bear it: the poor contributed enough if they reared children. This indulgence of the senate produced such harmony in the state, despite the hardships of blockade and famine, that nobles and commons alike abhorred the name of king. Demagoguery, in later years, never made a man so popular as good administration then made the whole senate.

Upon the approach of the enemy everyone retired from the fields into the city, which they surrounded with guards. Some parts of the city seemed secured by the walls, others by the river. The Sublician bridge almost gave the enemy entry into the city, were it not for Horatius Cocles, whom fortune appointed to be its bulwark that day. His post was at the bridge. When he saw the Janiculum taken by sudden assault, the enemy charging down from it, his own people, disorganized and terrified, deserting their arms and ranks, he seized hold of individuals, blocked their flight, appealed to the faith of gods and men, and assured them that flight was futile if they abandoned their posts: if they left the

[1]Livy, 2.9.

bridge behind as a passage, there would soon be more of the enemy on the Palatine and Capitoline than on the Janiculum. He admonished and charged them to demolish the bridge with steel or fire or however they could: he himself would receive the enemy's advance as far as one man might.

Horatius did withstand the onset of the Etruscans until his friends demolished the bridge, and then swam safely back to his own lines. Two other famous examples of Roman heroism are associated with this same war. Mucius Scaevola ("left-handed") undertook to enter the Etruscan camp singlehanded and kill the king. By mistake he killed a secretary instead, and when he was dragged before the king thrust his right arm into hot coals to show how little he valued safety. Porsinna was impressed with his gallantry and released him. The third instance was of the maid Cloelia, whom the Etruscans held as hostage and who led her fellow hostages, under a shower of Etruscan missiles, safe back to Rome. It is probable that these stories gloze over a serious Roman defeat which involved Etruscan occupation of their city. After peace was made with Lars Porsinna the tension between classes which his invasion had allayed broke out afresh.

[1]From the very beginning of the republic the strong were encroaching on the weak, and for this reason the people were alienated from the senate. After the expulsion of the kings the ruling classes exercised justice and moderation only till the dread of Tarquin and the fierce war with Etruria had subsided. From that time the patricians began to tyrannize over the plebeians as over slaves, to scourge and put them to death with virtually regal authority, to expropriate their lands, exclude them from government and monopolize it for themselves. Greatly oppressed by these severities and still more by the illegal interest on debts, the

[1]Sallust, fragment.

people had also to contribute taxes and personal service for incessant wars.

[1][Continued foreign wars and dictatorial authority kept the plebeians in check until, in 494 B.C.,] the consuls ordered the army to march out of the city on the pretext that the Aequians were renewing hostilities. This brought sedition to a head. . . . Without orders from the consuls the plebeians withdrew to the Sacred Mountain beyond the river Anio, three miles from the city. . . . In the city there was great panic; everything was at a standstill because of mutual apprehensions. The plebeians left behind feared violence from the senators, who in turn feared the plebeians remaining in the city, uncertain whether they should prefer them to stay or leave. "How long," they asked, "will the crowd of seceders remain quiet? What will happen if foreign war should break out in the meanwhile? Certainly the only remaining hope is harmony in the citizen body, and harmony must be achieved by fair means or foul." They decided to make their advocate Menenius Agrippa, an eloquent man, and a favorite of the plebeians because he was himself a plebeian born. When he was admitted into the camp he is said merely to have told this tale, in the unpolished old-fashioned style:

"Once when a man's parts did not, as now, agree together but each had its own program and style, the other parts were indignant that their worry and trouble and diligence procured everything for the belly, which remained idle in the middle of the body and only enjoyed what the others provided. Accordingly they conspired that the hands should not carry food to the mouth, nor the mouth accept it, nor the teeth chew it. But while they angrily tried to subdue the belly by starvation the members themselves and the whole body became dangerously emaciated. Hence it be-

[1]Livy, 2.30.

came evident that the belly's service was no sinecure, that
it nourished the rest as well as itself, supplying the whole
body with the source of life and energy by turning food into
blood and distributing it through the veins." By thus showing that the plebeians' anger against the senators was like
internal sedition in a body he swayed the men's minds.
Negotiations for concord were then undertaken. The terms
included a provision that the plebeians should have their
own magistrates, who should be sacrosanct and possess
power to aid the common people against the consuls; it
would not be lawful, moreover, for a patrician to hold
this magistracy. In this way tribunes of the people were
created.

*The new authority of the tribunes was particularly chaf-
ing to the patrician Gaius Marcius, surnamed Coriolanus
for a heroic exploit, and when he paraded his contumacy
he was banished. Coriolanus joined the Volscians, as perhaps other disgruntled patricians did also, and was made
their general for war against Rome (488 B.C.). Roman emissaries who attempted to recall him to his allegiance were re-
buffed. Then the women took over.*

[1]Now matrons collected in a crowd round Veturia, Coriolanus' mother, and his wife Volumnia; whether this was
official policy or woman's fear I cannot determine. In any
case they prevailed that the elderly Veturia and Volumnia
with Coriolanus' two small boys should go to the enemy
camp and with tearful prayers protect the city which her
men could not defend with arms. When they reached the
camp and were announced to Coriolanus . . . he sprang up
from his seat like a madman and offered to embrace his
mother. Instead of humility the woman showed anger: "Before I accept your embrace tell me, please, whether it is to
an enemy or a son I come, whether I am a captive in your

[1]Livy, 2.40.

18

camp or a mother. Has long life and unhappy age dragged me so far as to see you first an exile and then an enemy? Could you ravage this land which begot you and fed you? However hostile and vengeful your coming, did not your anger fall when you crossed its borders? Did it not occur to you when Rome came into sight, 'Within those walls are my home and gods, my mother, wife, and children'? If I had not given birth, it follows, Rome would not be under attack; if I had no son, I could die free in a free country. But any suffering of mine will bring you more disgrace than me unhappiness, and miserable as I may be I shall not be so long. Look to these others, on whom your stubbornness will bring untimely death or lasting slavery." Then Coriolanus' wife and children embraced him; the wailing of the crowd of women and their moans for themselves and their country finally broke the man's resolution. He embraced his family and sent them back, and withdrew his camp from the city.

But tension between the orders persisted, though the details of plebeian resistance to patrician arrogance which Livy records are probably retrojections of events during the Gracchan revolution three centuries later. In 451 and 450 instead of the regular magistrates a commission of ten was elected to codify the laws. The publication of the code known as the Twelve Tables was in the popular rather than the oligarchic interest. One of the ten, the arrogant Appius Claudius, claimed that a freeborn girl named Verginia was his slave and forcibly took her from her father and her fiancé. To protect her honor her father slew her, and the plebeians again showed their indignation by refusing military service and seceding to the Sacred Mountain. The consuls Valerius and Horatius elected in 449 enacted a series of popular measures, the most significant of which provided that laws enacted by the plebeian assembly should be binding upon the whole people. Another landmark in the rise of the plebeians was the Canuleian law of 445, which legalized marriage between plebeians and patricians. Since family connection was the single most important factor in political advancement at Rome it was inevitable that plebeians should now be admitted to all offices of state, and during the century following they were in fact given one office after another until in 340 the principle was established that one consul must, and the other might, be a plebeian.

The first significant step in the Roman march towards the unification of Italy was the conquest of the rich city of Veii, an Etruscan outpost about twelve miles from Rome. After blockading the city for ten years, during which their efforts were hampered by repeated class dissensions at home, the Romans appointed Camillus to prosecute the war (396 B.C.).

[1]Camillus perceived that it would be difficult to take the city by assault and therefore ordered mines to be dug; the ground near the city was easy to work to a depth which concealed the operation from the besieged. When the work had proceeded satisfactorily he attacked from the outside, to draw the defenders to the walls, while others made their way through the mine unperceived to the temple of Juno inside the citadel, the largest and most sacred building in the city. Here the king of Veii chanced to be sacrificing. On inspecting the entrails the soothsayer cried out in a loud voice that the goddess would give the victory to whoever completed the sacrifice. When the Romans in the mine heard this utterance they quickly tore up the floor and burst through with shouts and clashing arms. The enemy fled in terror; the Romans seized the offering and brought it to Camillus.

[1]Plutarch, Camillus, 5.3.

[1]When the Veians and their goods had been removed and disposed of, the Romans began to pull down the shrines of the gods and the gods themselves, but in the posture of worshipers rather than pillagers. The office of transporting Juno to Rome was assigned to young men chosen out of the whole army; they purified their bodies, put on white raiment, and entered the shrine with reverence. According to Etruscan practice, only a priest of a certain family could touch the image, and so at first they scrupled to handle it, but then one of the youths, whether by divine inspiration or in playfulness, said, "Do you wish to go to Rome, Juno?" —and the others cried out that she had nodded assent.

Plebeian discontent was exacerbated by the inequitable distribution of the spoils of Veii, and quieted by dispatching a colony to the Volscian country; neverthelesss the plebeians proposed a mass migration to Veii. Plebeian hostility towards Camillus was temporarily countered by his campaign against Falerii (394 B.C.), in the course of which he demonstrated the usefulness of his high principles.

[2]At Falerii it was the custom to employ the same person as schoolteacher and companion, and many boys were entrusted to his sole care, as is done in Greece to this day. The nobles' children, as was natural, were taught by their most eminent scholar. In peacetime this man had instituted the practice of taking the boys out into the country for play and exercise, and during the war he continued it. He would entertain them in short or long walks with games and stories, until one day he managed to bring them to the enemy outposts, then into the Roman camp, and then to Camillus' headquarters. His infamous deed he topped with a more infamous speech, saying that he was putting Falerii in the power of the Romans by delivering to them the children of the most influential Faliscans. Upon hearing this

[1]Livy, 5.22.   [2]Livy, 5.27.

Camillus replied: "Neither the people to whom you bring this blackguard's gift, you blackguard, nor their general is of your stripe. With the Faliscans we have no fellowship founded on men's covenants; but there is and there will continue to be between us the fellowship implanted by nature. War as well as peace has its laws, and we wage it with justice as well as vigor. Our arms we bear not against children, who are spared even when cities are stormed, but against men armed like ourselves, who attacked our camp at Veii without provocation. You have conquered them, as you think, by a scoundrel's trick; I shall conquer them, as I did Veii, in the Roman way, by courage, effort, weapons." He stripped the fellow, tied his hands behind his back, and gave him to the boys to drive back to Falerii, putting rods in their hands to scourge him as he went. . . . At Falerii, senate and market place rang with Roman integrity and their commander's justice. Unanimously they dispatched emissaries to Camillus' camp, and then by his permission to the senate at Rome, to surrender Falerii. This is reported to be their speech when they were introduced into the senate: "Senators, a victory which neither god nor man could begrudge, you and your general have won over us. We surrender to you because we believe (and what could be handsomer for a victor?) that life will be better under your administration than under our own laws."

But continued plebeian agitation forced Camillus into exile. A new peril arose when Clusium, a city of the powerful Etruscan confederacy, asked Rome for help against invading Gauls. The envoys whom Rome sent to Clusium only irritated the Gauls, who marched southward rapidly and inflicted a stunning defeat upon the Romans at Allia, only fifteen miles from Rome (390 B.C.). At Rome the young men retired to the citadel, the population scattered to the countryside, and the elders remained in the undefended city. The Gauls roamed through the deserted city, and then congregated in and about the Forum.

[1]There they found the plebeian houses boarded up, but the patrician mansions open, and were almost more timid to enter the open than the closed buildings. They were touched with reverence when they saw, seated in the vestibules, men whose decorations and apparel gave them a superhuman dignity, and whose noble visages and expressions a godlike majesty. As they stood gaping at these images one of them is said to have stroked the beard of Marcus Papirius—beards were worn long in those days—whereupon Papirius struck him on the head with his ivory staff. The angered Gaul slew him, and from this beginning the others were butchered where they sat. After the nobles had been murdered no one was spared; the houses were ransacked and, when they were emptied, burned.

Refugees congregated at Veii appointed Camillus, who had defeated a Gallic contingent at Ardea, dictator. Meanwhile the besieged Romans on the Capitoline had a narrow escape. On a dark night the Gauls scaled the hill so silently that not even the watchdogs were aroused.

[2]But the geese they did not elude. These had been left alive, despite the pressing dearth, because they were sacred to Juno, and this proved a salvation. Their cackling and clapping wings aroused Marcus Manlius, a stout soldier who had been consul three years before; he snatched his weapons, called others to arms, and, while they were still in confusion, with the boss of his shield dislodged a Gaul who had reached the summit. His fall knocked those behind him down and startled the others so that they dropped their weapons to cling to the rocks, where Manlius killed them.

Starvation forced the garrison to purchase the withdrawal of the Gauls at the price of a thousand pounds of gold.

[1]Livy, 5.41.   [2]Livy, 5.47.

KINGS AND EARLY REPUBLIC

[1]The transaction was disgraceful enough, but insult was added to indignity. The scales which the Gauls brought were dishonest, and when the tribune objected the insolent Gaul threw his sword into the scale and uttered the remark intolerable to Romans: "Too bad for the beaten!" But gods nor men would suffer Romans to live by payment. Providentially, before the unspeakable purchase had been consummated, when, because of the altercation, the gold had not all been weighed out, the dictator arrived and ordered the gold carried back and the Gauls removed. They objected that a bargain had been made: Camillus declared that no bargain made by an inferior officer after he himself had been created dictator could be binding, and bade them be ready to fight. . . . The excited Gauls seized their arms and charged the Romans with more passion than prudence. But now fortune had veered, now divine support and human intelligence favored the Romans. At the first encounter the Gauls were routed as easily as they had won at Allia.

After the departure of the Gauls Livy reports a movement to transfer the city to Veii, which was opposed by Camillus on the grounds that Rome's sacred origins and destiny were inextricably connected with its traditional site. It may well be that the arguments for retaining the ancient site were suggested by a movement in Livy's own day to remove the capital to the east.

The sack of Rome by the Gauls marks an epoch in Roman historiography as well as Roman history. Nineteenth-century criticism denied all validity to traditions concerning the earlier period, on the grounds that all records had been burned in the destruction of Rome. The stories in Livy were said to rest only on folk ballads, of the kind which Macaulay consciously tried to reproduce in his Lays

[1]Livy, 5.48.

of Ancient Rome. Contemporary criticism of the earlier traditions is not so ruthless, but agrees that beginning with the fourth century the ancient writers could use respectable historical sources.

At the beginning of the century Rome was in control of a League—Latin cities to the south and a portion of Etruria to the north. The first direction of expansion was southward, along the western shore. The Greek cities around the Bay of Naples were subject to constant raids by the Samnite mountaineers of the interior, and upon the invitation of Capua Rome fought the First Samnite War (343–341 B.C.), at the conclusion of which it gained control of most of Campania and granted citizenship to Capua and Cumae. The Latins resented their inferior position in the League, but a Latin War (340–338 B.C.) dissolved the League, most of whose cities were then incorporated in the Roman state. When Rome besieged the free Greek city of Naples, the Neapolitans obtained Samnite support, and thus the Second Samnite War began (326–304 B.C.), during which the Samnites received Etruscan and Umbrian assistance and inflicted a humiliating defeat upon the Romans at the Caudine Forks (321 B.C.). It was now clear that Rome was determined to dominate the peninsula, and in the Third Samnite War (298–290 B.C.) the Italic peoples were joined by Etruscans and Gauls in a vain attempt to stop Rome. In 282 B.C., when the Greek city of Thurii was harassed by Lucanian incursions, Rome's assistance was solicited. Tarentum, in the instep of the Italian boot, resented this interference in her sphere of influence, and invited the intervention of Pyrrhus of Epirus, who brought 25,000 soldiers trained in Macedonian tactics and twenty elephants (280 B.C.). After winning sundry "Pyrrhic" victories Pyrrhus returned to Greece in 275 B.C., and left Rome undisputed master of Italy and a recognized world power.

Stories told of the Pyrrhic War, for which Plutarch's Life of Pyrrhus is our principal source, indicate Rome's new awareness of its own distinction. When Pyrrhus sees the Roman army marshaled he realizes that they are no barbarians he has to deal with. His suave emissaries find the stalwart Romans proof against cajolery and bribery alike and too honorable to enter a plot to poison the enemy. Most significant of all, the blind Appius Claudius enunciates the principle that Rome will make no peace with an invader on Italian soil. Rome could in fact speak for Italy in a way that no other ancient imperial city could speak for the peoples it subjugated. By founding colonies, by extending Roman citizenship, by a system of alliances, by building roads Rome had incorporated rather than merely dominated Italy. Political unification was promoted by a system of roads, and local languages and customs gradually and without duress gave way to a common culture based on the Latin language and Roman law. An ancient invader could normally count on disaffection of subject peoples to support his campaigns: Hannibal was to find that the peoples of Italy were loath to be "liberated."

2. Mediterranean Conquests

The eastern Mediterranean, during the third century B.C., was divided among the successors of Alexander the Great, the Ptolemies in Egypt, the Seleucids in Syria, and the Antigonids in Macedonia. Italy faces west rather than east, and it was natural that Rome's first foreign contacts should involve the fourth great power, Carthage. As far back as the sixth century and again in 348 B.C. treaties regulated commercial intercourse between the two states and their respective subjects and allies. A third, concluded in 279 B.C., provided for military co-operation against Pyrrhus, but with the removal of the common enemy it was inevitable that the erstwhile allies should become rivals. About 284 B.C. a band of Campanian mercenaries called Mamertines had deserted Syracuse and seized neighboring Messana. In 265, when Hiero of Syracuse was about to take the city, Messana asked Carthage for a garrison, which Carthage was very ready to supply because it wished to limit Syracusan power. But the majority of Mamertines asked to be taken under Roman protection, and the Romans, well aware that the step implied war with Carthage, sent an expedition to Sicily nevertheless. But before we trace the course of Rome's most decisive war we must glance at the history, constitution, and character of the enemy.

[1]Carthage had been settled by the Phoenicians fifty years before the fall of Troy. Its founders were either Zorus and Carchedon, or, as the Romans and Carthaginians

[1]Appian, Punica, 1–2.

themselves hold, Dido of Tyre, whose husband had been secretly slain by the ruler of Tyre, Pygmalion. Informed of the murder through a dream, Dido took much wealth and such men as desired to escape Pygmalion's tyranny and sailed to Africa, where Carthage now stands. When the Africans repelled them they asked for only so much ground to settle in as an oxskin would hold. The request seemed ludicrously petty, and the Africans were ashamed to refuse such a trifle. They could not imagine how a city could be built on so tiny a spot, and out of curiosity they agreed, under oath, to give it them. The Phoenicians cut the hide into a very narrow single strip, of which they made a circle about the spot where the Carthaginian citadel stands; that is why the citadel is called Byrsa ["hide"; but in reality Byrsa is Semitic for "fortress"]. In due time they surrounded the citadel with a city. They were cleverer soldiers than their neighbors and, being Phoenicians, skillful sailors. As their power grew they mastered Libya and much of the Mediterranean and carried war into Sicily, Sardinia, and other islands of that sea, and also into Spain, and they founded numerous colonies. In power their state was equal to the Greek, in wealth second only to Persia.

[1]The Carthaginian government included kings, a senate as the aristocratic element, and the commons, which had authority in appropriate spheres; on the whole the balance of powers was very like that in Rome or Sparta. . . . In the conduct of war the Carthaginians are superior, as one would expect, in naval training and equipment; their seamanship is a long national tradition, and they have greater experience at sea than any other people. But for military service on land the Romans are much more efficient. To this they devote their whole attention, whereas the Carthaginians wholly neglect their infantry, though they do make some

[1]Polybius, 51–52,56.

slight provision for their cavalry. The reason for this is that they employ foreign mercenaries, but the Roman soldiers are natives and citizens. . . . At Carthage nothing is regarded as disgraceful if it brings a profit; at Rome nothing is more disgraceful than to receive bribes and make profit by improper means.

The Roman expedition to Sicily defeated the Carthaginians and Hiero separately, and in the year following entered into alliance with Hiero against the Carthaginians. To drive the Carthaginians from Sicily and protect their own coast the Romans required a navy. Within sixty days they built 120 ships, using a grounded Carthaginian vessel for a model, and trained crews to row on wooden stages erected on land. With this fleet they won a battle off Mylae (260 B.C.) and with another a greater battle off Ecnomus on the Sicilian coast (256 B.C.). Now the Romans could invade Carthage.

[1]The Romans then sailed to Africa with 350 ships, captured a number of towns, and left Atilius Regulus in command. Regulus took 200 additional towns, which went over to him out of hatred of Carthage, and ravaged the country as he went. The Carthaginians thought their reverses were due to bad leadership, and requested a commander of the Lacedaemonians; these sent them Xanthippus. . . . Xanthippus performed as expected; of the 30,000 men Regulus commanded only a few were able to escape to Aspis. All the rest were killed or captured, and among the latter was the consul Regulus himself. Not long afterwards the wearied Carthaginians sent Regulus to Rome along with ambassadors of their own, to obtain a truce or else to return. In private Regulus urged the Roman officials to press the war with vigor, and then returned to certain torture. The Carthaginians shut him up in a weasel trap stuck full

[1]Appian, *Punica*, 3–4.

of spikes and so killed him. For Xanthippus success was a prelude to disaster. In order that such an exploit might not be credited to the Lacedaemonians, the Carthaginians pretended to honor him with rich gifts and sent him back to Sparta with a flotilla whose skippers had orders to throw him and his Spartan comrades overboard.

The defeat of Regulus was followed by other reverses, on sea and land, but the Romans persisted. Their most formidable adversary was Hamilcar Barca, who occupied Mount Eryx near Panormus and delivered one telling stroke after another. In 242 a new Roman fleet destroyed a Carthaginian armada bringing supplies to Sicily, and the Carthaginians agreed to yield that island and pay a huge indemnity. While Carthage was engaged in putting down a revolt of mercenaries whom it was now unable to pay (241–238 B.C.), Rome seized Sardinia and Corsica, and when Carthage remonstrated Rome increased the indemnity. In 227 B.C. Sicily and Sardinia-Corsica became the first two Roman provinces.

Between the end of the First and the beginning of the Second Punic War troubles in Illyria and northern Italy demanded Roman attention. In Illyria a pirate kingdom had been ruining Roman trade and had mistreated Roman ambassadors sent to protest. Campaigns in 228 and again in 219 B.C. reduced Illyria to a tribute-paying dependency, though it was not organized as a province until after 167 B.C. In the north public lands belonging to the state had been pre-empted by noble squatters, to the dissatisfaction of the humbler citizenry. In 232 the tribune Gaius Flaminius carried a measure for distributing this land. The Gauls thought new settlements would endanger their own interests, and in 225, probably with fresh arrivals from across the Alps, made war on Rome. They were completely defeated by *Flaminius*, now a consul, in 222, and Roman authority was extended to the foot of the Alps.

Carthage, smarting at its losses, was vigorously creating a new empire in Spain, under the skillful leadership of Hamilcar Barca and his son-in-law Hasdrubal. Massilia, which was in alliance with Rome, protested Carthaginian encroachment on her interests. Roman envoys drew up a treaty specifying that Carthage was not to go north of the Ebro but that Rome would continue its alliance with Saguntum, which lay south of that river. The Carthaginians laid siege to Saguntum, however, and when Rome's protests were rejected war was declared (218 B.C.) It was the genius of Hannibal, Hamilcar's son, which made this war the most dangerous Rome ever engaged in.

[1]Upon his first arrival in Spain Hannibal became the center of attention in the whole army. The veterans imagined they had recovered a rejuvenated Hamilcar: they saw the same energetic expression, the same piercing eyes, the same features and visage. But very quickly his resemblance to his father was a negligible factor in winning approval. Never were high aptitudes for obeying and commanding—very different qualities—combined to such a degree in a single character. It was not easy to decide whether the general or the army loved him best. It was Hannibal that Hasdrubal chose to put in charge of any business that required courage and energy, and it was under Hannibal that the soldiers displayed greatest confidence and daring. He was fearless in undertaking dangerous enterprises, he was prudent in discharging them. Toil could not weary his body or subdue his spirit. Heat and cold he endured alike. He ate and drank to satisfy nature, not pleasure. Hours for sleeping and waking were not determined by the clock; whatever time was left after work was done he devoted to

[1]Livy, 21.4.

sleep. Nor was sleep wooed by soft couches and stillness; often he could be seen lying on the ground among the sentries and pickets, covered with a soldier's cape. His dress was no different from his contemporaries', but his arms and horses were pre-eminent. Among horse and foot alike he was far the best; he was the first to engage in a battle, the last to leave the engagement. But great as the man's merits were, his enormous faults were as great—inhuman cruelty, faith worse than Punic, no scruple for truth or sanctity, no fear of gods, no respect for oaths or religion.

The Romans thought the war would be waged in Spain, and the consul Publius Cornelius Scipio proceeded towards that country; but Hannibal was determined to carry the war to Italy and had brought his army across the Pyrenees to the Rhone before Scipio reached Massilia. Scipio sent his brother on to Spain and returned to Italy to meet Hannibal. Despite hostile nature and difficult terrain Hannibal reached the summit of the Alps, where he heartened his dispirited soldiers by showing them the Po Valley stretching before them.

[1]But the descent was even more trying than the ascent, for on the Italian side the Alps fall sheer. The whole way was precipitous, narrow, and slippery, so that they could not keep from slipping nor stick to their tracks if they stumbled: men and beasts rolled one on top of another. A cliff they reached was so narrow and perpendicular that a soldier without pack could scarcely lower himself by feeling his way and holding onto bushes and roots. A recent landslip had deepened the precipice to nearly a thousand feet. At this impasse the cavalry halted, and when Hannibal wondered what was delaying the column he was told that the rock was impassable. He went to inspect the situation in person and found the column would have to detour through a pathless

[1]Livy, 21.35.

and untrodden tract. But this was found impracticable. The first few who attempted to pass could find footing in the new snow which covered that hard packed below, but when the tramp of men and beasts ground this to slush they trod on the naked ice below. Men floundered and struggled. The slippery ice afforded no traction, and was the more treacherous as it was downhill; if a man rose on his hands or braced himself on his knees he would collapse together with his supports, and there were no stumps or roots against which he could buttress himself. They kept wallowing in the slush on the smooth ice. Sometimes the pack animals, stamping their hoofs against falling, broke through, and were stuck in the hard, deep-frozen ice as if trapped and fettered.

Hannibal cut through the rock with hot vinegar and made a zigzag path down the cliff. Scipio's attempt to stop him at the river Ticinus failed, and Hannibal crossed the Po. Sempronius, the other consul, was recalled from Sicily to join Scipio, and together they attacked Hannibal at the Trebia (December 218) and received a crushing defeat. The next spring Hannibal crossed the Apennines into Etruria; as he marched towards Rome he was followed closely by the consul Flaminius.

[1]The Carthaginians now reached a spot admirably suited for ambush, where Lake Trasimene is so near Mount Cortona that there is only space, which seems to have been left by design, for a very narrow road. Farther along the plain opens out, and then there are hills. Here Hannibal placed his camp in full view, and posted himself with his Africans and Spaniards. The Balearic and other light troops he concealed in the mountains, and the cavalry he posted under the cover of hills at the entrance of the defile, so that when the Romans had entered, the cavalry with the lake and the

[1]Livy, 22.4.

33

mountains would enclose them on all sides. Now though Flaminius had reached the lake at sunset of the preceding day he failed to reconnoitre but passed the defile before full daylight, and when his column debouched into the plain he saw only the enemy directly in front; the ambuscades to the rear and overhead were undetected. When the Carthaginian had his enemy where he wanted him, cut off by lake and mountain and surrounded by his men, he gave the signal for a co-ordinated attack. His men poured down by the shortest way. A mist from the lake which lay thicker on the lowland than on the hills heightened the shock and surprise to the Romans, whereas the enemy columns could see each other as they descended and regulate their pace. From the shouts which arose on all sides the Romans sensed they were surrounded before they could see the enemy, and fighting had begun in van and flanks before lines could be formed, armor adjusted, swords drawn.

Though consternation and panic were general, the consul was undaunted. The ranks had been disordered because the men turned to face the several shouts; Flaminius marshaled them, as time and place permitted, and wherever he could go or make himself heard he admonished them and bade them stand and fight: "We must get clear not by vows and praying the gods but by strength and courage; steel will cut a path through the lines; the less fear, the less danger." But noise and confusion rendered counsel and command inaudible; so far from recognizing their standards and ranks and positions, the men scarcely had presence of mind to don armor for fighting, but were rather hampered than protected by their equipment. Darkness made ears more useful than eyes. They turned their faces where there were groans of the wounded, buffets on body or armor, the mingled cries of attack and terror. Some in the act of flight ran into and joined groups who were fighting;

34

others, seeking to return to the fight, were diverted by bands of fugitives.

But wherever directed, sorties were futile; mountain and lake on the flanks, enemy battalions to the front and rear, shut them in. Salvation, it was plain, depended solely on a man's own right hand, own sword, and each became his own leader, his own encourager to strenuous action. A new and unorthodox battle began, not in lines marshaled according to the three grades nor with shock troops in front of the standards and the others behind, nor with soldiers keeping to their own regiment, company, and squad. It was chance that grouped them, and each man's temper posted him van or rear. So intense was their ardor, so single-minded their exertions, that none of the combatants noticed an earthquake which leveled large sections of Italian cities, diverted torrential rivers from their courses, carried the sea up into streams, and brought mountains down with huge uproar.

Flaminius' army was annihilated, and in consternation the Romans appointed a dictator, Quintus Fabius Maximus, whose strategy was to keep as near Hannibal as he could without risking an engagement. In the spring of 216 B.C. Hannibal, now in Apulia, was confronted by new consuls, Lucius Aemilius Paulus, an aristocrat, and Marcus Terentius Varro, a popular leader, upon whose rashness tradition laid the blame for Rome's greatest military disaster.

[1]Hannibal had pitched his camp near the village of Cannae, with the wind called Vulturnus at his back; the region is parched and dry, and the wind carries clouds of dust. The position was not only comfortable but would bring a distinct military advantage when they formed for battle, for they would have only their backs exposed to the

[1]Livy, 22.44–45.

blasts and fight against an enemy blinded by enveloping dust. The consuls were careful enough in scouting the route as they followed the Carthaginian, but when they arrived at Cannae and had the enemy in sight they built separate camps, at a considerable distance from one another, and divided their troops as they had done previously. The river Aufidus flowed past either camp and afforded approach to the watering parties of each, but they had to watch for opportunities and sometimes fight. The lesser camp was on the other side of the Aufidus, and there water could be fetched more freely because the enemy had no guard on the farther bank.

The terrain was suitable for cavalry action, in which arm Hannibal was invincible, and he conceived hopes that the consuls would afford him an opportunity for battle; he marshaled his forces, therefore, and provoked his opponents by flying charges of Numidians. Again the Roman camp was embroiled by insubordination and by disagreement between the consuls. Paulus chided Varro with the foolhardiness of Sempronius and Flaminius, and Varro instanced Fabius as the specious model for timid and slow-moving generals. He called gods and men to witness that it was in no way his fault that Hannibal had assumed squatter's rights in Italy: he was tied down by his colleague, and the soldiers who were indignant and eager to fight had sword and buckler taken from their hands. Paulus protested that if mischance befell the legions when they were exposed to ill-advised and imprudent battle he would be free of blame though he would share the consequences. Men whose tongues were so nimble and rash, he warned, must have hands equally vigorous when it came to fighting.

While the Romans were frittering time in altercation rather than deliberation Hannibal had kept his troops in formation till late in the day; now he withdrew them to his palisade and sent the Numidians across the river to attack a watering party from the lesser camp. This disorganized group the Numidians routed by their shouting and turbulence before they had well reached the opposite bank, and their rush carried them to an outpost in front of the rampart and even to the very gates of the camp. The Romans were outraged that their very camp should be menaced by a disorderly troop of mere auxiliaries; all that kept them from crossing the river forthwith and forming for battle was the circumstance that the supreme commander that day was Paulus. But on the day following, when it was Varro's turn, Varro posted the battle signal without consulting his colleague, formed his troops, and led them across the river. Paulus could refuse approval but not support, and so he followed.

For the battle which ensued Hannibal made his line strong at the wings but weak at the center, and posted strong reserves at the rear. When the Roman charge carried through the weak center, Hannibal's wings executed an encircling movement; the exhausted Romans were unable to break through the ring, and more than ninety per cent of their army was destroyed. Hannibal's brilliant victory entailed other consequences as serious. A number of allies defected to Hannibal, and the important city of Capua opened its gates to him; Philip V of Macedon made overtures for an alliance with him; and Syracuse, after the death of Hiero, went over to the Carthaginian side.

[1]But none of these disasters, none of these revolts of their allies, could so shake the Romans that they would ever think of peace, either before Varro reached Rome [Aemilius Paulus had fallen in action] or after his return quickened the sense of calamity. At that very juncture the state showed so lofty a spirit that upon his return from the huge

[1]Livy, 22.61.

disaster for which he himself was largely to blame throngs of all classes went out to meet him and to convey their thanks for his not having despaired of the state. If he had been a Carthaginian general he would inevitably have been crucified.

Rome's resilience was demonstrated by its energy in other theaters. In 212 B.C. Marcellus took Syracuse, despite the defensive engines designed by Archimedes; the city was sacked and became tributary to Rome. The same year the Romans blockaded Capua, and Hannibal marched on Rome to effect the recall of their army—in vain. Capua's polity was dissolved, its territory confiscated, its nobility executed. In pursuance of his alliance with Hannibal, Philip of Macedon attacked Roman possessions in Illyria, but Rome's control of the sea enabled her to checkmate Philip by supporting his Greek enemies. In Spain Gnaeus and Publius Scipio had been very successful from 218 B.C. on, until in 211 they were both killed and their armies crushed by Hannibal's brother Hasdrubal. Victories in Sicily and at Capua enabled the Romans to send reinforcements to Spain under Publius Scipio's like-named son, then twenty-four years old, who won brilliant successes. Foiled in Spain, Hasdrubal followed his brother's route to join him in Italy. The Roman general guarding Hannibal in Apulia intercepted Hasdrubal's letters; he left a skeleton force behind, hastened to join his colleague by forced marches, and together with him cut Hasdrubal's army to pieces at the river Metaurus (207 B.C.). Hannibal knew, when his brother's head was tossed into his camp, that his hopes were ended, and withdrew into the mountains of Bruttium.

In 205 the young Scipio returned from his conquest of Spain to take up the consulship, and proceeded to Sicily to prepare for the invasion of Africa. He defeated the Car-

thaginians and their Numidian ally Syphax, whom he replaced with a rival chieftain, Masinissa. An armistice was
drawn up and the Carthaginian forces recalled from Italy.
Hannibal's return emboldened the Carthaginians to violate
the armistice, and in the battle of Zama (202 B.C.) Hannibal was decisively defeated. Rome's terms limited Carthage
to its own environs, forbade it to wage war outside Africa
or even in Africa without Roman permission, deprived it of
its navy, and imposed heavy indemnities. But Hannibal had
proven to be not only Rome's most formidable enemy but
one of the greatest military geniuses of history.

[1]Who can help admiring this man's skillful generalship,
his courage, his ability, if he will consider the span of time
during which he displayed these qualities and imagine the
pitched battles, the skirmishes and sieges, the revolutions
and counterrevolutions of states, the vicissitudes of fortune,
in a word his whole grand design and its execution. For
sixteen years on end he maintained the war with Rome in
Italy without once releasing his army from service in the
field; he kept vast numbers under control like a good pilot,
without any sign of dissatisfaction towards himself or friction amongst themselves. And the troops under his command, so far from being of the same tribe, were of many
diverse races who had neither laws nor customs nor language in common.

Hannibal knew that Carthage could not save him from
Roman hatred, and fled to Antiochus of Syria, who was
entering upon a war with Rome. When peace was made
Hannibal took refuge with Prusias, king of Bithynia.
Flamininus came on a special mission to remonstrate with
Prusias for harboring an enemy of Rome, and Prusias be-
trayed his guest.

[1]Polybius, 11.19.

[1]Hannibal realized that all avenues were guarded, and so he called for the poison which he always had ready for such an event and said: "Let us relieve the Romans of their anxiety; they are too impatient to wait for an old man to die. It is no great or memorable victory Flamininus will win over a lone soldier, unarmed and betrayed. Roman character has indeed changed, as this day shows. Their fathers warned Pyrrhus, an armed invader in Italy, to beware of poison. This generation has sent an ambassador of consular rank to persuade Prusias villainously to murder his guest." Then he called curses down on Prusias and his kingdom, invoked the gods of hospitality to witness the breach of faith, and drank the cup off. This was the end of Hannibal's life.

Having attained unquestioned supremacy in the west, it was inevitable that Rome should be drawn into the affairs of the east. At the time of Zama an infant Ptolemy succeeded to the throne of Egypt, and Antiochus III of Syria and Philip V of Macedon, both energetic and ambitious kings, planned to deprive Egypt, Antiochus of Phoenicia, and Philip of the Aegean islands. Rhodes and Pergamum appealed to Rome for help. Partly out of philhellenism and partly to prevent the growth of a potentially dangerous sea power, Rome entered on the Second Macedonian War (200–196 B.C.), and with the aid of the Aetolians defeated Philip at Cynoscephalae. At the Isthmian Games of 196 the Roman consul Flamininus proclaimed the autonomy of the Greeks, who had been subject to Macedonia. The Aetolians were disappointed at not receiving the hegemony of Greece, and induced Antiochus to invade the country. The Romans defeated him at Thermopylae in 191, and when he failed to observe their terms crossed into Asia Minor, with the support of the Rhodian and Pergamene

[1]Livy, 39.51.

fleets, and crushed him at Magnesia (190 B.C.). Rome retained no territory for itself but strengthened Rhodes and Pergamum and so made it difficult for a single strong power to arise. When Philip's successor Perseus grew dangerously powerful Rome entered the Third Macedonian War (171–167 B.C.) and upon the defeat of Perseus by Aemilius Paulus (168) the Macedonian kingdom was divided into four disparate states. The Achaean League was suppressed and a thousand of its leading citizens (including the historian Polybius) were sent to Rome as hostages. Seventy cities of Epirus were sacked and 150,000 of their inhabitants enslaved, large indemnities enriched the Roman treasury, the Rhodians were punished for favoring an accommodation with Perseus. There could now be no doubt that Rome was the real sovereign of the eastern Mediterranean. Rome's peremptoriness and the acquiescence of the Hellenistic rulers are well illustrated by the story of Popilius Laenas' circle. During the Third Macedonian War Antiochus IV (against whom the Maccabees would shortly rebel) was on the point of taking Alexandria, and the Romans were disturbed at the prospect.

[1]When Antiochus was four miles from Alexandria he was met by the Roman commissioners. He saluted them and held his hand out to Popilius. Popilius asked him first to read a document which he handed him. He did so, and said he would call and consult with his ministers, whereupon Popilius with customary directness drew a circle around the king with the staff in his hand and said: "Give me your answer to the senate before you step out of this circle." The king was stunned by this peremptory order, but after hesitating a moment replied, "I will do as the senate bids." Popilius then deigned to give him his right hand, as a friend and ally. Antiochus departed out of Egypt.

[1]Livy, 45.12.

Meanwhile Rome was extending and consolidating its power in Italy and the west also. Cisalpine Gaul, over which Rome's control had loosened during the Hannibalic War, was recovered by wars with the Insubrians and Boii (198–191 B.C.), and new highways linked Rome with Ariminum, Placenta, and the Po Valley. During the same period Roman sway was extended over the Ligurian tribes through the Italian Riviera to Massilia. After additional campaigns against the Allobroges and Arverni the province of Gallia Transalpina or Narbononesis was formed in the Provence. The territory acquired from Carthage in Spain was organized into the provinces of Hither and Further Spain in 197, but the native tribes continued restive and serious revolts broke out between 197 and 179 and again from 154 onwards. After a number of serious Roman reverses the Romans elected Scipio Aemilianus, the last conqueror of Carthage, consul; in 133 B.C. Scipio destroyed Numantia, which was the seat of the war, and pacified all of Spain.

After Zama Carthage recovered enough prosperity to alarm Romans like Cato, who concluded all his speeches with the phrase "Carthage must be destroyed." An occasion for Roman intervention arose when the Carthaginians, whose treaty forbade them to take up arms without Roman consent, finally resisted the inroads of Masinissa. The apprehensive Carthaginians offered unconditional submission, and complied when they were told to surrender their arms. But when they were told that they must abandon their city and settle ten miles inland they manned their walls with improvised weapons and defied the Romans (149 B.C.). Incapacity of Roman generals extended the siege until 146, when an army restored to efficiency by Scipio Aemilianus assaulted the city.

[1][After penetrating into the city] Scipio turned his atten-
[1]Appian, Punica, 128.

tion to the citadel, its strongest point, where many people had taken refuge. Three streets leading from the market place to the citadel were lined on both sides with six-story houses, from which the Romans were pelted. They seized the first houses and used them as a base for attacking the next. From their roofs they made bridges of planks and beams to cross over to the next. While one battle was in progress on the roofs another was fought, against all comers, in the narrow street below. Everywhere there were groaning and wailing and shouting and agony of every description. Some were killed out of hand, some flung down alive from the roofs to the pavement, and of these some were caught on upright spears or sabers or swords. Fires were not set because of the men on the roofs, but when Scipio reached the citadel the three narrow streets were set afire simultaneously. Men were charged to level a path through the debris as the houses burned down so that the army's movements should not be obstructed.

This produced new scenes of horror. The fires spread devastation far and wide; the men did not pull buildings down piecemeal but applied great force and overthrew them in a mass. Crashes grew louder, and along with stones many corpses pitched to the ground. There were some living bodies too, mostly of old men, children, and women who had hidden in the inmost crannies of the houses; some were lacerated, some half burned, and all uttered distressing cries. Others, flung down from the great height along with timbers, stones, and burning brands, were broken and mangled and crushed into unnatural shapes. Nor did this end their trouble. Those told off to remove the debris with axes, crowbars, and boathooks and smooth a way for the infantry shoved the dead and those still living into holes in the ground, using their axes and crowbars and shoving and turning them with their tools like blocks of wood or stone.

Human beings were fill for gullies. Some were thrown in head down, and their legs, protruding from the ground, writhed for a considerable while. Some fell feet down, and their heads were above the surface. Their faces and skulls were trampled by the galloping horses, not through the riders' design but because of haste. Nor had the sweepers done their deed of design: there was the tension of battle, the expectation of quick victory, the excitement of the soldiery, the shouts of the criers and blasts of the trumpets, the commands of officers to advance or retire—all of which created a kind of madness and an indifference to what their eyes saw. Six days were spent on this effort. . . .

The city which had flourished for seven hundred years from its foundation, which had held broad dominion over lands and islands and seas, which had vied with the greatest of empires in its wealth of arms and ships and elephants and money, which had manifested extraordinary courage and fortitude by resisting a formidable enemy and famine for three years after it had been deprived of all its ships and arms—this city was now being utterly blotted out and destroyed. As Scipio looked on he is said to have wept and openly to have lamented the enemy's fate. For a long while he remained sunk in thought, reflecting that the fortunes of all cities and peoples and empires, like those of individuals, must change. Troy had fallen, once so prosperous a city; the empires of the Assyrians, and the Medes, and the Persians after them, had fallen, and so, lately, the Macedonian empire, the most brilliant of them all. Consciously or otherwise Scipio recited Homer's lines (*Iliad*, 6.448f.):

There will come a day when sacred Ilion shall perish,
And Priam, and the people of Priam of the strong ash spear.

An author of the fifth century A.D. has preserved the litany which the Romans used to invite Carthage's gods to desert their people:

[1]"If there is a god, if there is a goddess, who watches over the people and polity of Carthage, and in particular whichever one is its guardian, that deity I pray, supplicate, and petition: forsake the people and polity of Carthage, abandon all its houses, temples, shrines, and the city itself, desert them all; inspire this people and city with fear, terror, and forgetfulness; after leaving them behind come to Rome, to me and to mine. May our houses, temples, sanctities, and city be delightful to you and more commendable, so that we may know and understand that in future you will protect me, the people of Rome, and its soldiers. If you will do this I vow to found a temple to you and to celebrate games in your honor."

When Carthage was destroyed its site was declared accursed and its few survivors sold into slavery. The Carthaginian territory was organized as the province of Africa. In the same year another famous city was destroyed. After 196 Corinth had been head of the Achaean League, and when Rome found it necessary to punish the League the consul Lucius Mummius sacked and burned Corinth, sold its inhabitants into slavery, and carried its art treasures to Rome (146 B.C.). To point up the contrast with the finer sensibilities of the conqueror of Carthage the following anecdote is told:

[2]Mummius was so uncultivated that when, on the capture of Corinth, he was contracting for the transportation to Italy of the masterpieces of painting and sculpture of the greatest artists, he made a stipulation that if pieces were lost the carriers would have to make good by supplying new ones.

To regularize its actual control of the Aegean all Rome needed was sovereignty on the eastern shore, and this it acquired when, in 133 B.C., Attalus III of Pergamum died

[1]Macrobius, *Saturnalia*, 3.9.   [2]Velleius Paterculus, 2.13.

and bequeathed his kingdom to Rome. His motive probably was to forestall disputes over the succession which would have invited forcible conquest by Rome. Attalus' domain was organized as the province of Asia, and the increment to the Roman treasury provided the wherewithal for the social reforms which Gracchus envisaged and which will be dealt with in the chapter following.

3. A Century of Revolution

The distinction between patrician and plebeian which dominated Rome's internal politics during the first two centuries of the republic was virtually effaced when plebeians intermarried with patricians, gained access to the higher magistracies, and so attained social and economic equality. But the class struggle continued with a different alignment. Now the distinction was between an officeholding group, called nobiles or optimates, narrowly limited and bound together by family connections, and the rest of the citizen body, referred to as populares. The auctoritas ("prestige") which the nobles possessed was as tangible a thing, and as transmissible, as patrician birth. The popular leaders were themselves most often nobles. Some, like the Gracchi, were genuine reformers, concerned for the well-being of the body politic; others, like Marius, plainly exploited their leadership for personal aggrandizement.

Initially an outward manifestation of the party difference was the attitude towards internationalism. After the Hannibalic War the vogue for things Greek, naturally under upper-class leadership, became a flood, and Roman culture, from philosophy to cookery, was in effect revolutionized. The political opposition took the position of stalwart Romanism. The patron saint of the opposition was the Elder Cato, who had or affected a hearty contempt for all things Greek. In 155 B.C. the Greeks sent the heads of their philosophic schools as ambassadors to Rome, and while they awaited the senate's action they delivered public lectures on

47

philosophy. These, especially those of the Academic Carneades, were received with the wildest enthusiasm, and Cato was disturbed.

[1]Cato determined to clear the philosophers out of the city on any specious pretext. He arose in the senate and chided the magistrates for detaining at such length men capable of persuading anybody to do anything. "We ought," said he, "to decide and vote on this proposal at once, so that they can go back to their schools and lecture Greek children, and leave Roman young men to heed their own laws and magistrates as heretofore." It was not out of enmity to Carneades, as some think, that he did this, but because he despised philosophy and out of native pride scoffed at Greek culture and letters. He says, for example, that Socrates was a violent prattler who tried his best to make himself his country's tyrant by undermining its usages and subverting its citizens to opinions contrary to law. The school of Isocrates he ridiculed by declaring that pupils grew gray there, as if they were to practice their art and plead cases before Minos in Hades. To prejudice his son against everything Greek he indulged in an expression too vehement for his years, declaring in mantic and clairvoyant style that Rome would surely perish if it were infected with Greek literature. But time has proven his ominous prophecy vain, for while the city was rising to its greatest height it was making Greek learning and culture its own.

For the rise of party passions after the Hannibalic War Roman theorists offered an explanation which assumes the natural depravity of man. During the earlier republic (which they romanticized) men were constrained to political virtue by the pressure of external danger, but when this danger was removed they began to follow their own evil inclinations.

[1]Plutarch, Cato, 22.

[1]Partisanship and factionalism with their consequent evils originated in Rome as the result of peace and the abundance of all that men hold desirable. Before the destruction of Carthage Roman people and senate together managed the republic with prudence and moderation; there was no rivalry for glory and power in the citizen body. Fear of the enemy kept the state moral. But when that dread departed there entered the concomitants of prosperity, wantonness and arrogance. The peace they yearned for in adversity proved, when they got it, the harsher and crueler. The nobility turned its dignity and the populace its liberty into license, and every man robbed and pillaged and plundered for himself. The body politic was split into two parties, and between them the state was rent apart.

The nobility was powerful because of its organization; plebeian strength was less effective because it was not centralized but dispersed among a crowd. A handful of men manipulated policy at home and in the field; the treasury, the provinces, the magistracies, glories and triumphs, were their monopoly. The people were burdened with military service and poverty; the spoils of war generals divided with the few. In the meanwhile the parents of the soldiers and their little children were driven from their homes, the more powerful their neighbors the quicker. Along with power, then, there was an invasion of greed, measureless and ruthless; it tainted and spoiled everything, without scruple or reverence, until it hastened its own downfall. For as soon as nobles were found who preferred true glory to dishonest power the state began to stir and civil dissension to arise like an upheaval of the earth.

The nobles in question were the Gracchi, who initiated what proved to be a century of violent discord which ended

[1]Sallust, *Jugurtha*, 41.

only with the overthrow of the republic. The Gracchi were plebeians but noble, as an anecdote in Plutarch shows. When the proud Appius Claudius, sometime consul and censor, brought home the news that he had betrothed his daughter, his wife protested: "Why the hurry—unless you have got Tiberius Gracchus for our son-in-law." Tiberius' motives for reform were as much patriotic as social. The expropriation of the poor, described in the Sallust passage above, had greatly reduced the citizen rolls, and landless men were flocking to Rome to swell the mob of the idle.

[1]As Tiberius was passing through Tuscany on his way to serve in Spain he noticed that the country was depopulated and that those who worked the land or tended flocks were imported barbarian slaves. It was then that he conceived the policy which was to bring infinite trouble to him and his brother. . . . "The wild beasts that roam Italy," he would say in his speeches, "have their dens and lairs to shelter them, but the men who fight and die for Italy have nothing but air and light. Homeless and footless, they wander about with their wives and children. In battle their generals exhort them to defend their sepulchers and shrines from the enemy: they lie. Not one among the host of Romans has his ancestral altar or the tomb of his fathers: it is for the wealth and luxury of others that they fight and die. They are called masters of the world, they have no clod of earth to call their own."

The state possessed much public land, and according to a Licinian law of 367 B.C. no individual could use more than 500 acres of it. But the law was a dead letter; the public lands were occupied by noble squatters who treated it as their own domain. Tiberius' strategy was to have himself elected tribune (133 B.C.) and re-enact the Licinian law with the added provision that each of two sons of present

[1]Plutarch, *Tiberius Gracchus*, 8.

occupiers could occupy an additional 250 acres. The angry nobles induced Octavius, a tribune of their party, to veto the measure, and upon the advice of Tiberius the assembly deposed Octavius and passed Tiberius' law. A commission of three, Tiberius, his brother Gaius, and his father-in-law Appius Claudius, supervised its operation, using Attalus' legacy to equip the new farmers. To secure the continued effectiveness of his law Tiberius stood for re-election, but on election day a mob of nobles murdered him and 300 of his followers. The recall of Octavius may have been a drastic departure from custom; the killing of Tiberius was lynch law.

Ten years later Tiberius' brother Gaius became tribune and expanded his brother's program. Not only did he regularize the grain supply and make it available to the poor at reasonable prices and provide for colonization and road building in Italy, but he also took thought for the empire and settled a Roman colony in Carthage. His sharpest blow to senatorial power was in favoring the rich business class, called equestrians or knights. By providing that cases of malfeasance in provincial administration be tried before equestrian juries, that provincial governorships be designated before elections, and that equestrians be given a virtual monopoly of the lucrative business of tax farming, he strengthened the plebeian as he weakened the senatorial party. When Gaius proposed to extend Roman citizenship to the Latins and Latin rights to the Italian allies his followers were loath to share their new-won privileges, and when he failed of election to a third term (122 B.C.) he and 3000 of his followers were killed, this time with a show of legality: the senate declared martial law.

Senatorial rule now had a free hand, and displayed its incapacity and venality in the scandalous Jugurthine War in North Africa, in which, between 118 and 104 B.C., Jugurtha proved his convictions that "all things at Rome are for sale" by bribing one senatorial leader after another. Popular indignation raised Marius, a "new man" (i.e., one whose ancestors had not held high office), to the consulship (107 B.C.). Marius himself was not a reformer in the Gracchan sense, but merely wished to make his way into the governing class, as his famous speech shows:

[1]"I know, fellow citizens, that men generally use one mode in suing for office, and when they have obtained it another in administering it. At first they are diligent, humble, restrained; then they lead lives of indolence and arrogance. My view is the opposite. Because the totality of the state is greater than a consulship or praetorship, greater care should be bestowed on administering an office than on winning it. . . . You have charged me with the task of making war on Jugurtha, to the acute distress of the nobility. Consider well, I beg you, whether it would be better to change your minds and send on this or any similar mission one of that clique of nobles, a man with a long pedigree and many family portraits but no military experience, a man who would frantically bustle about in his ignorance—and find some commoner to manage his job. It has often happened that the man you chose to command has had to look for someone to command him. I myself know of cases, fellow citizens, where men began to read history and Greek military treatises after they became consuls. They put the cart before the horse: a man does a job after he is elected to it, but he should know how first.

"Compare me, the 'new man,' my fellow citizens, with those proud nobles. What they know from lectures and books I have myself seen, myself done. What they learn from handbooks I know from service. They despise me for an upstart, I despise their worthlessness. They can taunt me

[1]Sallust, Jugurtha, 85ff.

with my social position, I them with their infamies. My own belief is that men are born equal and alike: nobility is achieved by bravery. If the ancestors of Albinus or Bestia could be asked whom they would prefer for a descendant, myself or them, what do you suppose they would answer except that they wished the best men for their progeny? If they are right to despise me they should despise their ancestors whose nobility began, like mine, with achievement. They begrudge me my office: let them begrudge the toil, the uprightness, the perils, which gave me that office. Spoiled by pride, those fellows live as if they scorned the offices you give; they campaign for them as if their lives were unblemished. . . . I cannot, to win your credit, display portraits and triumphs and consulships belonging to my ancestors, but, if occasion demands, I can show military awards and medals and scars on my breast. These are my busts and my patent of nobility, not inherited, as theirs are, but won by my own many exertions and dangers.

"My expressions are not elegant; I don't care. Merit itself makes a sufficient show. It is they who need art to gloze baseness with rhetoric. I never learned Greek; I never wanted to, for Greek did little for the character of its professors. I did learn things far more useful to the state—to strike the enemy, to be vigilant on guard, to fear nothing except disgrace, to endure heat and cold alike, to sleep on the ground, to bear privation and fatigue at the same time. . . . They say I am vulgar and unmannerly because I cannot give a dainty dinner, that I have no entertainer or cook that costs more than a farm steward. I am happy to admit the charge, fellow citizens. From my father and other righteous men I learned that daintiness is appropriate to women, strenuousness to men, that good men ought to have more glory than riches, that weapons, not furniture, is the true ornament. . . .

"With the gods' help everything is ready to hand—victory, booty, glory. Even if they were uncertain or remote, all good men should support the state. Cowardice never conferred deathlessness; no parent has ever prayed for his children to live forever; he prays that the lives they live be worthy and honorable. I would say more, fellow citizens, if words could make cowards brave. For the strenuous I think what I have said is plenty."

Rome had need of a man of Marius' type. Before the Jugurthine War was finished Celtic and Germanic tribes, particularly the Cimbri and Teutones, had descended into southern Gaul and in 105 B.C. destroyed 60,000 Roman soldiers at Arausio (Orange), the greatest Roman defeat since Cannae. Instead of proceeding to Italy the invaders spent the next three years raiding Gaul and Spain; and thus Marius, who was re-elected consul year after year, had time to reorganize the army. In two battles, 102 and 101 B.C., he annihilated the invaders, and in 100 Marius served his sixth consulship.

Among Marius' reforms of the army one had great significance for the future course of Roman policy. Instead of a citizen militia serving for single campaigns and in the intervals returning to civilian life, the army was now professional, with enlistments running for sixteen or twenty years. The primary loyalty of the soldiers was now not to the state but to the general, to whom they looked for bonuses and veterans' benefits, and if the general was at odds with the government they did not hesitate, as in the cases of Sulla's and Caesar's armies, to march on the capital to assert his and their claims. Generals of the old militia could not have so used their troops. This move in the direction of the general-emperor was reinforced by another tendency. It was obviously impractical for provincial governors engaged in extended military operations to be changed annually, and therefore their commands were "prorogued." This meant that the power of a commander who held supreme authority in a distant province for a considerable period tended to become independent of and even superior to that of the home administration, which was inevitably swayed by the wishes of the general. Sulla partially and Caesar wholly revolutionized the government at Rome by bringing to bear the power they had acquired in provincial commands.

To obtain land for his veterans (a problem which all subsequent generals had to face) Marius allied himself with two violent popular leaders, Saturninus and Glaucia, and when their further measures (cheap grain, colonies abroad, extension of citizenship) seemed extreme Marius yielded to the senate's behest to use force against them. The men surrendered but were lynched. In 91 B.C. the tribune Marcus Livius Drusus, himself an optimate and the son of Gracchus' opponent, advocated a number of reforms, the most striking of which were the enlargement of the senate and the enfranchisement of the Latin and Italian allies; he was murdered before the end of his term of office. The disappointed Marsians and Samnites of central Italy seceded from their alliance, founded a new state called Italia with Corfinium as its capital, and offered citizenship to all who would join them. Rome was able to conclude the so-called Social War (90–88 B.C.) which followed only by offering citizenship first to those who had not seceded and then to the rest. The most successful Roman general in the Social War was Sulla, who had been Marius' adjutant against Jugurtha. The one who finished the war was Pompey, who was to prove Caesar's principal opponent.

During the years of disorder at Rome the brilliant Mithradates IV Eupator of Pontus, on the southern shore of the Black Sea, had grown very powerful, and at his instigation, on a day in 88 B.C., 80,000 Italian residents of Asia Minor were murdered—a sufficient indication of the esteem in which Roman publicans were held. Mithradates then murdered the Italian commercial colony on Delos and continued to Athens. Rome was threatened with the loss of all her possessions east of the Adriatic. Sulla, who was consul for 88 B.C., was given the command for the Mithradatic War. But Sulla was known to have strong aristocratic sympathies, and while he was with the army at Nola, partisans of Marius, now aged sixty-eight, passed a law to transfer the command to Marius.

[1]When Sulla heard of this he decided to settle the issue by war, and called his troops to a meeting. These were greedy for the Mithradatic campaign because they thought it would be profitable and feared Marius would enlist other soldiers than themselves. Sulla spoke of Marius' outrageous conduct, and without making his meaning explicit (he did not dare speak openly of such a war) urged them to be ready to execute his orders. They understood what he meant and, as they were afraid of missing the campaign, spoke out what Sulla had in mind and encouraged him to lead them to Rome. Sulla was delighted, and marched six legions to Rome. . . . At dawn [after his victory] he summoned the people to an assembly, deplored the condition of the state which had so long been given over to demagogues, and said he had done what he had done out of necessity. He introduced a measure that nothing should be brought before the people which had not previously been approved by the senate, an ancient practice which had fallen into disuse; also that voting should be not by centuries but by tribes, as King Tullius had ordained. By these two laws, that the senate must give prior approval to measures brought before the people, and that voting should be in the hands of the wealthy and conservative instead of the poor

[1]Appian, Civil Wars, 1.57.

and radical, they thought occasion for civil discord would be
eliminated. . . . [The leaders of the opposition were outlawed.] Marius escaped to Minturnae, without aides or
orderly. The magistrates respected the official proclamation
but were timid about themselves killing a man who had
held six consulships and performed many brilliant exploits.
While Marius was sleeping in a darkened room they sent a
local Gaul with a sword to dispatch him. As the Gaul approached the pallet in the dark, it is said, he was terrified at
the gleam and flash of fire he thought was darting from
Marius' eyes; Marius himself rose on his bed and roared
at him, "Do you dare kill Gaius Marius?" The Gaul turned
and dashed through the doors like a man possessed, crying,
"I cannot kill Gaius Marius."

*Marius made his way to Africa, and upon Sulla's depar-
ture for the east the popular leaders recalled Marius to help
overthrow the aristocratic regime. Aristocrats were murdered, their property plundered, their heads nailed to the
rostra. Marius apparently went berserk.*

[1]In a word, so insatiable a passion for bloodshed seized
Marius that, when he had killed most of his enemies and
because of excitement could remember no one else he
wished to destroy, he passed the word to his soldiers to slay
every passer-by, one after another, unless he extended his
hand to him. To such a state had things come in Rome that
men died not only without a trial and without a quarrel but
simply because that man's hand was not extended to them.
Naturally in the great crowd and confusion it was not only
a matter of indifference to Marius, but he could not have
used his hand freely however much he may have wished to.
Hence many whose deaths he did not in the least desire
died needlessly. The total number of killed on this occasion

[1]Dio Cassius, 30, frg. 102.10.

cannot be determined, for the slaughter continued for five whole days and nights.

In January 86 B.C. Marius entered upon his seventh consulship, and died a few days later. His successor Flaccus was sent to supersede Sulla, but was killed. An army mustered to oppose Sulla in Macedonia mutinied at Brundisium and killed its general, Cinna. Carbo, the remaining consul, prevented the senate from yielding to Sulla's demands, and prepared to resist any hostile move Sulla might make upon his return.

In the east Sulla had been brilliantly successful. In 86 he took Athens, after a long siege, and destroyed Mithradates' remaining forces in Greece in battles at Chaeronea and Orchomenus. With the aid of his quaestor Lucius Lucullus, who commanded a fleet, he invaded Asia Minor, and forced Mithradates to surrender the Roman possessions he had taken and to pay a huge indemnity. To pay their heavy fines for having supported Mithradates the cities of Asia Minor had to borrow from Roman bankers, and at so usurious a rate that the indebtedness soon amounted to six times the loan. The peace Sulla made with Mithradates he knew was a makeshift, but he was eager to return to Italy, where he landed, at Brundisium, in 83. Here he was met by senatorial leaders, including the still youthful Pompey, and with their assistance defeated the very considerable forces of the popular party in several battles and finally crushed them at the Colline Gate in Rome (82 B.C.).

[1]When Sulla learned that the greater part of the enemy had been destroyed and the remainder had fled to Antemnae, he came to Antemnae at dawn. When 300 of the inhabitants sent a herald, he promised them safety if they would do some mischief to his other enemies before coming over. They took him at his word, attacked their fellows,

[1]Plutarch, Sulla, 30.

and many on both sides were cut down. Nevertheless Sulla collected these and other survivors to the number of 6000 in the hippodrome, and convoked the senate in the nearby temple of Bellona. As he began to speak, those assigned to the task began to butcher the 6000. Naturally the shrieks of such a multitude being slaughtered in so small a space carried, and the senators were startled. Sulla continued his speech with a calm and unconcerned expression, and bade the senators pay attention to his speech and not busy themselves with what was going on outside: some naughty people were being admonished at his orders. Even the stupidest Roman could now realize that they had changed tyrants, not escaped tyranny. . . .

Slaughter now became Sulla's business, and murders without number or limit filled the city. Private animosities doomed many who had no relations with Sulla; he consented to gratify his associates. Young Gaius Metellus made bold to ask Sulla in the senate what end there would be to these evils and at what point he might be expected to stop. "We do not ask you," he said, "to free from punishment those you are resolved to kill, but to free from suspense those you are resolved to save." Sulla said he did not yet know whom he would spare, whereupon Metellus said, "Then tell us whom you are going to kill." . . . At once, without communicating with any official, Sulla proscribed 80 persons. Despite general indignation he proscribed 220 more on the following day, and as many again on the third day. In a public address on the subject he said he was proscribing as many as he could remember; those who escaped his memory for the present he would proscribe another time. Further, he penalized humanity with death, proscribing any who harbored or protected a proscribed person, making no exception of brother, son, or parents: the prize for killing a proscribed person was two talents, if a

slave murdered his master or a son his father. What seemed
the greatest injustice of all, he canceled the civil rights of
sons and grandsons of proscribed persons and confiscated
their property. Proscriptions were the rule not only in Rome
but in every city of Italy; neither temple of god nor hearth
of hospitality nor ancestral hall was unstained by bloodshed;
husbands were slaughtered in the arms of their wives, sons
in the arms of their mothers. The victims of political passion or private animosity were nothing compared to those
slaughtered for their property. Even the executioners were
moved to say that his fine house killed this man, his garden
that, his warm baths the other. Quintus Aurelius, who had
no political connections but thought that his only concern
with the misfortune was to condole with those affected by
it, walked into the Forum and read the list of the proscribed. He saw his own name, and said, "Too bad. My
Alban farm has condemned me." He had not gone far before he was overtaken and massacred. . . .

Aside from the bloodshed, Sulla's other acts also gave
offense. He proclaimed himself dictator, reviving this office
after a lapse of one hundred and twenty years. There was
also voted him immunity for all past actions, and for the
future power of life and death, confiscation, colonization,
founding or demolishing cities, withdrawing or bestowing
kingly office at his pleasure.

Sulla's program as a whole was to curtail the political
rights of the people and center authority in the senate. He
fixed the ages for holding various offices, prescribed the
intervals between offices, made tribunes ineligible for other
magistracies. He laid a foundation for the imperial civil
service by regularizing the tenure of provincial governorships. These were to be held by retiring praetors and consuls; commanders for military expeditions were to be
appointed by the senate. In 79 B.C., somewhat surprisingly,

Sulla laid his dictatorship down, and upon his death in the year following his work was promptly undone.

One of the principal objects of Sulla's system was to prevent successful generals from dominating the government. His own lieutenant Pompey was the first of a series of generals who did dominate the government. The consul of 78 B.C., Lepidus, sought to restore the distribution of cheap grain which Sulla had suppressed, to recall the Marian exiles, and return their confiscated lands. As proconsul of Cisalpine Gaul in the year following he marched on Rome to enforce his demands. He was defeated by Pompey, who was appointed to a special command for the purpose, and the defeated Marians joined their comrades who had assembled in Spain. Here Sertorius, who had been duly appointed governor in 83, was able to hold his own against senatorial armies and against Pompey himself, who was given the command in 78, until 72 B.C., when Sertorius was assassinated by a jealous subordinate.

Pompey returned to Rome in time to complete the suppression of the revolt of the gladiators under Spartacus. The fact that mutinous gladiators could in a few months in 73 B.C. collect 70,000 desperate runaway slaves and defeat two Roman armies is a comment on social conditions. It was Crassus, another of Sulla's former lieutenants, who cornered the main body of the rebels, before Pompey cut off the body that escaped to North Italy.

In the east Mithradates was restive and his ally, Tigranes of Armenia, had annexed Syria and Greater Cappadocia (83 B.C.). In 75 B.C. Nicomedes III of Bithynia bequeathed his kingdom to Rome, but Mithradates championed the claim of Nicomedes' son against the Romans. Mithradates had the help of pirates, of whom we shall hear more presently, and was supplied with officers by Sertorius. In 74

Mithradates invaded Bithynia, but was driven from there and his own kingdom of Pontus by Lucullus, and took refuge with Tigranes in Armenia. Lucullus took Tigranes' capital, but his soldiers were disaffected because of his strict discipline, and the financial interests in Rome hated him.

[1]In an interval of leisure [71–70 B.C.] Lucullus turned his attention to further justice and law in the Asiatic cities. Long lack of these had subjected the province to indescribable and incredible misfortunes. Plundered and enslaved by taxgatherers and moneylenders, people perforce sold their handsome sons and virgin daughters, and cities their dedications, pictures, and sacred statues. In the end they were bound to their creditors as slaves, but what came before was worse—tortures of rope, barrier, and horse, exposure in the blazing sun, being thrust into mud or ice, so that slavery brought relief and peace. Such were the evils which Lucullus found in the cities, and in a short time he relieved them of all these abuses. In the first place he ordered that interest be reckoned at no more than one per cent monthly; secondly, he cut off all interest that exceeded the principal; third and most important, he ordained that the creditor should receive not more than a fourth of the debtor's income, and a creditor who added interest to principal was deprived of the whole. In less than four years, as a result, the debts were all paid and properties returned to their owners unencumbered. This public debt resulted from the fine of 20,000 talents which Sulla had imposed on Asia. Twice the sum had been repaid to the moneylenders, but usurious interest had brought the debt up to 120,000 talents. The creditors considered themselves outrageously used; they vociferated against Lucullus at Rome, and bribed some of the tribunes to proceed against him.

As a result Lucullus was deprived of his command

[1]Plutarch, *Lucullus*, 20.

(66 B.C.). *By the terms of the Manilian law he was super-seded by Pompey. At Rome Lucullus consoled himself for his political humiliation by luxury which has come to be called Lucullan.*

[1]In the life of Lucullus, as in Old Comedy, the first part contains statecraft and generalship and the latter drinking parties, feasting, orgies, torch races, and all manner of frivolity. Under this heading I would include his extravagant building, his cloisters and baths, particularly his pictures and statues and his devotion to such objects, which he collected at lavish expense, bestowing on them the rich treasure he had accumulated in his campaigns. Even now when luxury has so multiplied the gardens of Lucullus are reckoned the most sumptuous of the imperial gardens. On the seashore and near Naples he suspended hills over vast underground structures, encircled his houses with moats and channels for breeding fish, and built open-air banqueting casinos. When the Stoic Tubero saw them he called Lucullus Xerxes in a toga. . . . His daily meals suggested the new-rich. His purple coverlets, his jeweled flagons, his professional dancers and entertainers, and even more the variety and exquisite elaboration of his cuisine made him the envy of the vulgar. . . . Once when he was dining alone and was served a simple and moderate meal he angrily summoned the butler in charge. The butler said he did not think Lucullus would want anything lavish, for no company was invited. "What do you mean?" he retorted. "Don't you know that Lucullus is dining with Lucullus today?" . . . His furnishing of a library, on the other hand, deserves warm praise. He collected many choice manuscripts, and the use he put them to was more admirable than his acquisition of them. His libraries and cloisters and study rooms were freely accessible to Greeks, who resorted to

[1]Plutarch, *Lucullus*, 29.

them as to an asylum of the Muses. . . . In general his house was home and headquarters for Greeks who came to Rome.

At the conclusion of the Gladiatorial War Pompey and Crassus became consuls (70 B.C.), though their candidacy was a violation of the Sullan constitution and their ambitious designs were distrusted by the senate. To win the support of the populares they restored the tribunate to its former privileges, and thus completed the overthrow of the Sullan constitution. Upon the conclusion of their consulship they refused proconsular appointments because none available offered sufficient scope for their ambitions. Pompey's chance came when the plague of Cilician pirates became so troublesome as to interrupt importation of grain to Rome.

[1]The power of the pirates was at first based on Cilicia, and at the beginning it was precarious and clandestine, but during the Mithradatic Wars it was proved useful to the king's service and so took on confidence and boldness. Then when the Romans were embroiled in civil wars at the gates of Rome the sea was left unguarded and little by little they were drawn on so that they not only attacked shipping but devastated its lands and coastal cities. Soon men of large means and proud family and superior intellect embarked with the pirates and shared their enterprises as though this occupation conferred respectability and reputation. In many places there were erected piratical naval stations and signal towers, and the fleets that put in were speedy and maneuverable and well equipped for their work, and had practiced crews and expert skippers. Even more than the terror, the odious ostentation of these pirates aroused indignation. They had gilded masts and purple sails and silvered oars, as if they reveled in their iniquity and preened themselves on

[1]Plutarch, Pompey, 24.

it. Their fluting and psaltery and drinking along the whole
coast, their kidnapings of important personages and holding captive cities for ransom were a disgrace to Roman
leadership. Their vessels numbered more than a thousand,
and the cities they took four hundred. . . . Most insulting
of all was this practice: whenever a captive cried that he
was a Roman and gave his name, they pretended to be
stunned and terrified and smote their thighs and groveled
before him, beseeching forgiveness; and when the victim
saw them humble and suppliant he believed they were in
earnest. Then some would put Roman shoes on his feet and
others throw a toga about him, to prevent further mistakes,
they said. They carried the joke on and got their fun out of
the man, and then put a ship's ladder down in mid-ocean
and bade him disembark and go on his way rejoicing; if he
did not wish to go they shoved him over and drowned him.

*It was the tribunate which he restored to power that gave
Pompey the authority he craved. Against the opposition of
the senate the tribune Gabinius, in 67 B.C., carried a law
conferring on Pompey extraordinary authority superseding
all other officers in the whole Mediterranean for three years.
He did his work so systematically that he cleared the Mediterranean in three months, and showed true statesmanship
by resettling instead of executing the pirates he captured.
Pompey's authority still had three years to run, and he was
anxious for new laurels. Opportunely the dissatisfaction with
Lucullus was at its height, and again against the opposition
of the senate, the tribune Manilius carried a bill which conferred upon him full authority over the affairs of Asia
(66 B.C.).*

*Again he worked systematically and well. He drove
Mithradates from Pontus to Armenia and defeated him,
whereupon Tigranes submitted to Pompey and became a
Roman ally. In 64 he organized Syria as a Roman province,*

and in 63 settled a dynastic quarrel in Judaea, nominated a high priest to be head of the local government, and annexed the country to Syria. Mithradates, in the meanwhile, had projected an invasion of Italy with the Celts of the Danube Valley, but committed suicide when his army deserted him for his son Pharnaces. Pharnaces made peace with Pompey, who in 62 B.C. brought his rich spoils and victorious army back to Italy.

At Rome Pompey's successes brought uneasiness not only to the senate but to his rivals for political supremacy—Crassus, his former colleague, whose chief resource was his enormous wealth, and Julius Caesar, whose magnetism and political astuteness made him leader of the old Marian faction. Many men whose fortunes had been ruined by proscriptions and counterproscriptions would scruple at nothing which would bring them wealth or office. In 64 B.C. two of these, Catiline and the like-minded Gaius Antonius, were supported for the consulship by Caesar and Crassus. The third candidate was Cicero, a "new man" and therefore distasteful to the optimates, but they supported him nevertheless as the lesser evil, and so won his adherence to the optimate cause. Cicero was elected with Antonius, who promised not to oppose him in return for the proconsulship of Macedonia (for 62) which had fallen to Cicero's lot. In the consular elections of July 63 Catiline was again a candidate, this time without the support of Caesar and Crassus, and was defeated.

[1]From this time Catiline turned his back on politics because it involved envy and strife and was not the speediest and most effective means for attaining absolute power. He obtained quantities of money from women who hoped their husbands would be killed in a revolution, conspired with a number of senators and knights, and collected plebeians,

[1]Appian, Civil Wars, 2.2.

foreigners, and slaves. Lesser leaders of the conspiracy were
Cornelius Lentulus and Cethegus, then praetors. To the
Sullans up and down Italy who had squandered their profits
and were eager for similar doings he sent messengers, Gaius
Mallius to Faesulae in Etruria and others to Picenum and
Apulia, and these quietly enrolled an army for him. These
facts were still secret when they were communicated to
Cicero by Fulvia, a woman of position. Her lover Quintus
Curius had been expelled from the senate for scandalous
behavior, and merited inclusion in Catiline's pact. With
lightheaded braggadocio he intimated to his mistress that
he would soon be in a position of power. By now rumors of
what was going on in Italy were getting around. Cicero
posted guards at intervals throughout the city and sent
many of the nobility to keep an eye on what was happen-
ing in the suspected localities. [On 7 November 63 Cicero
delivered an invective against Catiline in the senate]:

[1]"How much further, Catiline, will you abuse our forbearance? How much longer will your recklessness baffle our
restraint? Will your unbridled audacity stop at nothing? Do
the night watches on the Palatine, the sentinels posted
in the city leave you indifferent? Are you not moved by the
alarm of the people, the rallying of all good men, the precautions of this meeting, the look and expressions of all
assembled here? Can't you see your plot is exposed, don't
you realize that all of us here assembled know the details of
your conspiracy? Do you suppose there is a man here who
does not know what you did last night and the night before,
where you were and with whom, and what plans you laid?"

*The Catilinarians in Rome were arrested and brought to
trial; Caesar argued for leniency but the upright if quixotic
Cato, great-grandson of the Elder Cato, insisted upon capital punishment and carried the day. Catiline and his main*
[1]Cicero, *I Catiline*, 1.

body tried to make their way north and died fighting.

It was expected that Pompey would emulate Sulla and march on Rome, but he disbanded his army, and requested the senate to ratify his eastern arrangements and grant his veterans allotments of land. But the senate, no longer in fear, was dilatory. Caesar, returned in 60 from a governorship in Spain, formed a secret coalition with Pompey and Crassus; together the triumvirate could dominate the government and satisfy the desires of each. For 59 B.C. Caesar was elected consul, but his colleague was the optimate Calpurnius Bibulus. So ineffective was Bibulus' opposition that wags dated the year "the consulship of Julius and Caesar." By appealing directly to the popular assembly Caesar carried the measures Pompey desired, procured for Crassus' benefit a remission of one third the contract price for the revenues of Asia, and for himself a general command of both Gauls and Illyria to run for five years from March 59 B.C. The unofficial triumvirate had proven stronger than the state and its members determined to continue their arrangement. Pompey married Caesar's daughter Julia, and Caesar married the daughter of Calpurnius Piso, whom the triumvirate had supported for the consulship. Their two most vocal opponents, Cicero and Cato, the triumvirate removed from Rome. Cato was given an assignment in Cyprus, which his Stoic conscience did not permit him to refuse. Cicero was exiled as result of a bill which outlawed persons responsible for the execution of Roman citizens without trial. To pass this bill Clodius, who hated Cicero for private reasons, had himself adopted into a plebeian family to make himself eligible for the tribunate. In 58 B.C. Caesar proceeded to his Gallic conquests. Caesar's generalship—and his detachment in speaking of it—may be illustrated by his account of his relief of Cicero, the orator's brother, who was in command near Brussels and was under *siege by the Nervii; if Caesar had failed at this point his whole enterprise would have collapsed.*

[1]As the assault on Cicero's camp daily grew heavier and more ruthless, chiefly because many of the defenders were wounded and few left fit for duty, messengers and dispatches were sent to Caesar in more rapid succession. Some were caught and tortured to death in sight of our soldiers. There was one Nervian in the camp, Vertico by name, a man of good birth who had taken refuge with Cicero at the beginning of the blockade and had proven his loyalty to him. This man offered his slave freedom and generous rewards if he would take a message to Caesar. The slave attached the message to a pike and, being himself a Gaul, moved among the Gauls without arousing suspicion and made his way to Caesar. It was from him that Caesar learned of the danger to Cicero and his legion.

It was about five in the afternoon when Caesar received the dispatch. At once he sent a messenger to the quartermaster Crassus, whose winter quarters were in the country of the Bellovaci twenty-five miles away, and ordered him to march at midnight and join him at once. Crassus set out promptly. Another aide Caesar sent to Gaius Fabius, the lieutenant general, to bid him bring his legion into the country of the Atrebates, through which he himself would have to march. To Labienus he wrote instructing him to bring his legion to the country of the Nervii if he could do so without prejudice to their cause. For the rest of the army he did not think it wise to wait, for they were rather remote; but he did collect about 400 horse from nearby cantonments.

About nine in the morning his scouts informed him of the approach of Crassus, and he moved forward twenty miles that day. He left Crassus in command at Samarobriva

[1]Caesar, *Gallic War*, 5.46–48.

and assigned him a legion, as he was leaving behind the baggage, public hostages, documents, and the grain which he had brought to last the winter. Fabius and his legion joined Caesar on the march, as ordered. Labienus had learned of the death of Sabinus and the massacre of his cohorts . . . and advised Caesar that it would be dangerous for him to withdraw his legion. This decision Caesar approved, and though he had two legions instead of the three he expected, he regarded speed as the sole salvation of the common cause. He proceeded to the country of the Nervii by forced marches, and there learned from captives how matters stood at Cicero's camp and how dangerous the situation was. He induced a Gallic trooper, by a large reward, to take a letter to Cicero; this he wrote in Greek characters, so that the enemy might not learn of our plans if it were intercepted, and he instructed the man, if he could not penetrate to the camp, to tie it to the thong of a javelin and throw it inside the entrenchments. The letter said that Caesar and the legions would arrive very shortly and encouraged Cicero to be true to himself. The Gaul was afraid of the risk, and threw the javelin, as he had been instructed. As it happened the javelin stuck in a tower, where it was not noticed by our men for two days; but on the third day a soldier sighted it, took it down, and brought it to Cicero. Cicero glanced through it and then read it out to a parade of his troops, to their intense joy. Soon the smoke of distant fires was visible, and this banished all doubt that the legions were coming.

[1]In the nine years of his command in Gaul this in brief is what Caesar accomplished. All Gaul which is bounded by the Pyrenees, the Alps, and the Cévennes, and by the Rhine and Rhone rivers, a circuit of some 3200 miles, he organ-

[1]Suetonius, *Julius*, 25.

ized as a province, excluding allies and states which had rendered good service, and imposed a tribute of forty million sesterces annually. He was the first Roman to attack the Germans beyond the Rhine; he built a bridge for the purpose and inflicted heavy losses upon them. He also invaded the Britons, a people previously unknown, defeated them, and exacted money and hostages. With all these successes he encountered reverses only three times: in Britain his fleet was nearly ruined by a storm; at Gergovia in Gaul a legion was routed; and in Germany his lieutenants Titurius and Aurunculeius were killed in an ambush.

The political uses to which Caesar immediately began to put his new wealth and prestige disquieted his colleagues. Pompey was veering to the optimate cause, and supported Milo against Clodius to procure Cicero's recall. There was virtual anarchy in the city; the streets were dominated by the rival gangs of Clodius and Milo. A near famine gave Pompey a proconsular commission for five years to ensure the grain supply; this was in effect another extraordinary military command. A coolness had arisen between Pompey and Crassus. Cato returned from Cyprus in 56 and gave the optimates needed leadership. In view of these strains, Caesar summoned his colleagues to a conference at Luca (56 B.C.), where they renewed their arrangements for another five years. Caesar would retain his Gallic command, Pompey receive Spain and Libya, and Crassus Syria, each for five-year periods. Pompey and Crassus were to be consuls for 55, but since it proved too late for them to file, they forcibly prevented elections from being held, and the next year they forced other candidates to withdraw and so were elected for 54.

From the first it was clear that the separate ambitions of Pompey and Caesar could not be reconciled, and the death of Julia removed the personal tie between the men. Instead of proceeding to his province Pompey governed it through legates, and himself remained to watch developments in the capital. Crassus, delighted to have a major command like his colleagues, departed for the east and made an unprovoked attack on the Parthians. The Parthians led him on into the desert where their numerous and skillful mounted archers could work their will on the legionaries with impunity. In despair Crassus consented to meet with the Parthian general at Carrhae to discuss capitulation.

[1]The first of the barbarians to approach him were two mongrel Greeks who leapt from their horses and made obeisance. Speaking in Greek, they urged him to send his aides forward to satisfy themselves that Surena and his party who were approaching had no weapons or armor. Crassus answered that if he were in the least concerned for his life he would not have put himself in their hands, but he nevertheless sent the two Roscius brothers to ask how and in what numbers they should meet. These Surena immediately seized and detained, and himself with his chief officers galloped forward and said: "What is this? The Roman imperator on foot and we mounted?" He ordered a horse for Crassus, who declared that neither was at fault for each was following the custom of his country. . . . There was a horse with a golden bridle, upon which the grooms lifted and mounted Crassus, and then they whipped the horse up to run. Octavius was the first to seize the bridle, and after him Petronius, a captain, and then the rest surrounded the horse, trying to stop him and pulling away the men crowding on Crassus from either side. There were shoving and confusion and blows, until Octavius drew sword and killed one of the barbarian's grooms and was himself cut down from behind by another. Petronius had

[1]Plutarch, *Crassus*, 31.

no weapon; when he was struck in the breastplate he jumped away unhurt. Crassus was killed by a Parthian named Pomaxathres. . . . Surena ordered the other Romans to come down without fear. Some did and surrendered, and the others scattered during the night. Of these only few were saved; the others Arabs hunted down and killed. It is reported that 20,000 were killed and 10,000 taken alive.

Crassus' head and hand Surena sent to Hydrades in Armenia, but he sent messages to Seleucia that he was bringing Crassus alive, and got ready a ludicrous procession which he mockingly called a triumph. He dressed Gaius Paccianus, the captive who most resembled Crassus, in an elegant woman's dress, conducted him on horseback, and instructed him to answer to the title of Imperator Crassus. Before him were trumpeters and lictors mounted on camels; money-bags were fastened to the lictors' staves and severed Roman heads to their axes. Behind followed Syrian courtesans and musicians who sang many ribald and absurd songs directed at Crassus' effeminacy and cowardice. Everyone looked at the spectacle.

[1]To the many Crassus affords an illustration of Fortune, but to the wise an example of foolish ambition which would not let him rest content to be the first and greatest among myriads of men, but made him think that because he was judged inferior to only two men he had nothing.

Apparently of intent, Pompey permitted chaos to rage in Rome until he was named sole consul to restore order. At the same time Pompey was governing important provinces through his personal agents, held the extraordinary commission for the grain supply, and armies maintained at public expense. This combination approached the power Augustus was later to assume. But Pompey was content with
[1]Plutarch, Crassus, 27.

the role of Indispensable Man, and the senate willingly co-operated with him to suppress the more dangerous radicalism of Caesar. The issue which precipitated civil war was the consulship for 48 B.C. Caesar felt, justifiably, that his safety demanded that his authority continue without interruption, but a law newly reinforced for the purpose by Pompey required that he lay his command down before offering himself for re-election. Caesar's request that he be allowed to run in absentia, and other overtures—that he would retain only Cisalpine Gaul and part of his troops, or that he would resign his provinces and disband his troops if Pompey would do the same—were similarly rejected. In January 49 the senate declared Caesar a public enemy and instructed Pompey to protect the state, and Caesar crossed the Rubicon, that is, passed out of his authorized province into territory where it was unlawful for him to appear under arms. Pompey mustered his forces in southern Italy; a letter to Cicero, inviting him to come to Luceria, shows his optimism:

[1]"Today, 10 February, Fabius Vergilianus has joined me. From him I learn that Domitius [Ahenobarbus, whom the senate had designated to supplant Caesar] with his eleven cohorts and fourteen others that Vibullius has brought up is on his way to me. It is his intention to start from Corfinium on the thirteenth, and Hirrus will follow with five cohorts. I give my opinion that you must come to us at Luceria; here you will be perfectly safe."

But Caesar's speed confounded Pompey's optimism. Domitius, besieged at Corfinium, asked Pompey for help, and Pompey had to leave Domitius to his fate:

[2]"Today, 17 February, I received your communication informing me that Caesar has invested Corfinium . . . and I am much disturbed by it. I cannot sufficiently trust the

[1]Cicero, *To Atticus*, 8.11A.   [2]Cicero, *To Atticus*, 8.12D.

loyalty of my soldiers to stake the country's fortunes on a single battle; the consuls' conscripts have not yet joined. Make every effort to extricate yourself, and if you can do so come to me here as soon as possible, before the enemy can collect all his forces. New recruits cannot be obtained here on short notice, and if they could you must know how little confidence we can put in these men who barely know one another against experienced regiments."

Pompey's decision was to withdraw from Italy; he had strong forces in Spain and controlled the sea, and his plan was to launch a co-ordinated attack upon Caesar from east and west. Caesar's attempt to forestall Pompey's departure to Greece failed.

[1]Following is a chronological summary of Caesar's movements after crossing the Rubicon. He occupied Umbria, Picenum, and Etruria, captured and released Lucius Domitius, who had illegally been appointed his successor and was holding Corfinium with a garrison, and then hastened along the Adriatic to Brundisium where Pompey and the consuls had taken refuge with the intention of crossing to Epirus as soon as possible. Caesar's efforts to prevent their departure were unsuccessful. He convoked a senate to deal with public business and proceeded to Spain to attack Pompey's very strong forces there under Marcus Petreius, Lucius Afranius, and Marcus Varro. To his friends he remarked that he was going against an army without a general and would return against a general without an army. Though his progress was delayed by the siege of Massilia, which shut its gates against him, and by extreme shortages of provisions he nevertheless won a complete victory. He then returned to Rome.

Despite the watchfulness of Pompey's navy Caesar ferried his army over to Epirus in November 49. Pompey had

[1]Suetonius, *Julius*, 34.

at his disposal the rich resources of the east, and his lieutenants showed little scruple in exploiting them.

[1]Upon receiving sundry defeats near Mount Amanus [in Syria, Pompey's lieutenant] Scipio gave himself the title of Imperator. This done, he requisitioned large sums from cities and kings and exacted from the taxgatherers of his province the moneys due for two years and forced them to advance him the amount for the year following. He also requisitioned cavalry from the entire province. Having made these collections, he left behind him the Parthian enemy which had lately killed the imperator Crassus and held Marcus Bibulus under siege, and marched his legions and cavalry out of Syria. The province was filled with anxious apprehension of a Parthian war and soldiers were heard to say they were ready to march against an enemy if such were their orders, but would not bear arms against a fellow citizen and consul. But Scipio took them to Pergamum, quartered them in luxurious cities, bestowed bountiful largesse upon them, and to exercise their soldiership gave them cities to plunder.

In the meanwhile the moneys requisitioned in the whole province were collected ruthlessly. Many novel devices for satisfying greed were contrived. A poll tax was imposed on all individuals, slave and free. Column taxes, door taxes, grain, soldiers, weapons, rowers, artillery, vehicles were requisitioned. Anything for which a name could be invented seemed appropriate for exacting money. Individual prefects clothed with military authority were placed in charge not only of cities but of villages and hamlets, and these were esteemed good and stalwart citizens to the degree that they behaved like cruel martinets. The province was full of general officers and their orderlies, teeming with prefects and collectors. Besides the moneys requisitioned

[1]Caesar, Civil War, 3.31.

these looked out for their private purses also. To cover shameful conduct with a decent title they kept repeating that they had been expelled from home and country and were in need of every necessity. The burden was compounded by usurious interest rates, as generally happens in war when all moneys are confiscated. In such circumstances the postponement of a day was called a gift. In that span of two years the indebtedness of the provinces was multiplied.

At Dyrrhachium Caesar boldly drew a seventeen-mile line of circumvallation around Pompey's forces.

[1]This was an unprecedented mode of warfare. . . . Ordinarily when a blockade is attempted it is by an army superior in horse and foot against one demoralized and weakened by defeat or other reverse, and the ordinary motive for blockade is to cut the enemy off from supplies. But here Caesar with inferior numbers was blockading a fresh and unbeaten army which was abundantly supplied. Ships from all quarters brought stores daily; whatever the wind, it was favorable from some accessible direction. But Caesar himself was in great straits, for to a great distance about him the grain was used up. . . . Some of his men not otherwise occupied found a root called chara, of which there was an abundance. Mixed with milk, it could be made into a kind of bread and it relieved their need greatly. When the Pompeians in conversation with our men taunted them with hunger, they would toss loaves of this bread at them to spoil their hopes.

The blockade failed, and both armies moved north to Thessaly, where they met at Pharsalus. Against his better judgment Pompey was provoked into giving battle by the politicians in his camp.

[2]When Pompey was deliberate in his measures these men declared that the business could be finished in a day but

[1]Caesar, *Civil War*, 3.47.   [2]Caesar, *Civil War*, 3.82.

that he was reveling in his authority and enjoyed treating consulars and praetorians like menials. They were already openly disputing about offices and priesthoods, filled consulships for years to come, clamoring for the houses and goods of the men in Caesar's camp. . . . In a word they were all preoccupied with offices or monetary gain or furthering private quarrels, and put their minds on the uses to which they would put victory, not how they could win it.

Caesar won the battle of Pharsalus on 9 August 48 B.C. If he had not, it is clear, Caesarism would still have prevailed. Pompey made his way to Egypt, and was murdered by order of the youthful Ptolemy as he was being rowed ashore.

[1]Caesar followed Pompey to Alexandria, and learned he had been killed. He saw that Ptolemy was plotting his own destruction also and waged against him a war made extremely difficult by the terrain and the season. It was winter and he was inside the walls of an opulent and crafty enemy, whereas he was himself unready for war and without supplies. Caesar won, and turned the rule of Egypt over to Cleopatra and her younger brother; he hesitated to make a province of it because under a headstrong governor it might become a source of rebellion. From Alexandria [after dallying with Cleopatra for some months] he crossed to Syria and thence to Pontus upon the urgent news that Pharnaces, son of Mithradates the Great, had seized the opportunity to make war and was growing bolder with success. Within five days of reaching Pontus and four hours of sighting him Caesar routed him in a single engagement.

It was on this occasion that Caesar sent his famous dispatch: Veni, vidi, vici. He returned to Rome in the autumn of 47, restored order in the city, and forgave the Pompeians who gave up resistance. Among these was Cicero, who wrote
[1]Suetonius, Julius, 35.

*his friend Atticus an account of a visit Caesar paid him in
December 45:*

[1]"What a formidable guest! But I cannot complain; he
was in a mellow mood. After his arrival at Philippus' on the
second evening of the Saturnalia the whole establishment
was so crowded with soldiers that even Caesar's dining
room could not be kept clear; there were no fewer than
2000 men. Naturally I was nervous how it would fare with
me the next day, but Cassius Barba came to my rescue by
setting guards. The camp was pitched outdoors; my villa
was made secure. On the third day of the Saturnalia he
stayed at Philippus' till nearly one, closeted on business
with Balbus; then he strolled on the beach. At two he
bathed; the Mamurra business left him noncommittal. After
dressing he sat down to dinner. He was under a course of
emetics, and so ate and drank freely and with satisfaction.
Everything was good and well served . . . and I think I
made a good host. But the guest was not the sort to whom
you would say, 'Do stop in again on your way back'; once
is plenty. Our talk was not serious but mainly literary. In
a word, he was pleased and seemed to enjoy himself. He
told me he would be at Puteoli one day, and the next near
Baiae. There you have the story of his visit, or, as I may
call it, his billeting."

*But there were Pompeians who did not give up resistance,
some, like the Stoic Cato, for doctrinaire reasons, most because they had a more tangible stake in the old order.*

[2]In body Pompey was no more, but his name was still
alive everywhere. Strong partisanship for his cause precipitated war in Africa, fomented by King Juba and Scipio, the
consular whom Pompey, two years before his death, had
chosen for his father-in-law. Their forces were augmented
by Cato, who had brought his legions through enormously

[1]Cicero, *To Atticus*, 13.52.   [2]Velleius Paterculus, 2.54.

difficult and desert terrain. The soldiers offered that honest man the supreme command, but he preferred to give obedience to his superior in rank. In keeping with my promise of brevity I must pass over details rapidly. Africa had been in possession of the Pompeian forces since the death of Curio, the leader of the Caesarian party, and so Caesar, following his fortune, proceeded to Africa. After initial reverses he recovered his stride and routed the opposition [at Thapsus, in April 46]. To the vanquished he showed the same clemency as he had done previously. After his victory in Africa Caesar was confronted by a more serious war in Spain. This had been fanned to formidable proportions by Cnaeus Pompey, the energetic son of Pompey the Great, who was reinforced by men from all parts who cherished his father's greatness. Caesar's fortune attended him in Spain also, but never had he engaged in a more bitterly contested and dangerous battle [than at Munda, in March 45]. . . .

Victorious over all his enemies, Caesar returned to Rome and, a thing incredible, pardoned all who had borne arms against him. He entertained the city lavishly with magnificent spectacles of gladiatorial shows and sham battles of ships, cavalry, infantry, elephants, and with public banquets extending over many days. He celebrated five triumphs. The furnishings for his Gallic triumph were of citrus, for his Pontic of acanthus, for his African of ivory, and for his Spanish of polished silver. The proceeds of the spoils, carried in triumph, amounted to more than six hundred million sesterces.

But only five months of peaceful rule fell to the lot of that great man who used his victories so mercifully. He returned to the city in October, he was cut off on the Ides of March [15 March 44 B.C.]. The leaders of the conspiracy were Brutus and Cassius. A promised consulship had not conciliated the former, the postponement of his candidacy had alienated the latter. Privy to the assassination also were some of his intimate friends, such as Decimus Brutus and Gaius Trebonius, whom the success of his party had raised to high position. Mark Antony, his colleague in the consulship and a man who could venture anything, had brought great odium upon Caesar by placing the emblem of royalty upon his head as he sat before the rostra at the Lupercalia. The crown Caesar thrust aside, but showed no displeasure.

Since crossing the Rubicon Caesar had scarcely sixteen months in Rome, and his achievements during that short span are remarkable. Like Alexander or Augustus, the eminence he attained by ruthlessness he exploited with statesmanship. He extended citizenship to Cisalpine Gaul and enrolled Gauls in the senate, abolished tax farming in Asia, regulated municipal constitutions, inaugurated a public works program, reduced debts, reformed the calendar. His powers rested ultimately on his sole control of army and treasury, and he dictated elections to important magistracies. The senate was reduced to being a mere advisory council (as in theory it had always been) and the magistrates to being agents of Caesar. Though he refused the crown and royal title, he accepted the other symbols of royalty—purple robe, a temple to his Clementia, statues, portraits on coinage. The show of monarchy was perhaps more offensive to traditionalists than its substance. Augustus, whose authority was as complete, was more careful of appearances and could claim that he was "restoring the republic."

The conspirators had assumed that upon the death of Caesar the republic would of itself spring back to life. But the republic was dead. Antony fired popular indignation against the assassins, and took possession of Caesar's papers and money. Lepidus, Caesar's surrogate as dictator, had a legion under his command and numerous veterans at his disposal. Antony and the senatorial opposition reached a compromise: the conspirators would go unpunished, but Caesar's acts, even those still unpublished, would be ratified. The principal conspirators uneasily left Rome for their provincial assignments, and Antony proceeded to establish himself as Caesar's successor. The tyrant was dead, tyranny marched on. Within five weeks Cicero wrote Atticus:

[1]"Ah, friend, I fear the Ides of March have given us nothing beyond the pleasure and the satisfaction of our hatred and indignation. What news I receive, what sights I see! 'Lofty was that deed, aye, but bootless.' "

Now a sickly youth of eighteen, Caesar's grandnephew and adoptive son Octavius entered the scene and proved himself one of history's greatest political geniuses. Against his family's advice he came to Rome to claim his inheritance, and when Antony refused to hand over Caesar's fortune, he discharged Caesar's lavish bequests with his own and borrowed money and so secured the loyalty of the veterans. The republicans were glad to exploit the rift between the Caesarians, and conferred consular authority upon Octavian (his proper style after his adoption was formalized) so that he could co-operate with their armies to defeat Antony at Mutina (44–43 B.C.). At the instigation of Cicero, now leader of the republicans, Antony was declared a public enemy. Cicero thought "that stripling must be praised, used, got rid of," but the stripling marched upon and occupied Rome and had himself elected consul with the sole charge of defending Italy. He then combined with Antony and Lepidus (whom he, it developed, would use

[1]Cicero, To Atticus, 14.12.

and get rid of) to form a triumvirate which, unlike the unofficial coalition of Caesar, Pompey, and Crassus, had formal and virtually unlimited authority to regulate the state
for a term of five years.

[1]As soon as the triumvirs were together alone they wrote
the names of those to be killed, listing men suspected because they were powerful and also personal enemies. They
traded their own relatives and friends for liquidation, both
then and later when they made new lists, one after another,
proscribing some for enmity or mere friction, some because
they were friends of enemies or enemies of friends, or very
wealthy. They needed much money for the war; revenues
from Asia had been paid to Brutus and Cassius, and kings
and satraps were still making contributions. And since
Europe, and especially Italy, was exhausted by wars and
taxes, the triumvirs in their need levied very heavy contributions on the common people and women, and con-
templated imposts on sales and rents. And now a man
would be proscribed for a villa or house. The number of
senators condemned to death and confiscation was about
300, and of the equestrians about 2000. The lists included
brothers and uncles of the proscribers, and also some of the
officers, who had been at odds with their superiors or fellow
officers. The greater number they postponed proscribing,
when they left the meeting for Rome, but twelve (some
say seventeen) of the most powerful they decided to send
men to kill at once. Among these was Cicero.

[2]Then Octavian and Antony transported their armies to
Macedonia and fought Brutus and Cassius near the city of
Philippi [42 B.C.]. The wing under Brutus' command de-
feated Octavian's army and captured his camp. . . . But
Cassius' wing was roughly handled [by Antony] and fled to
higher ground. Cassius supposed his colleague had met simi-

[1]Appian, Civil Wars, 4.5.   [2]Velleius Paterculus, 2.70.

83

lar fortune. When he saw a force of men moving in his direction he sent a veteran to identify them for him. The man was slow in reporting. The column was advancing at a run and now very close, but dust prevented recognition of their personnel and standards, and Cassius supposed they were the enemy charging. He covered his head with his cloak and calmly extended his neck for his freedman to strike. The head had fallen when the veteran returned to report that Brutus had won. When he saw his general lying dead, he said, "My slowness killed him, I must follow," and so fell upon his sword. A few days later Brutus fought again and was beaten. At nightfall he withdrew to a hill and prevailed upon his intimate Strato of Aegaeae to lend a hand for his death. He raised his left arm above his head and with his right hand held the point of Strato's sword near the left nipple where the heart throbs; then he lunged to open a wound, was transfixed by the stroke, and died at once.

Philippi marked the end of organized resistance to the triumvirs, but the triumvirs still had to settle matters amongst themselves. For administering the empire they agreed that Octavian was to have the western, Antony the eastern provinces, and Lepidus Africa. To seal the bond between the major triumvirs Antony married Octavian's sister Octavia. There were many urgent problems. Sextus Pompey, the surviving son of Pompey the Great, controlled the sea with a privateer navy (which had rescued many threatened victims of the proscription): the triumvirs came to terms with him until in 36 B.C. they were able to defeat him. Next Lepidus made claims upon Sicily and was eliminated from the triumvirate, and left Octavian and Antony to confront one another. In Italy disturbances in the north, and 170,000 veterans clamoring for land allotments, had to be pacified; in the east the Parthians were threatening war. Italy was the more difficult and for the time less attractive post, but the essential one for a man aspiring to sole rule. In the east Antony had divorced Octavia and married Cleopatra and was assuming the airs of an oriental monarch. Octavian exploited these derelictions of his rival to the full, to destroy Antony's very great popularity and represent himself as the defender of Roman tradition. In 38 the term of the triumvirate had been extended another five years, to expire in 33. In 32 Octavian published what purported to be Antony's will, in which the east was bequeathed to Cleopatra. In 31 B.C. he blocked the huge armada which Antony and Cleopatra were bringing against Italy at Actium, across the Adriatic.

[1]That was a day of great decision, on which Octavian and Antony brought their fleets out to fight, one for the salvation and the other for the ruin of the world. . . . The conflict began; one side had everything, a leader, rowers, soldiers; the other only soldiers. Cleopatra was the first to flee, and Antony chose to be companion of the fleeing queen rather than of his fighting soldiers. The general who should have castigated deserters turned deserter of his own army. It persevered in the fight long after its head was gone and struggled on to the death with no hope of victory. Octavian was eager to assuage with words men he could put to the sword; he shouted and pointed that Antony had fled, and asked them for whom and with whom they were fighting. When they had fought long for their truant general they reluctantly surrendered their arms and acknowledged defeat. Before they could bring themselves to beg quarter Caesar promised them life and forgiveness. Clearly, the soldiers had played the part of a good general,

[1]Velleius Paterculus, 2.85.

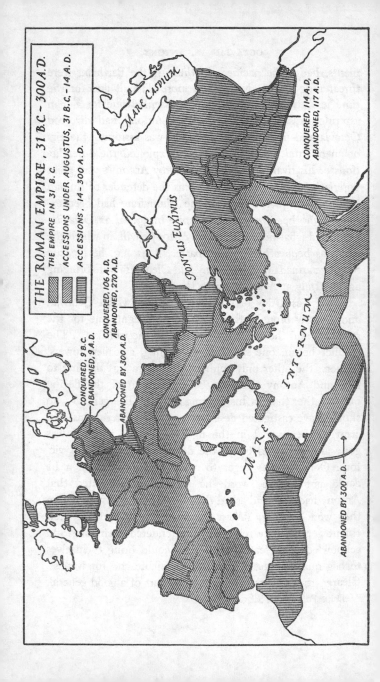

THE ROMAN EMPIRE, 31 B.C. – 300 A.D.

THE EMPIRE IN 31 B.C.
ACCESSIONS UNDER AUGUSTUS, 31 B.C. – 14 A.D.
ACCESSIONS, 14 – 300 A.D.

MARE CASPIUM

CONQUERED, 114 A.D.
ABANDONED, 117 A.D.

PONTUS EUXINUS

CONQUERED, 106 A.D.
ABANDONED, 270 A.D.

CONQUERED, 9 B.C.
ABANDONED, 9 A.D.

ABANDONED BY 300 A.D.

MARE INTERNUM

ABANDONED BY 300 A.D. →

the general of a cowardly soldier. One might well wonder whether a man who followed Cleopatra's decision in running away would have followed his own or her decision in using a victory. The army posted on land behaved similarly when Canidius fled headlong after Antony. Who could venture, in so brief a work as this, to express the benefits that day conferred upon the world or the improvement in the fortunes of the state? . . .

The following year Octavian followed the queen and Antony to Alexandria and there put the last touch to the civil wars. Antony manfully slew himself, so that his death redeemed him from charges of unmanliness. And Cleopatra gave up the ghost without womanish fears; an asp was smuggled past the baffled guards and stung her with its venom. It was appropriate to Octavian's fortune and clemency that none of those who had borne arms against him were killed by his hand or order. . . .

The throngs that went forth to meet Octavian on his return to Italy, the affection with which people of all classes, ages, and positions welcomed him, the magnificence of his triumphs and the lavishness of his spectacles—cannot be described adequately. Nothing man can desire of the gods, nothing the gods can vouchsafe man, nothing that wish can conceive or felicity bring to pass, did Augustus fail to bestow, at his return to the city, on the commonwealth, the Roman people, and the world. After twenty years civil wars were ended, foreign wars buried, peace recalled, the frenzy of arms everywhere lulled to sleep. Their force was restored to the laws, authority to the courts, dignity to the senate. The power of the magistrates was confined to its original limits, except only that two praetors were added to the eight existing. The traditional and revered form of the republic was restored.

Actium was a crowning mercy. Popular relief at the end

of the war is expressed in an ode of Horace, which, significantly, is discreetly silent about Antony and gloats only over Cleopatra:

> [1]Drink we now, and dancing round,
>   Press with footsteps free the ground;
>   Pour we now the rosy wine,
>   And, in honour of the gods,
>   Comrades, in their own abodes
> Pile we the banquet on each holy shrine.
>
>   Sin it were ere now to pour
>   Forth the cellar's generous store;
>   While the haughty queen of Nile,
>   With her base and scurvy crew,
>   Dared unbridled to pursue
> Wild hopes, and drunk with Fortune's favoring smile,
>
>   Madly dreamed the Capitol
>   Soon should totter to its fall,
>   And the Empire's self should die;
>   But her spirit quailed awhile,
>   When of all the ships of Nile
> From Rome's avenging fires scarce one could fly. . . .

[1]Horace, Odes, 1.37 (trans. Earl of Derby).

4. The Early Empire

In 27 B.C. Octavian Caesar rendered an account of his actions to the senate, surrendered his extraordinary powers, and restored the state to the senate and Roman people. His motive, as Dio Cassius (53.2) writes, was "that he might have his sovereignty voluntarily confirmed by the people, so as to avoid the appearance of having forced them against their will."

[1]During the reading of his speech and afterwards people shouted appeals for monarchical rule and reinforced them with every kind of argument until they "forced" him to assume autocratic power. Immediately he procured a vote granting his bodyguard twice the pay of other soldiers, to give him an alert watch. This shows that he really desired to set up monarchy. When he had his supremacy ratified in this way by senate and people he still wished to appear democratic. He accepted the care and full oversight of public business on the ground that they required his attention, but declared that he would himself not govern all the provinces, and not retain permanently those he would govern. The weaker provinces he returned to the senate, on the ground that they were peaceful and in no danger of war; but the stronger ones he retained, on the ground that they were insecure and dangerous, either because there were enemies on the frontiers or they themselves were capable of serious uprisings. Ostensibly the senate would thus enjoy the fairest part of the empire undisturbed and he him-

[1]Dio Cassius, 53.11ff.

self would have all the toil and danger, but in fact this was a pretext to keep them unarmed and incapable of war while he himself possessed arms and maintained soldiers. . . .

In reality Caesar was to have sole control of everything always because he commanded the soldiers and ruled the treasury; nominally public moneys were kept separate from his own, but in fact he had discretion over the expenditure of the former also. When his ten-year term expired he was voted another five, another five, after that ten, and again ten, and another ten for the fifth time, so that by the succession of ten-year terms he was sole ruler for life. That is why subsequent emperors, though they are not appointed for a designated period but for life tenure at once, nevertheless hold a celebration at ten-year intervals as if renewing their sovereignty; this is done even now.

Even at the beginning, when his rejection of monarchy and distribution of provinces were under discussion, Caesar had received many distinctions. He was voted the right to place laurels before the royal residence and to hang the oak crown [the Roman equivalent of the Victoria Cross] above them as a symbol that he was always victor over his enemies and savior of his fellow citizens. The royal residence is called Palatium not because there was ever a decision that it should be so named but because Caesar lived in the Palatine and had his headquarters there; the whole hill possessed a kind of distinction because Romulus had lived there. Hence even if the emperor resides elsewhere his house is called the Palatium. When Caesar had actually carried his arrangements out, the name Augustus was conferred upon him by the senate and people. They wished to give him some distinctive title, and various suggestions were proposed and urged. Caesar himself was eager to be called Romulus, but he sensed that this would raise a suspicion that he coveted kingship, and so he desisted and accepted instead Augustus, which signifies something superhuman; the most precious and sacred objects are called augusta. In Greek he was addressed as Sebastos, from the verb meaning "to revere."

So then the whole power of people and senate was transferred to Augustus, and thenceforward Rome was literally a monarchy; even if later two or three persons held power simultaneously the term "monarchy" is still accurate. The name "monarchy," to be sure, the Romans so detested that they did not call their emperors dictators or kings or anything similar; but since absolute authority over the state rested upon them, they could only be kings. The constitutional magistracies are still maintained, except the censorship, but they are held and administered wholly in accordance with the wishes of the ruler. But in order that their power may seem to derive from the laws rather than from their personal sovereignty, the emperors have usurped the powers which the democracy used to delegate, along with their titles, except that of dictator. They frequently become consuls, and are always called proconsuls outside the city limits. All hold the title imperator for life, whether or not they have won victories in battle, to symbolize their absolute sovereignty. "Imperator" has displaced "king" and "dictator," which have never been employed once they fell out of official usage; but their functions are secured by the title of "imperator." In their various capacities they can make levies, collect moneys, declare war, make peace, rule foreigners and citizens alike always and everywhere, even to the extent of putting equestrians and senators to death even within the city limits, and exercise all the functions in the province of the consuls and other magistrates of independent authority. By their exercise of the censorship they scrutinize our lives and morals, make census rolls, and at their discretion include or eject individuals from the senatorial or equestrian class. Because they are consecrated as priests and can bestow priesthoods on others . . . they are sovereign over all things sacred and holy. The so-called tribunician powers . . . enable them to veto acts of any other official which they do not approve and protect them against insult: if they think they are in the slightest degree injured, even by word let alone deed, they can destroy the culprit without trial as one accursed. . . . The usages of these several offices they took over from the democracy along with their names, to give the impression that their authority was legitimate. Furthermore they have acquired another prerogative, which none of the ancient Romans possessed outright, which would enable them to exercise the powers mentioned and any others in addition: they are released from the laws . . . and bound by no written code.

Thus the government was reorganized to improve it and assure its security, for it was no doubt impossible for a democracy to provide security. And yet events after the reorganization cannot be recorded in the same way as events before it. Formerly everything was reported to senate and people, even from remote places; everyone knew and many recorded what took place, and therefore, however much fear or favor, friendship or enmity, affected a report, the truth could always somehow be discovered from other reports of the same events and from public records. But from this time forward things were done secretly and kept concealed, and even what is published is distrusted because it cannot be verified. There is always a suspicion that every act and word is dictated by the wishes of those in authority and their associates.

Though some of the details in this account represent later developments it is on the whole a just presentation of the revolution effected by Augustus. Augustus himself, towards the end of his life, drew up an account of his stewardship to be engraved on bronze tablets in front of his mausoleum on the Campus Martius. Copies of this document were inscribed on the walls of the temples of Rome and Augustus in the east, on the outside in the Greek which the people read, and on the inside in Latin. The fullest copy was found at Angora (whence it is called Monumentum Ancyranum). Here are some selections:

[1]At the age of nineteen, on my own initiative and expense, I raised an army with which I restored liberty to the state when it was oppressed by a domineering faction. . . . The people elected me consul and triumvir for regulating the state. The men who murdered my father I drove into exile and punished them by legal action; afterwards, when they took the offensive against the state, I defeated them twice. I waged wars, civil and foreign, on land and sea, throughout the world. All citizens who asked pardon I spared in my victory; foreign nations who could safely be forgiven I preferred to save than destroy. . . . For successes by land or sea achieved by myself or under my auspices the senate decreed thanksgiving to the gods 55 times; the days celebrated by these thanksgivings amounted to 890. . . . During a severe shortage I did not refuse to supervise the grain supply, and so administered the office that in a few days and at my own expense I freed the whole people from fear and actual danger. . . . I refused to accept authority [as overseer of morals] contrary to ancestral usage, but administered the things the senate wished me to. . . . As I write this I have been chief of the senate forty years. I have been pontifex maximus, augur, [and member of various priestly colleges.] . . . I increased the number of patricians, upon instruction of people and senate. Three times I revised the senate roll. [In 28 B.C. the census included

[1]Res Gestae Divi Augusti, 1ff.

93

4,063,000 citizens, in 8 B.C. 4,223,000, in A.D. 14 4,937,000.]
By new laws I restored ancient patterns falling into disuse
[these concerned sumptuary laws, laws, governing sexual
morality, encouraging marriage and the rearing of children,
and the like], and I myself established precedents for posterity to imitate. By decree of the senate, consuls and priests
undertook vows for my health every four years. . . . Moreover, all the citizens with one accord, individuals and
municipalities, offered sacrifices for my health at all *pul-
vinaria*. . . . It was legally enacted that I should be sacrosanct in perpetuity and that I should hold the tribunician
power for life. . . . My sons, the Caesars Gaius and Lucius,
whom fortune snatched from me in their youth, the senate
and people designated as consuls, each in his fifteenth year,
to do me honor, with the intention that they should assume
the office after five years. . . .

There follow enumerations of Augustus' largesse to plebe-
ians, municipalities, and the public treasury, of his building
operations, of the spectacles he provided for public enter-
tainment, of his military campaigns and successes, of his
relations with peoples outside the empire. He then con-
cludes:

In my sixth and seventh consulships [28–27 B.C.] when
I had quenched the civil wars and had obtained complete
control of affairs by universal consent, I transferred the
commonwealth from my own dominion to the authority of
the senate and the Roman people. For this favor on my part
I received by decree of the senate the title Augustus: the
doorposts of my house were officially decked with laurels, a
civic crown was fixed above my door, and in the Curia Julia
was placed a golden shield whose inscription testified that it
was given me by the senate and Roman people in recognition of my valor, clemency, justice, and piety. After that
time I took precedence over all others in prestige, but of

power I held no more than those who were my colleagues in any magistracy. While I was serving my thirteenth consulship, [2 B.C.] the senate and equestrian order and whole Roman people gave me the title Father of His Country, and decreed that it should be inscribed on the vestibule of my house, in the senate, and in the Forum Augustum under the chariot erected to my honor there by decree of the senate. When I wrote this I was in my seventy-sixth year [A.D. 13; Augustus died A.D. 14].

The use made of this document indicates a reasoned plan to associate the genius of the emperor with that of Rome itself and to give the same religious sanction to both. In each of 265 precincts of Rome there was a shrine to Rome and Augustus. Poets like Vergil and Horace were genuinely converted to the new order, and under the patronage of Maecenas, who was a sort of minister of public information, celebrated the new patriotism and glorified the new regime as the instrument of providence to bring the blessings of the Roman peace to the world. The prime object of the Aeneid was to show that Rome's mission was divinely ordained from the beginning of time and that Augustus was divinely appointed to lead the Romans to its fulfillment. The heart of the Aeneid is the solemn passage where Anchises, in the Elysian Fields, declares Rome's destiny:

[1]There is the man, there is the leader so often promised, Augustus Caesar of divine lineage; he shall once again establish a golden age in the fields Saturn once ruled. He shall extend our bounds beyond the Garamantes and the Indians. . . . Others will breathe life into bronze with more delicate art—I know it well—will carve marble into the visage of life, will plead cases better, will chart the orbits of the stars and foretell their risings. But your task, Roman, is this: to rule the peoples. This is your special genius: to enforce the

[1]Vergil, *Aeneid*, 6.791ff.

habits of peace, to spare the conquered, to subdue the proud.

In literature in particular the Augustan is the Golden Age; Vergil and Livy, Horace and Ovid, were never surpassed in their kind. Not only the production but the study of Latin literature received imperial encouragement; before the end of the century the Roman emperor would endow professorships of rhetoric. Quintilian, the first and most distinguished of these professors, wrote a competent treatise on the education of the orator, in the course of which he suggests reading programs. His list of standard authors and his judgments on their merits constitute a kind of canon, which maintained its validity throughout the empire and was received as authoritative by the Renaissance. The presence of this canon is as perceptible in Roman history as is the presence of the Old Testament in the history of New England, and hence it deserves to be recorded as a historical document.

[1][Having indicated what Greek authors are profitable for the intending orator] I shall now treat of Roman authors. As Homer provided an auspicious opening for my Greek list so Vergil does for the Latin, for he is without doubt second only to Homer in all epic, Greek or Latin. I shall apply the words I heard in my youth from Domitius Afer. When I asked him what poet he would place next to Homer he replied, "Vergil is second, but much nearer first than third." We must indeed yield to Homer's superhuman and celestial stature, but Vergil shows greater application and precision, perhaps because his was the harder task. For Homer's unrivaled flights we may find Vergil's uniform excellence an adequate balance. All the others follow at a great interval. Macer and Lucretius should be read . . . but

[1]Quintilian, 10.1.85ff.

the former is undistinguished and the latter difficult. Varro of Atax achieved his reputation through translations of others' work: he is not negligible, but neither can he enrich one's diction. Ennius we should revere as we do venerable groves whose great gnarled trunks inspire religious awe rather than aesthetic satisfaction. More nearly contemporary poets are more useful for our objective. Ovid is frivolous even in epic and too much enamored of his own talent, but some of his work is admirable. . . . In elegy we can challenge the Greeks. To me Tibullus seems the most concise and polished, but some prefer Propertius. Ovid is more wanton than either, and Gallus more austere. Satire is wholly Roman. Lucilius is so admired that his devotees make bold to rank him not only above other satirists but above all other poets. In my judgment they are as far astray as is Horace, who speaks of Lucilius' "muddy flow" and says he needs pruning. Lucilius is remarkable for being outspoken as well as learned, and this gives his satire both edge and wit. Horace is terser and more precise and, unless affection misleads me, deserves first place. Persius' one book has earned him his high reputation. . . . In lyric Horace is virtually the only poet worth reading. On occasion he can soar, and he is full of pleasantry and charm, uses a large variety of figures, and is bold and apt in his choice of words. Of our classics in tragedy Accius and Pacuvius are outstanding for serious moral reflections, weighty language, and dignified personages. Their works lack the finishing touches of the expert hand, however, though this may be the fault of their age rather than of themselves. . . . Comedy is where we stumble. Though Varro quotes Stilo's declaration that if the Muses chose to speak Latin they would use the language of Plautus, though the ancients extolled Caecilius, and though Terence's plays (which are the most elegant of their kind and would be even finer if they kept to iambic trimeters) are attributed to Scipio Africanus, we scarcely attain a faint shadow of the charm of Greek comedy. Our language is not capable of it, and even among the Greek dialects only the Attic proved to be. . . . But our historians need not yield to the Greeks. I should not hesitate to confront Thucydides with Sallust, and Herodotus would be content to accept Livy as his peer. His narrative is marvelously agreeable and lucid, his speeches indescribably eloquent. The words are suited to the circumstances and personages; as to the emotions, particularly the more agreeable ones, I may say in a word that no historian has surpassed Livy in treating of them. Thus by merits of a different kind Livy has achieved the high reputation Sallust won by his superb rapidity. . . . But it is our orators above all who put Roman achievement on a par with the Greek. Cicero I would match against any of them with perfect assurance. I am aware that this will raise angry protest, especially since it is not my plan to introduce a comparison with Demosthenes at this point. To do so is beside the point, for I hold that Demosthenes should be our principal text and even be learned by heart. In their qualities—judgment, arrangement, distribution, preparation, demonstration—I find similarity between Demosthenes and Cicero. In style there is a difference. Demosthenes is concentrated, Cicero diffuse; Demosthenes' periods are short, Cicero's ample; Demosthenes' weapon is the rapier, Cicero's often the bludgeon; from the one nothing can be subtracted, to the other nothing can be added; one is more studied, the other more natural. . . . But it must be granted that Demosthenes has priority, and so was largely responsible for Cicero's attainments. Cicero devoted himself wholly to imitating the Greeks, and I think he has reproduced the energy of Demosthenes combined with the spaciousness of Plato and the sweetness of Isocrates.

But though the new order encouraged literature it fettered it too, as it constricted all forms of individual expression. A patriotic Roman writing more than half a century after Augustus could see the darker side of the brilliant pax Romana.

[1]When the slaughter of Brutus and Cassius left the state without an army, when Sextus Pompey was crushed in Sicily, and when the relegation of Lepidus and the death of Antony had left Augustus sole leader of the Caesarian party, he dropped the title of triumvir and advertised that he was consul and content with tribunician authority for protecting the people. And when he had enticed the soldiers with largesse, the people with grain, and everyone with the sweets of repose, he rose by degrees and concentrated in himself the functions of senate, magistrates, and laws. None opposed, for the most spirited had fallen in battle or proscription, and the remaining nobles waxed in wealth and honor according as they were complaisant to slavery; revolution had exalted them, and they preferred the safe present to the perilous past. Nor did the provinces dislike the innovation; rivalries of potentates and rapacity of governors had rendered the rule of senate and people suspect, and the laws, subverted by violence, intrigue, and bribery, were powerless to protect. . . .

The state was thus revolutionized; not a shred of the old morality was left. With equality gone, all looked to the emperor's bidding, and there was no apprehension, as long as Augustus was in his prime and could maintain himself, his house, the peace. But with his advancing age and bodily exhaustion the end drew near and with it new expectations. A few spoke of the blessings of freedom—in vain; more feared war, and some desired it.

[1]Tacitus, *Annals*, 1.2.

Augustus (and all his successors) was not only commander-in-chief of the armies and in direct charge of the border provinces but also in control of foreign policy. He reduced the armies swollen by the civil wars and made them more professional, and his military operations, which were not more ambitious than the resources of the state could easily bear, were directed towards achieving easily defensible frontiers and consolidating the power of the state. The subjugation of Spain was completed, the restive Alpine peoples pacified, Caesar's Gallic conquests more completely organized, the territory between the Rhine and the Elbe conquered, the peoples of the middle and lower Danube subjugated, and the Roman boundary carried to the Drave. The simultaneous conquests in Germany and Pannonia are the best proof of Augustus' efficient organization. The one frightening disaster was the uprising of the German nationalist leader Arminius in A.D. 9 and the massacre of a complete Roman army under Varus in the Teutoberg Forest.

[1]Varus' birth was distinguished rather than noble. His nature was mild, his manners quiet, he was inclined to passivity in mind as in body, and more accustomed to peacetime service than to active campaigning. That he did not despise money he showed in Syria; the province was rich and himself poor when he came to govern it, and the roles were reversed when he left. When he took command of the armies in Germany his notion was that the Germans were human only in respect to voice and limbs and that these people whom swords could not cow could be gentled by law. With such a program he marched into the heart of Germany as if among men enjoying the repose of peace, and he wasted the campaign season by conducting legal business in due form from a judge's tribunal. But, as only

[1]Velleius Paterculus, 2.117–119.

those who have had experience of them realize, the Germans are as crafty as they are savage; lying is native to them. They trumped up a series of fictitious lawsuits, now inciting one another to altercations and now thanking the Romans for just decisions, for mollifying their barbarism by a novel method which they had not known, and for settling by law disputes which they used to settle by weapons. To such a degree of negligence did they reduce Varus that he believed that he was a judge holding court in the Forum, not a general commanding an army in the heart of Germany.

Then there appeared a young man, noble, brave, alert, clever beyond the ordinary barbarian, whose name was Arminius. He was son of Sigimer, a prince of that nation, and his expression and glance showed the fire of his spirit. He had been associated with us in previous campaigns, and had attained Roman citizenship and equestrian rank. Arminius exploited the general's negligence for treachery, rightly perceiving that a man who fears nothing is easiest to overwhelm and that a sense of security is the commonest prelude to disaster. At first he admitted a few, then more, to share in his designs; he showed them and convinced them that the Romans could be crushed. Theory he followed with practice, and he fixed a day for his plot. Varus was informed of the matter by Segestes, a compatriot of Arminius who was distinguished and loyal and who demanded that the conspirators be thrown into chains. . . . But Varus refused to believe and declared that he judged the German's good will by the scale of his own deserts. After this first warning no time was left for a second. . . . By the negligence of its general, the perfidy of the enemy, and the unkindness of fortune the bravest of all Roman armies, outstanding in energy and experience, was surrounded and denied the opportunity it desired to fight or extricate itself on other than uneven terms; indeed some were severely punished for using Roman weapons and Roman courage. The men were hemmed in by forests and marshes and ambuscades and massacred by an enemy they were in the habit of slaughtering like cattle and of giving or denying quarter according as they were moved by anger or pity. The general had more heart for dying than for fighting; he followed the example of his father and grandfather and ran himself through.

The anomaly of an autocrat who pretended to be a republican magistrate entailed serious awkwardness in determining the succession. Augustus sought to meet the problem by conferring upon the person of his choice such distinctions—a proconsular imperium and tribunician power —as would make the succession automatic. He chose first his nephew Marcellus, who died in 23 B.C., then his general and son-in-law Agrippa, who died in 12 B.C., then his third wife Livia's sons, Lucius and Gaius, who died in A.D. 2 and A.D. 1. His only daughter Julia was exiled for gross immorality, the more heinous in view of her father's efforts to raise the moral tone of society; her daughter, also called Julia, later met a like fate for a like offense. Augustus' last and reluctant choice was his eldest stepson Tiberius, who was fifty-six at Augustus' death in A.D. 14 and ruled to A.D. 37.

Mutinies in Illyricum and on the Rhine at the inception of Tiberius' reign were quelled by his adoptive son Germanicus, but when Germanicus wished to proceed with the conquest of Germany he was recalled by Tiberius, who opposed expanding the empire. Germanicus was then sent on an expedition to Armenia (A.D. 17–19), where he died under suspicious circumstances. The only other external disturbances during Tiberius' reign were an uprising in Gaul (A.D. 21) and a longer struggle with the refractory African chieftain Tacfarinas (A.D. 17–24).

But within the imperial family the anomaly of autocracy without provision for succession was bound to generate dangerous intrigue. Germanicus' widow Agrippina plotted to secure the purple for her sons Drusus and Nero, but was forestalled by Tiberius' unscrupulous pretorian prefect Sejanus, who imprisoned her and her sons, after having poisoned Tiberius' son Drusus and become the lover of Drusus' widow Livia. It was Sejanus who enlarged the pretorian guard and concentrated it in Rome, and so gave it decisive power in future successions to the purple. In 31 Tiberius became aware of Sejanus' designs, and he and his supporters were executed. Possibly it was the incipient coup of Sejanus which sharpened the law of laesa majestas, formally confined to actual treason, and broadened it to include every show of disrespect to the emperor or his family.

[1]A man had removed the head from a statue of Augustus to substitute another. The case was tried in the senate, and since the facts were uncertain evidence was obtained by torture. When the defendant had been condemned this kind of accusation proceeded to the point where it became a capital offense to beat a slave near a statue of Augustus, to change clothes there, to carry a ring or coin bearing his image into a privy or brothel, or to express an adverse opinion upon any utterance or act of his. A man was even put to death for permitting an honor to be voted him in his own town on the same day that honors had once been voted to Augustus.

[2]In the consulship of Cornelius Cossus and Asinius Agrippa [A.D. 25], Cremutius Cordus was arraigned on a new charge, never previously recorded. He had published a history which praised Brutus and called Cassius the last of the Romans. The plaintiffs were Satrius Secundus and

[1]Suetonius, Tiberius, 18.　　　　[2]Tacitus, Annals, 4.34.

Pinarius Natta, creatures of Sejanus. This and Caesar's lowering expression as he listened were fatal, but Cremutius, knowing that he was doomed, made his speech:

"It is my words, Senators, that are condemned; of deeds I am guiltless. But my words do not touch the emperor or his mother, where the law of *majestas* applies. It is said that I praised Brutus and Cassius; many have written their histories, none has named them without respect. Livy, distinguished for style and accuracy, so praised Pompey that Augustus called him a Pompeian, but this was no hindrance to their friendship. Livy nowhere refers to Scipio, Afranius, this same Cassius and Brutus as brigands and traitors, as is the present style, but repeatedly calls them distinguished men. Asinius Pollio's writings glorify their memory, and Messala Corvinus was proud to call Cassius his general: both these writers retained their wealth and honors undiminished. Cicero's treatise raised Cato to the stars; and the dictator Caesar was content to answer in a written speech, as if he were pleading before a jury. The letters of Antony, the harangues of Brutus contain many bitter (and false) reproaches against Augustus, and the widely read poems of Bibaculus and Catullus are filled with insults to the Caesars; but the Divine Julius and the Divine Augustus tolerated their books and allowed them to survive. This may have been forbearance, or it may have been wisdom: what is disregarded grows stale, resentment implied recognition.

"Among the Greeks not only liberty but license was condoned, or if anyone did take offense he used words to punish words; I say nothing of them. But amongst ourselves it has never been blameworthy to speak freely of those whom death has exempted from hatred or favor. Are Brutus and Cassius holding the field of Philippi under arms and are my harangues rousing the populace to rebellion? Did they not die seventy years back? Do we not know them by statues which not even the conqueror destroyed and from the memoirs of historians? Posterity gives every man his due, and if I am doomed there will be those who will remember me along with Brutus and Cassius."

He stalked out of the senate and starved himself to death. The senators voted that the aediles burn his books. But copies were concealed and then published. It is ludicrous folly to suppose that despotism in the present can extinguish a remembrance for posterity.

Perhaps the most significant index of the shift in the character of Rome is that the historians of the empire focus their attention exclusively on the Palatine hill; the rest of the empire, including Rome itself, becomes a vague background, attended to only as it affects the ruling house and its rivals. As in the ancient Near East, history tends to become a dynastic chronicle; this is plain in Suetonius, plainer in his successors, the writers of the so-called Augustan history, and it is sensed by Tacitus himself, when he apologizes for the dreary succession of prosecutions and suicides with which he must conclude his account of the reign of Tiberius:

[1]I am quite aware that what I have related and have yet to relate seems too trifling to record. But one must not compare my chronicle with what the historians of ancient Rome have written. They told of great wars, the storming of cities and subjugation of kings, or, when they turned to internal history, rivalry of consulate and tribunate, agrarian legislation, the struggle between plebs and optimates, and all with free scope. My task is confined and lowly: a lifeless peace only slightly pricked, dismal gloom in the city, and a prince indifferent to carrying the empire forward.

Actually Tiberius' administration, though not spectacu-

[1]Tacitus, Annals, 4.32.

lar, was efficient and economical. In A.D. 26 he retired to
Capri, where he spent the remainder of his reign in morose
addiction to sexual vices—or so the historians partial to the
aristocracy say. In their tradition his career is summarized
as follows:

[1]Tiberius distinguished his career by great indolence, excessive cruelty, unprincipled avarice, and abandoned licentiousness. He died in Campania in the twenty-third year of
his reign and the eighty-third of his age, to the great joy of
all men.

If the tradition denigrated Tiberius, his grandnephew
and successor Gaius Caligula (A.D. 37–41) could not be
painted blacker than he was. Suetonius' Life of him (the
relevant sections of Tacitus are lost) is one long catalogue
of sadistic enormities. He was undoubtedly deranged, and
if there was method in his madness it was a determination
to throw off Roman tradition and openly flaunt the pomp
as well as the absolution of oriental kingship. He was the
first emperor to demand deification in his lifetime, and this
aroused the resistance of the Jews in particular. He ordered
Petronius, his legate of Syria, to erect his statue in the
temple at Jerusalem, but Petronius prudently temporized
until the emperor died. In Alexandria the order caused riots,
and Philo headed a delegation to intercede with the emperor. Caligula was murdered by officers of the pretorian
guard; the senate proclaimed them "restorers of liberty"
and debated reinstituting the republic.

But it was to the interest of the pretorians to have an
emperor, and so they dragged from his hiding place and
saluted as emperor Claudius (A.D. 41–54), the surviving
brother of Germanicus, then fifty-one years old, and the
senate could only acquiesce. Claudius was ungainly, para-

[1]Eutropius, 7.11.

lytic, and in his youth his family had been embarrassed to let him be seen in public. He had the reputation of being a learned fool, but it may be that he consciously fostered this reputation as a protective coloring. Seneca's savage satire on his deification (called "The Pumpkinification of Claudius") attacks three idiosyncrasies in particular: his devotion to historical study, his concern for law courts, his opening the senate to Gauls; the satire is rather a reflection on its author. But to check on the calumnies of Seneca, and of Tacitus and Suetonius, we have a large number of his enactments in inscriptions and on papyri, whose style proves their words are his own and not a secretary's, which show profound understanding for the problems of the empire and great capacity for administering it. A letter of his to the turbulent Alexandrians, dated A.D. 41 and extant on papyrus, shows his understanding and his firmness.

[1]"Tiberius Claudius Caesar Augustus Germanicus Imperator, Pontifex Maximus, of tribunician power, consul designate, to the city of Alexandria, greeting. [I grant the request, proffered by your embassy, to honor me with statues and the like] but I deprecate appointing a high priest and building temples to me, for I do not wish to trouble my fellow men and I hold that in every age temples and similar distinctions have been granted only to gods. Concerning your petitions, these are my decisions: For all who have become ephebes [and so qualified to receive citizenship] up to my principate, Alexandrian citizenship with all its rights and privileges is confirmed, except for any of slave birth who contrived to become ephebes. I desire further to confirm favors granted to you by former princes and kings and prefects, as the Divine Augustus confirmed them. I desire that the overseers of the temple of the Divine Augustus in Alexandria be chosen by lot as those of the temple of the

[1]P. London, 1912; Edgar and Hunt, L.C.L., 212.

said Augustus in Canopus are chosen by lot. Your proposal that the civic magistracies be made triennial I approve; they will administer their offices with moderation for fear of having to render an accounting for bad rule on the expiry of their term. Concerning the senate, I cannot say what the usage was under your ancient kings, but you know well that there was none under former Augusti. This is then a novel proposal, and it is not clear whether it is expedient for the city and for my government; I have therefore written to Aemilius Rectus to examine the matter and inform me whether it is proper for a senate to be constituted, and if so, the proper mode for doing so.

"Which party was responsible for the rioting and street fighting (or rather the war, if truth be told) with the Jews I have not wished to make a strict inquiry, though your ambassadors, and especially Dionysius son of Theon, argued vehemently against their opponents; but I have stored up unappeasable anger against whichever party renews the turbulence. I tell you plainly that unless you stop this ominous passion against one another I shall be compelled to show how a benevolent prince can be turned to righteous anger. Again I adjure you, therefore: the Alexandrians must conduct themselves gently and benevolently towards the Jews who have for many years lived in the same city and not dishonor their religious observances but permit them the usages they practiced in the time of the Divine Augustus, which I too, when I had heard both sides, confirmed; and the Jews I explicitly forbid to agitate for more than they formerly had, and, in future, to send separate embassies as if they lived in a separate city. Such action is unprecedented. Nor must they force their way into games reserved for full citizens, for they enjoy as their own the abundance of advantages of a city not their own. Nor must they bring in or introduce Jews sailing down from Syria or Egypt; this

would force serious suspicions upon me. Otherwise I shall
take all measures against them as awakening a disease affect-
ing all the world. If both parties desist from these practices
and are willing to live in mutual gentleness and benevolence, I too will take thought for the city, as I and my
ancestors have long done. I testify that my friend Barbillus
has always shown concern for you in my presence and that
he has been your zealous advocate in the present case; I
testify also for my friend Tiberius Claudius Archibius. Fare-
well."

The empire was not only well administered under Claudius, it was also significantly enlarged. Britain was conquered and made into a province, as were also Thrace and
the two Mauretanias.

It was doubtless to secure administrative efficiency that
Claudius first raised freedmen, such as his chief ministers
Narcissus and Pallas, to high position. Tacitus may nevertheless be right in charging that Claudius was too susceptible to their influence, as he certainly was to the influence of his wives. At his accession he was married to his
third wife, Messalina, who bore him Octavia (later married
to Nero) and Britannicus (whom Nero poisoned). Messalina's profligacies and her contempt for her husband went
so far that she reportedly went through a marriage cere-
mony with her paramour, the consul-elect Silius.

[1]It must seem incredible, I know, that people could show
such assurance in a city which knows everything and talks
about it. Yet on a day announced and before accredited witnesses the consul designate and the emperor's wife foregathered as for a legitimate marriage, heard and acknowledged
the solemn formula, offered sacrifice to the gods, reclined
with guests, exchanged kisses and embraces, and passed the
night with conjugal freedom. But I have not invented the
[1]Tacitus, *Annals*, 11.27.

story to shock; I report what I have heard and my predecessors have written.

The imperial household was in consternation, and especially those in power who dreaded revolution. Now there were no whispered conversations but open complaints: "When an actor trod the emperor's bed there was scandal but no catastrophe. But now a young, handsome, and intelligent noble, soon to be consul, is girding himself for higher expectations. The next step after such a marriage is easy to divine." The thought of Claudius' stupidity and uxoriousness, and of the many murders Messalina had suborned, doubtless heightened their alarm. On the other hand, Claudius' gullibility raised the hope that if they could overwhelm him with the enormity of the charge Messalina could be crushed before she was heard. The crucial point was that he must not hear her defense or even her confession. . . . Narcissus watched for an opportunity, and while Claudius lingered at Ostia, he induced two courtesans with whom Claudius frequently consorted to be the emperor's informers by offering large bribes and promises and showing that their power would rise if the empress were expelled.

As soon as the courtesan Calpurnia retired with Claudius she threw herself at his knees and cried out that Messalina had married Silius; at the same time she asked Cleopatra, who waited nearby for the purpose, whether she had heard the news. When Cleopatra nodded confirmation he ordered Narcissus summoned. Narcissus begged pardon for having in the past kept silent about such lovers as a Vettius or Plautius, nor, said he, would he now charge adultery, as if to recover house, slaves, and other furnishings of wealth. Let Silius keep these but let him give back the wife and destroy the marriage contract. "You are divorced," he said, "do you know it? People, senate, and soldiery saw

Silius married; if you do not act promptly the new husband possesses Rome. . . ." It is reliably reported that Claudius was so terrified that he repeatedly asked whether he was still the ruler, whether Silius was still a subject. Messalina, more dissolute than ever, was celebrating a mock vintage festival at home. Presses were trodden, must flowed, women girt with skins leapt about like bacchants at their orgies. She herself with hair loosed brandished the thyrsus, and at her side Silius, crowned with ivy and wearing the buskin, tossed his head as the lewd chorus chanted. They say that Vettius Valens climbed a high tree in sport, and when he was asked what he saw, he said "a terrible storm from Ostia." It may be he did see a cloud, or his expression may have been an unwitting presage of Claudius' arrival from Ostia.

Narcissus did prevent a confrontation, and Messalina was executed. Claudius' fourth wife was his niece Agrippina, who induced him to adopt her son Nero as guardian for his own son Britannicus. In A.D. 54 Agrippina fed Claudius poisoned mushrooms, and in the first year of his rule (A.D. 54–68) Nero poisoned Britannicus. Nero was only sixteen when he assumed the purple, and the first five years of his reign, under the tutelage of Seneca the philosopher and Burrus the pretorian prefect, were a golden age.

¹In guiding the youthful emperor these men showed a unanimity which is rare when power is shared. In their different ways, Burrus in military discipline and strict manners and Seneca in polished language and dignified courtesy, each was effective, and they supported one another in allowing the youth certain pleasures, when he chafed at stern virtue, in order to control his mercurial temper. Each had to oppose the truculence of Agrippina, who was enamored of domineering and abetted by Pallas, under whose influence

¹Tacitus, *Annals*, 13.2.

Claudius had ruined himself by an incestuous marriage and a lethal adoption.

They indulged Nero in his devotion to literature, music, horses, and the freedwoman Acte, and were responsible for good legislation and capable provincial administrators— Galba, Suetonius, Paulinus, Vespasian, and Corbulo. But Seneca retired and Burrus died, and in A.D. 59 Nero became his own master and made his indulgences his chief business. His personal appearances on the concert stage outraged conservative sentiment. At the instigation of Poppaea, wife of Otho, he murdered his mother, divorced and subsequently murdered Octavia, and married Poppaea. In A.D. 64 Rome was devastated by a fire.

[1]Whether the disaster was accidental or the wicked doing of the emperor is uncertain (authorities give both versions), but the fire was the most violent and destructive that had ever befallen the city. It began in the part of the circus adjacent to the Palatine and Caelian hills. It started in shops stacked with combustibles, was sped by the wind, and at once seized the whole length of the circus. There was no masonry of houses or walls of temples to retard it. First the blaze ran through the level areas, then rose to the hills and devastated the hollows. Its velocity outstripped preventive measures, for old Rome with its winding streets and irregular plan was vulnerable. Aggravating the evil were terrified and shrieking women, the feeble old and inexperienced young, people saving themselves or others, dragging the infirm or waiting for them, hurrying or delaying. While they looked back they were cut off in front and flank, when they reached a refuge this too caught fire, and they discovered that places they believed remote were involved in the conflagration. . . .

All this time Nero was in Antium, and did not return

[1]Tacitus, Annals, 15.38.

to Rome until the fire approached his house, which connected the palace with the gardens of Maecenas. But it could not be stopped; the palace, house, and surrounding buildings were destroyed. To relieve the homeless refugees Nero threw open the Campus Martius, the buildings of Agrippa, and his own gardens, and erected temporary shelters for the multitude. Provisions were brought in from Ostia and neighboring towns, and the price of grain was sharply reduced. But these popular measures did not counteract the rumor that while the city was in flames Nero appeared on his private stage and performed the Fall of Troy, making the ancient calamity fit the present. . . .

To allay the rumor [that he was responsible for the fire] Nero fastened the guilt and inflicted exquisite tortures upon a people hated for their wickedness, vulgarly called Christians. The name was derived from Christ, who was executed by Pontius Pilate in the reign of Tiberius. Checked for the moment, the mischievous superstition broke out again, not only in Judaea, the source of the evil, but even in Rome, into which everything infamous and abominable from all quarters flows and flourishes. First some were seized and made confession, and then upon their information a huge multitude were convicted, not so much for the crime of arson as for their hatred of the human race. Mockery was added to their deaths. They were covered with animal skins and torn to pieces by dogs, many were crucified or burned, and some were set afire at nightfall to serve for illumination. For the spectacle Nero offered his gardens, and he presented horse races in addition. In the dress of a charioteer he himself mingled with the crowd or stood up in his sulky. Hence, though the victims were guilty and deserved extreme punishment, nevertheless they aroused compassion, for it was not for the public good but for one man's savagery that they were being destroyed.

His cruelty to Christians, more than anything else, has given Nero the black name he bears in all literature. Here is a typical Christian characterization of him:

[1]Christians were to be found in Rome from the time of Claudius. But when the name of Christ spread more and more among the nations there rose against it the old envy of the serpent, and the heart of an emperor was filled with savage malice. Licentious, vain, and arrogant Nero, who abandoned himself to males and abused them in turn, the foul violator of his mother, sisters, and all his close female relatives, crowned his wickedness by becoming the first to raise persecution against true believers and oppose the worship of Christ. He had with him Simon Magus, who was steeped in evil and a master of wizardry. This man was rejected by the Lord's apostles Peter and Paul. Against them the emperor was angry because they preached Christ the Son of God and scorned to worship idols; he ordered Peter crucified and Paul slain with the sword.

Even the authors who hint (quite unjustly) that Nero was responsible for the fire have only praise for his rational replanning and rebuilding of the city. But the elegance of his own Golden House did arouse resentment.

[2]Prodigal as Nero was in other luxuries, his building was most ruinous of all. He had built a house from the Palatine to the Esquiline, which he called Passage House; when it was burned down and rebuilt he called it Golden House. Its size and elegance can be sufficiently indicated by the following details. Its vestibule was of a size to contain a colossal statue of himself 120 feet high. It was so spacious that it had a colonnade of three rows a mile long. There was a pond, more like a sea, surrounded by structures to represent cities, and there were rustic stretches with alternating plowland, vineyards, pastures, woodland, with numerous

[1]Gregory of Tours, 1.25.   [2]Suetonius, Nero, 31.

animals of all kinds, wild and domestic. In the rest of the house everything was overlaid with gold picked out with gems and mother-of-pearl. The dining rooms had ceilings coffered with ivory panels which revolved to scatter flowers and tubes to sprinkle perfume. The main dining hall was round and revolved constantly, day and night, like the heavens. His baths had running sea water and sulphur water. When the building was finished and he dedicated it, he expressed his approval only by remarking that at last his house was fit for a human being.

Opposition to Nero's highhandedness raised conspiracy in Rome and rebellion in the provinces. The suppression of Piso's ambitious conspiracy in A.D. 65 involved many executions. Among those ordered to take their own lives was Nero's former tutor, the philosopher Seneca.

[1]Seneca calmly requested tablets for making a will, and on the centurion's refusal turned to his friends and declared that as he was prevented from showing gratitude for their deserts he would leave them his only, but fairest, possession, the pattern of his life; if they heeded this they would win a reputation for good character and the reward of steadfast friendship. At the same time, now by persuasion and now by rebuke, he led them from tears to fortitude, asking them repeatedly, "Where are those philosophical precepts, where the logic you have so long studied for just such an event? Has Nero's savagery been a secret? After the murders of mother and brother it is natural that he should add the death of his guardian and tutor."

When he had discoursed in this fashion to all in common he embraced his wife. He relaxed his stern fortitude to beg and implore her to temper her grief and not nourish it forever but rather to find honorable solace for the loss of her husband by contemplation of a life spent in virtue. In

[1]Tacitus, *Annals*, 15.62.

return she declared that she too had resolved to die, and asked for the executioner's stroke. Seneca would not oppose her nobility and would not leave behind for insult one he dearly loved. "I have shown you a cushioning for life," said he, "but you prefer the glory of death. I do not begrudge you the gesture. Let the constancy of our departure be alike for both of us, but greater fame in your end." Then with the same stroke they severed the arteries of their arms.

It was disorder in the provinces that finally brought Nero down. Parthian resentment at Roman aggressiveness in Armenia was allayed when, in A.D. 66, Nero crowned Tiridates, brother of the Parthian king, king of Armenia. At the same time Judaea revolted, and Vespasian was sent to subjugate it. In Britain Queen Boudicca led an uprising in which 70,000 Romans were killed and London destroyed; Boudicca was defeated by Paulinus and took poison. But when Nero compounded the disgrace of a theatrical tour in Greece (during which he left a freedman to govern Rome) with the execution of successful and popular generals like Corbulo and the Scribonii, rebellion flared up among his own officers. In A.D. 68 Vindex in Gaul, Clodius Macer in Africa, and Galba in Spain revolted, and the latter bribed the pretorians to proclaim him emperor. To forestall a worse fate Nero committed suicide, exclaiming, as he died, "What an artist is lost!"

A.D. 68–69 is the year of the four emperors. The pretorians found Galba too strict and stingy, killed him, and selected Otho, former husband of Poppaea (January 69). But the troops on the Rhine had proclaimed their general Vitellius emperor and marched with him on Rome. In April 69 Vitellius defeated Otho, who committed suicide. In the east the soldiers besieging Jerusalem proclaimed Vespasian emperor, and Vespasian cut off Rome's grain supply by seizing Egypt. Meanwhile legions from the Danube marched on Rome and killed Vitellius. Early in A.D. 70 Vespasian came to Rome where the senate duly conferred the imperial authority upon him. "The secret of empire had been discovered," remarks Tacitus, "emperors could be created elsewhere than in Rome."

5. Flavians and Antonines

Rome needed just such an honest and industrious country-
man as Vespasian (A.D. 69-79) to restore sanity and effective government after the caprices of Nero and the civil
wars. Vespasian exercised strict control over the imperial
administration, rehabilitated the bankrupt treasury by an
upward but equitable readjustment of taxes, extended and
consolidated the frontiers in Britain and Germany by building roads and erecting forts, promoted romanization of
backward areas by establishing colonies. For all his reputed
frugality he built generously but, unlike Nero, for the public benefit; the site of Nero's private lake, for example, he
used for the Colosseum, built for public enjoyment. He was
the first emperor to endow state professorships; the rhetorician Quintilian was the first holder of such a professor-
ship. In constitutional matters Vespasian introduced no significant changes. Though he had no slightest connection
with the Julio-Claudian dynasty he assumed the name of
Caesar, thus assuring its use as a title for all succeeding emperors. He also delegated a large part of his duties to his
son, thus assuring his regular succession, and provided that
Titus should be succeeded by Domitian.

Two troublesome wars were in progress when Vespasian
assumed the purple. In lower Germany a chief called Civilis
started a nationalist uprising which proved the more dangerous as the legionaries expected to control it had themselves been recruited in Germany. A similar uprising of
Gauls was centered in Trèves. Both were suppressed by

energetic action on the part of Vespasian, and in future legionaries never served in the provinces of their origin. The Jewish War had broken out in A.D. 66. Among the Jews devotion to religion involved national loyalty, with a consequent sensitivity to alien infringement, and although the upper classes, which Rome favored, were content with Roman rule, the zealots continued restive and at last fomented revolt. In A.D. 70, when Vespasian returned to Rome, he left his son Titus to besiege Jerusalem.

[1]Titus pitched his camp before the walls of Jerusalem, and displayed his legions in battle order. The Jews formed their line close under the walls, to venture forward if successful, assured of a refuge if they should be repulsed. A charge of cavalry and light armed infantry was indecisive, but soon the enemy retreated. A series of battles was fought before the gates on the days following until continual losses forced them within the walls. The Romans then turned to assault; they disdained to starve the enemy out and demanded the path of danger, some for bravery's sake, many because of ferocity and greed. Titus himself had Rome and its wealth and pleasures before his eyes; unless Jerusalem fell at once these would be deferred. But the city was steep, and it had been fortified with enormous works which would offer adequate defense even on a plain. Two towering hills were fenced in by walls, skillfully curved inward so that the flanks of assailants were exposed to attack. The edge of the cliff was sheer; where the mountain helped the towers were raised to a height of 60 feet, in the hollows they were 120 feet. They made a wonderful appearance, and from the distance looked uniform. Within, other walls surrounded the palace. The tower Antonia, so called by Herod for Mark Antony, rose to a conspicuous height.

The temple had its own walls, like a citadel, more

[1]Tacitus, Histories, 5.11.

elaborate than the others; the colonnade which surrounded the temple formed an excellent outwork. There were an ever flowing spring, underground excavations in the hills, and pools and cisterns for holding rain water. The founders had foreseen frequent wars because of differences from other peoples, and had prepared for protracted siege. After the incursion of Pompey [63 B.C.], fear and experience taught them much. The avarice of the Claudian era enabled them to purchase the privilege of building fortifications in peace as if for war. Their numbers were increased by a huge rabble from the overthrow of other cities. . . .

Prodigies had occurred, but this people so bound by superstition and hostile to religion did not hold it lawful to expiate them by sacrifice and prayer. There were appearances of armies clashing in the skies, ruddy arms, the temple illuminated by a sudden glow from the clouds. The doors of the shrine suddenly flung open, and a voice greater than human cried that the gods were departing; at the same time there was a great stir as of departure. A few interpreted these portents as fearsome, but most were convinced that the ancient priestly writings foretold that at this time the east would grow powerful and that men from Judaea would gain mastery. These were enigmatic allusions to Vespasian and Titus, but the crowd, with characteristic human ambition, interpreted this mighty destiny to apply to themselves, and no reverses could turn them to the truth. It is recorded that the besieged, of every age and both sexes amounted to 600,000. All who could bore arms, and the number of those who dared do so was larger than the normal proportion. Men and women showed equal perseverance: they feared life more than death if they should be forced to leave their country. It was against such a city and people that Titus Caesar, since the terrain forbade normal tactics, determined to employ earthworks and mantlets.

*Despite furious resistance the Romans succeeded in pene-
trating the outer fortifications and set fire to the gates of the
temple precinct. At this point Titus called his staff officers
to a council to determine whether the fire should be allowed
to destroy the temple.*

[1]Some held that the law of war should apply, for the Jews
would never cease from rebellion so long as the temple, to
which they gathered from all points, remained intact.
Others advised to save it if the Jews abandoned it and
placed no weapons upon it, but if they occupied it for fighting to burn it down; in that case it would be a fortress, no
longer a temple, and the impiety would then rest not upon
the Romans but on those who forced the act. Titus, however, declared that not even if the Jews occupied it for fighting would he take vengeance on inanimate objects instead
of men or ever burn down so grand a structure. The loss
would be the Romans', for if it survived it would be an ornament to their sovereignty. Thus heartened, Fronto, Alexander, and Cerealis supported this view. Titus then dismissed the council, directed the officers to give the other
soldiers a respite to recruit their vigor for action, and
ordered the men chosen from the cohorts to open a road
through the ruins and extinguish the fire. . . .

About the fifth hour of the following day the Jews were
overpowered and shut up in the inner court of the temple,
whereupon Titus withdrew, resolved to attack the following dawn with his whole force and gain the temple. . . .
But on the withdrawal of Titus the rebels again attacked
the Romans, after a short respite, and there was fighting
between the temple garrison and the men extinguishing the
fire; these routed the Jews and pursued them to the sanctuary. Here one of the soldiers, awaiting no order and feeling no dread at such a deed but yielding to some demonic

Josephus, *Jewish War*, 6.239.

impulse, snatched a brand from the burning timbers and, hoisted up by a comrade, hurled the fire through a little golden door which gave access to the rooms around the sanctuary on the north. As the flames shot up the Jews raised a cry worthy of the disaster and scurried to the rescue, oblivious now to any thought of preserving life or husbanding strength, for the object of their past viligance was vanishing.

Someone ran to tell Titus, who was resting from the battle in his tent. He sprang up, just as he was, and ran to the temple to stop the fire. Behind him followed all the officers, and these were accompanied by excited privates and there was the noise and confusion incident to the disorderly movement of so large a force. With voice and hand Caesar signaled the fighters to put out the fire, but they could not hear his shout for the greater din which preempted their ears, nor notice his gesture for their preoccupation with fight or fury. Neither admonition nor threat checked the onset of the rushing legionaries; their sole general was passion. Packed close about the entrance, many were trampled down by their fellows and many stumbled on the hot and smoldering ruins of the colonnades and suffered the woes of the vanquished. When they neared the sanctuary they pretended not to hear Caesar's command and urged those in front to throw the fire in. The rebel were now wholly helpless, and there was general slaughter and rout. Most were ineffectual and unarmed civilians, who were slaughtered where they were caught. Around the altar a heap of corpses was piled up, a stream of blood flowed down the steps of the sanctuary, and the bodies of those killed above rolled down.

Caesar was unable to restrain the frenzy of his soldiers and the fire got the upper hand. With his officers he stepped in and saw the holy of holies and its contents which far surpassed its reputation among foreigners and was fully equal to our own boasts. . . . One of the men who had made his way in, when Caesar sprang forward to restrain them, thrust a brand into the hinges of the gate. At once a flame shot up from the interior and Caesar and his officers withdrew; now there was no one to prevent those outside from spreading the fire. And so, against Caesar's wishes, the temple was burned down.

In A.D. 73 Titus with his father Vespasian celebrated a magnificent triumph over the Jews (of which the Arch of Titus, above the Roman Forum, is a memorial) and upon Vespasian's death in 79 he succeeded to the purple. Titus was a general favorite (he was called "the darling of the human race") and his short reign (A.D. 79–81) includes only one event of interest to posterity: this is the eruption of Vesuvius which buried Pompeii and Herculaneum. On this subject we have a letter from the Younger Pliny, whose uncle died in the catastrophe, addressed to the historian Tacitus:

[1]"My uncle was in command of the fleet at Misenum. On August 24 [A.D. 79], about one in the afternoon my mother called his attention to a cloud of unusual size and aspect. He had taken the sun, bathed, reclined for lunch, and was then studying. He asked for his shoes and climbed to a point which offered a good view of the phenomenon. At a distance it was not clear from what mountain the cloud issued; later it was found to be Vesuvius. Its shape might best be represented by a pine tree; it rose to a great height, like a trunk, and then spread into branches. . . . At one moment it was white, and then murky and spotted, as if it had carried up earth or cinders.

"My uncle's scientific interests prompted a closer view. He ordered a light boat and gave me permission to come

[1]Pliny, 6.16.

along. I replied that I preferred to study; it happened that he had given me a composition to write. As he was leaving the house he received a note from Rectina wife of Bassus who was terrified by the imminent danger, and begged that he save her villa; it lay close to the mountain, and the only escape was by boat. My uncle changed his plan: what he had started for scientific interests he performed for humanitarian reasons. He launched warships and embarked to save not only Rectina but many others, for many people lived on that agreeable coast. He hurried to the spot from which others were flying and steered directly into the danger, so intrepid that he dictated and noted down the changing phenomena. The ashes which fell upon the ships grew hotter and thicker the nearer he approached, and now there were pumice and stones blackened, scorched, and cracked by fire, and now the sea suddenly ebbed and landslips from the mountain blocked the shore. He hesitated a moment whether he should veer away, as his pilot was urging, and then said, 'Fortune favors the brave; make for Pomponianus'.' . . . Broad flames were shooting from Vesuvius in many places and their brilliant glow shone out in the night's darkness. To reassure Pomponianus' household my uncle kept repeating that these were fires and farmhouses the terrified country folk had left burning. Then he went to bed and really slept, for his breathing, which was heavy and deep because of his corpulence, was distinctly heard. But the court which led to his rooms was now so deep in a mixture of pumice and ashes that if he remained in his bedroom any longer it would be impossible to leave. He was aroused, and rejoined Pomponianus and the others who had stayed awake. They deliberated whether they should keep indoors or wander about in the open. Now the house was tottering with frequent and violent tremors and seemed to sway back and forth as if torn from its foundations. In the open there was the fall of pumice, though it was light and porous, to fear; but a comparison of the dangers made this preferable. For my uncle's part it was a balance of calculations, for the others a balance of fears. They tied pillows upon their heads with towels to protect them from the downfall.

"By now it was daylight elsewhere, but there night blacker and thicker than any other; this was relieved by numerous torches and other lights. They decided to go down to the shore and see at first hand whether they could put out to sea, but it continued wild and contrary. There my uncle lay down upon a discarded sail and twice asked for cold water and drank it. Then flames presaged by a sulphurous smell turned the others to flight but only roused him. He arose, leaning on two slaves, and then collapsed. . . . When day returned (the third from that he had last seen) his body was found without lesions, its clothing undisturbed; its posture was more like sleep than death."

[1]The disaster caused by Vesuvius was unprecedented. Titus relieved the situation, at his own expense and without troubling others, by every kind of assistance. He himself took care of the sick and comforted the bereaved. He lived forty-one years and died [A.D. 81] of a fever at the same Sabine farm where his father died. The grief his death brought to city and provinces is indescribable. They called him "darling of the human race," and wept for him as if the world had been orphaned of its permanent guardian.

Domitian, son of Vespasian and the freedwoman Domitilla and brother of Titus, ruled fifteen years [A.D. 81–96]. At first he made a show of clemency and was energetic in domestic and military affairs. He vanquished the Chatti and the Germans, was very just in judicial matters, and constructed or completed many buildings in Rome. He rebuilt

[1]Aurelius Victor, 10.

the libraries which had been burned down, seeking models the world over, especially from Alexandria. He was so skillful an archer that his arrows would fly between the extended fingers of a man standing at a distance. But later he turned despotic, began to execute good men, and like Caligula demanded to be addressed as Lord and God. He amused his leisure, when he was alone, by hunting swarms of flies. Hence, when someone inquired whether anyone was in the palace, he was told, "Not even a fly." He was furiously lascivious, and called his foul practices by the Greek name "bed-wrestling exercise." Antonius, governor of Upper Germany, was so incensed by Domitian's savagery and scurrilous language (he had called him "harlot") that he rebelled. When Antonius had been defeated in battle by Norbanus Lappius, Domitian raged with bestial savagery against the whole human race, even his own kin. Fear of this cruelty and their own guilty conscience brought a number of persons to conspire against him. The instigators were his chamberlain Parthenius and Stephen, and next Clodian, who suspected punishment for diverting funds; the tyrant's wife Domitia was also made an accomplice because she dreaded torture because of an affair with the actor Paris. They struck Domitian down with many wounds, when he was forty-five years old. The senate ordered him a gladiator's funeral and erased his name from public monuments. Up to this time emperors had been of Roman or Italian birth; henceforward they were foreigners. It was by the merits of outsiders, then, that Rome flourished. Could anyone be more prudent or moderate than Nerva, more divine than Trajan, more excellent than Hadrian?

[1]Domitian fancied that the voice of the Roman people, the liberty of the senate, the conscience of the human race were obliterated; he banished teachers of philosophy and

[1]Tacitus, *Agricola*, 2.

exiled every noble pursuit, so that nothing honorable might anywhere be encountered. We did provide a wholesale example of submission; as a former age saw the extreme of liberty, so we witnessed the extreme of servitude, when investigations abolished free communications. We should have lost our memories as well as our voices if it were as easy to forget as to keep silent. Now at last our spirit has returned. At the very beginning of our most felicitous era Nerva combined things once irreconcilable, sovereignty and freedom, and Trajan is daily increasing our age's blessings. Public safety has not only our hope and prayer but the confidence of vigorous fulfillment. Yet in the nature of human frailty remedies are slower than diseases; just as our bodies grow slowly, but perish in an instant, so it is easier to crush than to revive genius and its pursuits. Inertia itself becomes attractive, and we end by loving the sloth we hated. During those fifteen years, a large segment of a man's life, many died by fortune's lot but the ablest by the savagery of the emperor; only few of us have survived not only the departed but ourselves. Out of the heart of our lives there have been cut away the many years which brought youth to old age and old age to extinction in dumb silence.

Emperors with autocratic tendencies regularly suspected that the "philosophers" might nurture subversion; Domitian showed his character by reviving ancient measures for their suppression.

[1]In the consulship of C. Fannius Strabo and M. Valerius Messala [161 B.C.] the senate passed a decree on Latin philosophers and rhetoricians: "M. Pomponius, praetor, put the question. The matter of philosophers and rhetoricians having been introduced, the senators decreed that M. Pomponius, praetor, should take measures appropriate to the welfare of the state and his own position to ensure that

[1]Aulus Gellius, 16.

they should not remain at Rome." Some years after this senatorial decree the censors Cn. Domitius Ahenobarbus and L. Licinius Crassus [92 B.C.] promulgated an edict to suppress Latin rhetoricians: "It has come to our attention that certain men have set up a new kind of instruction and are receiving our youth as students, that they have assumed the title of Latin rhetoricians, and that young men waste whole days in idleness in their schools. Our ancestors have established what the young should learn and what schools they should attend. These new teachers, contrary to the traditional norms of our ancestors, are not approved and not desirable. We therefore feel bound to declare, to those who conduct such schools and those who attend them, that they do not meet with our approval." But not only in the crude ages when people had not been refined by the cultural influences of Greek education were philosophers ejected from Rome: even in the reign of Domitian the senate decreed their expulsion from the city and Italy and forbade them to return. It was because of that decree that the philosopher Epictetus removed from Rome to Nicopolis.

The death of Domitian afforded the senate an opportunity to name the emperor; their choice fell upon Nerva (A.D. 96–98), who was seventy years old at his accession. Nerva's reputation was in jurisprudence, and he showed his anti-autocratic leanings by exempting senators from imperial inquisition and thus giving the senate a measure of autonomy, and by adopting and so designating as his successor the efficient but relatively unknown Trajan rather than one of his own relatives. Trajan (A.D. 98–117) was of Spanish birth and a "new man," and proved an admirable emperor. He confirmed the privileges of the senate, reduced the power of the pretorians, extended social benefits, and built the most magnificent of the Roman fora, with the hundred-foot column celebrating his victories over the Dacians at its center. His conquest of Dacia (A.D. 101–106), which he made into a province, provided necessary protection for the Danubian frontier. He strengthened the Roman occupation of Numidia by founding the cities of Thamugadi and Lambaesis. In about 112 Chosroes of Parthia drove Rome's vassal from Armenia and made his own son king. Trajan reduced not only Armenia (which was incorporated with Cappadocia) but Mesopotamia also. But Chosroes was able to recover his capital Ctesiphon, and Trajan was recalled from his eastern campaigns by disturbances in Africa, Britain, and along the Danube. He died en route to Rome in A.D. 117.

Trajan's conscientiousness and efficiency as an administrator is illustrated by correspondence with the Younger Pliny, who was governor of Bithynia (about A.D. 110). Especially interesting is the exchange on the subject of the Christians. Here is Pliny's inquiry:

[1]"It is my rule, sire, to refer questions upon which I am in doubt to you: who could better guide my uncertainty or inform my ignorance? I have never been present at trials of Christians, and therefore do not know the method and limits to be observed in investigating or punishing them. I have been in no little doubt whether age is to be considered or the very young treated like the adult, whether recantation secures pardon or it is of no avail to desist being a Christian if a man has ever been one, whether the name of Christian itself even when no crime is involved or the crimes associated with the name is the punishable offense.

"In the meanwhile I have observed the following procedure in the cases of alleged Christians. I asked whether they were Christians, and if they confessed it I repeated the question a second and third time, with a threat of capital

[1]Pliny, 10.96.

129

punishment. If they persisted I ordered them executed, for whatever their profession might be there could be no doubt that obdurate contumacy should be punished. Some who possessed the privileges of Roman citizenship were touched by the same madness; these I remanded to Rome for trial.

"Because the investigation was in hand it was natural that charges should proliferate, and a variety of matters came up. An anonymous placard containing many names was posted. Those who denied they were or had been Christians, who repeated after me an invocation to the gods and offered incense and wine to your image (which I had ordered brought in with the images of the deities for the purpose), and who, moreover, cursed Christ—it is said that no real Christian can be forced to do these things—I thought it right to dismiss. Others named in the placard said they were Christians but soon denied it: they had been Christians, they said, but had ceased being so, some three years before, some many years, and a few as much as twenty-five years. They all venerated your statue and the images of the gods and cursed Christ.

"They asserted that the sum of their fault or error was that they were accustomed to assemble before dawn on a fixed day, pronounce a formula to Christ as to a god, and bind themselves by oath, not for criminal purposes but never to commit theft, brigandage, adultery, prevarication, and never to refuse a deposit on demand. When they had done this it was their custom to separate and then reassemble to take food, but of an ordinary and harmless kind. Even this they ceased to do after the publication of an edict in which, according to your mandates, I forbade secret societies. For this reason I thought it essential to determine the truth of the matter, even by torture, from two female servants who were called deaconesses; but I discovered nothing more than a depraved and excessive superstition.

"I have therefore adjourned the proceedings and have resorted to consulting you. The matter seemed sufficiently important to refer to you, especially in view of the large numbers involved. People of every age and rank and of both sexes are and will continue to be gravely imperiled. The contagion of that superstition has infected not only cities but villages and hamlets; but it seems possible to check and correct it. It is clear, at least, that the temples which had been deserted are again frequented, and the sacred festivals long intermitted are revived. Sacrificial victims for which purchasers have been rare are again in demand. This makes it easy to conjecture what a host of people can be reclaimed if opportunity for recantation is offered."

And this is Trajan's reply:

[1]"You have followed a correct procedure, my dear Pliny, in sifting the cases of those who were reported to you as Christians. No universal rule of fixed form can be set up. No search is to be made for these people; if they are reported and proven guilty they must be punished, with this proviso, however: if a man denies that he is a Christian and makes it plain that he is not, that is, by worshiping our gods, then however suspect he may have been in the past his recantation shall secure him pardon. Anonymous accusations must not constitute an indictment. That is a wicked procedure, and not in keeping with the spirit of our age."

Later antiquity rated Trajan as the next great emperor after Augustus, partly because his conquests were in an area which particularly concerned them, and partly because of the visible evidences of his achievements.

[2]When [on his visit to Rome in A.D. 357] the emperor Constantius reached the Forum of Trajan, a structure unique under heaven, I believe, and admirable even in the

[1]Pliny, 10.97.   [2]Ammianus Marcellinus, 16.10.15.

judgment of the gods, he stood transfixed with astonishment as he observed the colossal complex of buildings, an indescribable phenomenon never again to be striven for by mortal man. He was disabused of any hope of attempting anything of the kind, and said that he would and could copy only Trajan's horse, which is situated in the middle of the main court, carrying Trajan himself. The Persian prince Ormisda, who was standing with him, remarked with his native wit, "First, Emperor, order a like stable to be built, if you can. The horse you propose to fashion should have as free a range as this one we see."

On his deathbed Trajan adopted his kinsman, ward, and principal commander Hadrian (A.D. 117–138), like himself of Spanish origin and a remarkably gifted man.

[1]Hadrian was so thoroughly imbued with Greek literature that many called him The Greekling. He was steeped in Athenian pursuits and habits and possessed not only their language but also their other disciplines. He was expert in song, lyre, and medicine; he was musician, geometer, painter, and a sculptor in bronze or marble second only to Polycletus and Euphranus. In addition he was also witty, so that humanity would seem to have rarely discovered anything more elegant. His memory was incredible; he could list places, transactions, soldiers, even when they were absent, by name. His energy was prodigious; he traveled through all the provinces, outstripping his suite, and restored and enlarged all their towns. He organized carpenters, stone-masons, architects, and every kind of builder and decorator into cohorts on the model of a military legion. He was various, manifold, and multiform. He possessed a native control over vices and virtues and could govern his impulses by artifice: he cleverly concealed a nature

[1]Aurelius Victor, 14.

that was envious, gloomy, wanton, and inclined to inordinate display; he simulated continence, courtesy, and clemency, and dissimulated his ardent passion for glory. He was extremely sharp in repartee, and could retort equally to serious remarks, jests, or curses; he could cap poem with poem and saw with saw so that you would suppose he had studied them in advance. His wife Servilia he abused like a slave and drove her to suicide. He openly boasted—and this proves his monstrous character—that he had taken care she should not become pregnant by him, to the ruin of mankind. He was struck down by a subcutaneous disease which he endured patiently for a long while, but then his acute pain and discomfort cost the lives of many senators. He secured peace from several kings by secret bribes, and then openly boasted that he had achieved more by peace than others had by arms. His organization of public, palace, and military offices has persisted, with minor changes introduced by Constantine, to this day. He lived sixty-two years and was carried off by a wretched death, suffering such severe torments in all his members that he repeatedly begged his faithful servants to kill him: only the vigilance of his intimates prevented him from doing violence to himself.

On the frontiers Hadrian's policy was to retrench to easily defensible lines, and to improve the military establishment. The only serious uprising was that of Bar Kochba in Judaea; this was crushed mercilessly and a temple to Jupiter Capitolinus erected in Jerusalem. Besides his administrative reforms and his generous building program, his main contribution of significance to posterity was his patronage of the codification of the Roman law by Salvius Julianus and of a revival of Greek literature and art almost as marked as that of the Renaissance. His passion for and deification of his beloved Antinous is a less attractive aspect of his Hellenism; more attractive are the un-Roman lines he recited at his death:

> [1]O blithe little soul, thou, flitting away.
> Guest and comrade of this my clay,
> Whither now goest thou, to what place
> Bare and ghastly and without grace?
> Nor, as thy wont was, joke and play.

When he fell sick in A.D. 136 Hadrian adopted Aelius and clothed him with tribunician power, and himself retired to his fabulous villa at Tibur. But Aelius died at the beginning of 138, and Hadrian then adopted Antoninus Pius, who in turn adopted Lucius Verus, the son of the deceased Aelius, and his wife Faustina's nephew, Marcus Annius Verus, later called Marcus Aurelius. Antoninus Pius (A.D. 138–161) was so upright and benevolent that he was called a second Numa.

[2]When he was made emperor Antoninus Pius supplanted none of the officials Hadrian had appointed, and was so steadfast that he retained good men as provincial governors for seven- or nine-year terms. He waged several wars, through legates. Through Lollius Urbicus he defeated the Britons, and after driving the barbarians back built a second wall of turf [from the Firth of Forth to the Firth of Clyde]. Through other legates and governors he forced the Moors to sue for peace, and subdued insurgent Germans, Dacians, other tribes, and also the Jews. He suppressed rebellions in Achaea and Egypt also, and several times checked the hostile intentions of the Alans. His procurators he ordered to levy only moderate tribute, and those who exceeded the measure he bade render an account of their deeds; gain from

[1]Historia Augusta, Hadrian (trans. A. O'Brien-Moore).
[2]Historia Augusta, Antoninus Pius, 5.

provincial oppression never pleased him. He was willing to hear complaints against his procurators.

He asked the senate to pardon men whom Hadrian had condemned, saying that Hadrian himself had been about to do so. The imperial pomp he reduced to an ordinary citizen level. This won him credit, though the court attendants objected; since he used no intermediaries they could not terrorize people or sell information which was not kept secret. To the senate he deferred as much as he wished another emperor to defer to him when he was a senator. . . . He governed the people subject to him with great diligence, and cared for all things and persons as if they were his own. All the provinces prospered in his reign. Informers were abolished. Confiscations were rarer than ever, and only one man was found guilty of aspiring to the throne.

It was the healthy state to which Hadrian had brought the empire that made Antoninus' benevolent reign possible. By the end of that reign there were serious rumblings on the frontiers of the empire and within it with which his successor would have to deal. Antoninus married his daughter to Marcus Aurelius, the elder of his adopted sons, and in A.D. 147 conferred upon him the title of Caesar, which all heirs destined to become Augustus would henceforth bear. Upon the death of Antoninus, Marcus Aurelius (A.D. 161–180) succeeded, and at once made his adoptive brother Lucius Verus (A.D. 161–169) his associate; for the first time two Augusti shared power. Verus was an ineffectual profligate, and only added to Marcus Aurelius' heavy burdens. These burdens he bore with qualities approaching saintliness; never has so spiritual a man carried the highest secular responsibility in the world. Only because he surrendered himself wholly to the will of Stoic providence could the frail and sensitive and peace-loving recluse steel himself to spend his winters fighting in the cold north.

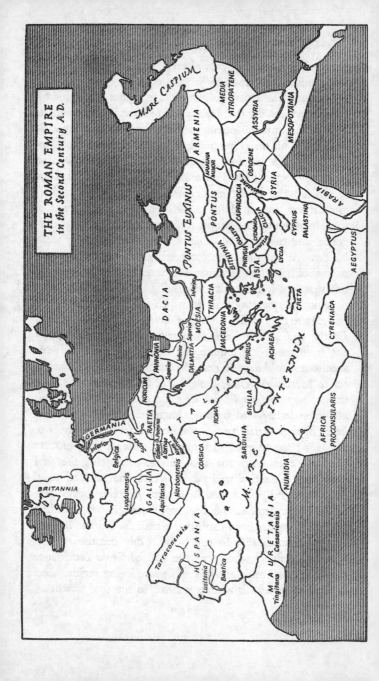

THE ROMAN EMPIRE
in the Second Century A.D.

The new regime began with calamities—flood in Rome, earthquake in Cyzicus, famine in Galatia, revolt in Britain, invasions of the Chatti in Germany, and disasters to Roman armies in Parthia. Verus was sent to the east, and despite his fecklessness his efficient generals made Mesopotamia a Roman protectorate. Verus' troops brought back with them a plague which decimated Europe. About A.D. 166 German tribes poured across the Danube and even penetrated to northern Italy. The invaders came to terms at Aquileia. The death of Verus in 169 was a relief to Marcus. The safety of the empire demanded that central and southeastern Europe be subjugated, and from 170 to 174 Marcus fought the Marcomanni, Quadi, and Sarmatians, but economic exhaustion and the revolt of Cassius in Syria and Egypt prevented complete success. To obtain funds Marcus held public auctions of the palace treasures in the Forum of Trajan. Cassius was murdered, but in 176 Marcus was forced to undertake a campaign in Egypt. Cassius' uprising had been occasioned by a false report of Marcus' death, and to prevent similar attempts in the future Marcus made his worthless and probably mad son Commodus an Augustus to share his power (A.D. 177). The Danubian area had been settled with semiromanized tribesmen for the defense of the frontier; this was the first step in the deromanization of the frontier provinces. In 178 the Marcomanni and Quadi again threatened the Danube; Marcus marched north and defeated them, but before he could reduce their territory to provinces he died. Partly for economy but mainly to hurry back to his singular diversions, Commodus patched up an inconclusive peace and returned to Rome.

[1]Commodus [sole emperor A.D. 180–192] was a greater plague to the Romans than any pestilence or crime. Among
[1]Dio Cassius, 73.15.

other things, the honors they voted to the father out of affection they were forced to assign to him out of fear, by command. He ordained that Rome itself be called Commodiana, the legions Commodian, and the day on which these honors were voted Commodiana. He assumed many names, including that of Hercules. Rome he styled the "Immortal Fortunate Colony of the Universe," for he wished to make it seem his own settlement. A gold statue weighing a thousand pounds represented him with a cow and a bull. Finally all the months were given his names, so that they were listed Amazonius, Invictus, Felix, Pius, Lucius, Aelius, Aurelius, Commodus, Augustus, Herculeus, Romanus, Exsuperatorius. These names he assumed at different times, but Amazonius and Exsuperatorius he applied to himself regularly, to show that in every respect he surpassed all mankind superlatively; so superlatively mad was that scum. His messages to the senate were in this form: "The Emperor Caesar Lucius Aelius Aurelius Commodus Augustus Pius Felix Sarmaticus Germanicus Maximus Britannicus, Pacifier of the Universe, Invincible, the Roman Hercules, Pontifex Maximus, Holder of the Tribunician Authority for the eighteenth, Imperator for the eighth, Consul for the seventh time, Father of his Country, to consuls, praetors, tribunes, and the fortunate Commodian senate, Greeting." Quantities of statues represented him as Hercules. It was voted that his age should be named Golden and so be entered in all written records. . . .

Before entering the amphitheater he would put on a sleeved tunic of white silk picked out with gold, in which he received our salutations; as he entered he put on a robe all of purple with gold fringes, with a Greek cape of the same color and a crown made of Indian gems and gold, and he carried a staff like Mercury's. The lion skin and club were carried before him in the street, and in the amphitheater they were placed on a gilded chair, whether or not he was present. He himself would enter the arena dressed as Mercury, and then fling his other garments off and begin his exhibition barefoot and in his tunic. . . . We would shout out whatever we were commanded, and particularly and continually this: "You are lord, you are first, you are most fortunate. You are victor, you will be victor; from everlasting, Amazonian, you are victor." Many of the common people did not go to the amphitheater, or passed on after looking in, partly from shame at the proceedings and partly from fear, for word spread that he meant to shoot a few people as Hercules did the Stymphalian birds. The story was believed because he had once collected everyone in the city who had lost a foot by disease or accident, fastened serpentlike trappings about their knees, given them sponges to throw instead of stones, and then killed them by striking them with his club, pretending they were giants.

The fear was shared by us senators as well as the rest. He did another such thing to us which gave us lively apprehensions. He killed an ostrich, cut off its head, and came towards us with the head in his left hand, brandishing his bloody sword in the right. He said nothing, but grinned and wagged his head to show he would do the same to us. Many would have succumbed to the sword on the spot for laughing at him (it was laughter rather than indignation that seized us), but I started to chew bay leaves from my garland and persuaded my neighbors to do the same; the motion of our jaws concealed the evidence of laughter.

[1]At the outset Commodus showed how he was likely to turn out. When his father in his last moments admonished him not to allow the barbarians who were now crushed to

[1]Aurelius Victor, 17.

recuperate their forces, he answered that a sound body could accomplish something, however slowly, but a dead one nothing. He surpassed all others in lust and greed and cruelty; he kept faith with no one, and showed the fiercest savagery against those he had exalted with high dignities and large gifts. So depraved was he that he often fought in the arena as a gladiator. He was wholly captivated by Marcia, a beautiful and accomplished wanton of freedman birth; she handed him a cup of poison as he left the bath, and then a powerful wrestler was sent in to throttle him. He died in his thirty-second year [A.D. 192].

If a date can be fixed for the decline of the Roman empire it would be the reign of Commodus. With Marcus Aurelius the principate as founded by Augustus ended, and the way was paved for the military despotism of the later empire. Commodus' successor Pertinax was chosen by the pretorians, but after three months they wearied of his prudent measures to restore discipline and economy, murdered him, and took a profitable if novel way of naming his successor.

[1]The pretorians placed upon their wall those of their number who had the strongest voices, who then called out that the imperial office was for sale; they undertook to deliver the office to the highest bidder and escort him safely to the palace. When this announcement was noised abroad the more dignified and reasonable senators, those of noble birth or wealth (a mere handful who survived Commodus' tyranny) neither went to the wall nor had any wish for an office which was to be chaffered for so indecently. But a certain Julianus, an ex-consul reputed to be very rich, was told of the soldiers' announcement late in the evening as he was feasting and drinking; he had no high reputation for

[1]Herodian, 2.21.

sober living. Upon the urging of his wife and daughter and a crowd of unruly guests he leapt from his couch and ran to the wall to see what was doing. All along the way they advised him to seize the cast-off rule: out of his abundant wealth he could outbid anyone, even if there should be rivals. When he got to the wall he shouted that he would give all they desired; he assured them that he possessed great wealth and treasuries filled with gold and silver. At the same time Sulpician, father-in-law of Pertinax, also an ex-consul, and prefect of the city, came to bargain for the emperorship. But the soldiers suspected him because of his relationship to Pertinax and feared some trick to avenge the murder of Pertinax.

So they put down a ladder and brought Julianus up to the wall, but refused to open the gates before they learned how much he would give. When Julianus climbed up he promised to renew the honors and statues of Commodus which the senate had pulled down, and to restore the privileges which the pretorians had enjoyed under Commodus. To each soldier he promised more money than they expected to ask or receive. Nor would there be any delay; he would send home for the money at once. The soldiers were persuaded and their hopes whetted. They hailed Julianus emperor and added Commodus' name to his own. Then they raised their standards, mounted Julianus' portraits upon them, and sought to form an escort for him. Julianus then offered the customary and also the royal sacrifices, and was led forth. His bodyguard was larger than customary, for he had acquired the emperorship through force, against the will of the people, by a shameful and indecent purchase, and so could reasonably fear that the people would oppose him. The soldiers in full panoply formed a square about him, ready to fight if need be. The king who was their own creature they placed in their midst, and raised their shields and spears over his head in case the procession should be pelted from the houses. Thus they escorted him to the palace. None of the people ventured to resist, but neither did any shout the felicitations which customarily greet kings. On the contrary, they kept their distance and muttered imprecations and recriminations for his having bought emperorship for money.

So dark is the picture of the emperors and their administration which our sources give that the observer may well wonder how the structure of the empire could survive even with no external enemies to shake it from without. But our principal sources for the early empire show a senatorial and hence anti-imperial bias (Tacitus and Dio were both senators), and all are primarily concerned with the personality of the emperor, not the state of the empire. That individual emperors were tyrannical or licentious or even demented is very probable, but the administration was not necessarily impaired, and the people appear to have been prosperous and content. The most persuasive argument for the benefits of Roman administration is the apparent satisfaction of the eastern half of the empire, which had enjoyed high civilization for centuries but had been troubled by local disturbances. A useful corrective for the gloom of the Roman writers is the Roman Oration of the Greek sophist Aelius Aristides. The speech is intended to please a Roman audience, and is lavish in its praise, but even a sycophant's adulation can serve as an index to his patron's ideals. Here are significant passages from the speech:

[1]"If one considers the vast extent of your empire he must be amazed that so small a fraction of it rules the world, but when he beholds the city and its spaciousness it is not astonishing that all the habitable world is ruled by such a capital. . . . Your possessions equal the sun's course. . . .

[1]Aelius Aristides, The Roman Oration, ed. J. H. Oliver.

You do not rule within fixed boundaries, nor can anyone dictate the limits of your sway. . . . Whatever any people produces can be found here, at all times and in abundance. . . . Egypt, Sicily, and the civilized part of Africa are your farms; ships are continually coming and going. . . .

"Vast as it is, your empire is more remarkable for its thoroughness than its scope: there are no dissident or rebellious enclaves. . . . The whole world prays in unison that your empire may endure forever.

"Governors sent out to cities and peoples each rule their charges, but in their relations to each other they are equally subjects. The principal difference between governors and their charges is this—they demonstrate the proper way to be a subject. So great is their reverence for the great Ruler, who administers all things. Him they believe to know their business better than they themselves do, and hence they respect and heed him more than one would a master overseeing a task and giving orders. No one is so self-assured that he can remain unmoved upon hearing the emperor's name; he rises in prayer and adoration and utters a twofold prayer—to the gods for the Ruler, and to the Ruler for himself. And if the governors are in the least doubt concerning the justice of claims or suits of the governed, public or private, they send to the Ruler for instructions at once and await his reply, as a chorus awaits its trainer's directions. Hence the Ruler need not exhaust himself by traveling to various parts to settle matters in person. It is easy for him to abide in his place and manage the world through letters; these arrive almost as soon as written, as if borne on wings.

"But the most marvelous and admirable achievement of all, and the one deserving our fullest gratitude, is this. . . . You alone of the imperial powers of history rule over men who are free. You have not assigned this or that region to this nabob or that mogul; no people has been turned over as a domestic and bound holding—to a man not himself free. But just as citizens in an individual city might designate magistrates, so you, whose city is the whole world, appoint governors to protect and provide for the governed, as if they were elective, not to lord it over their charges. As a result, so far from disputing the office as if it were their own, governors make way for their successors readily when their term is up, and may not even await their coming. Appeals to a higher jurisdiction are as easy as appeals from parish to county. . . .

"But the most notable and praiseworthy feature of all, a thing unparalleled, is your magnanimous conception of citizenship. All of your subjects (and this implies the whole world) you have divided into two parts: the better endowed and more virile, wherever they may be, you have granted citizenship and even kinship; the rest you govern as obedient subjects. Neither the seas nor expanse of land bars citizenship; Asia and Europe are not differentiated. Careers are open to talent. . . . Rich and poor find contentment and profit in your system; there is no other way of life. Your polity is a single and all-embracing harmony. . . .

"You have not put walls around your city, as if you were hiding it or avoiding your subjects; to do so you considered ignoble and inconsistent with your principles, as if a master should show fear of his slaves. You did not overlook walls, however, but placed them round the empire, not the city. The splendid and distant walls you erected are worthy of you; to men within their circuit they are visible, but it requires a journey of months and years from the city to see them. Beyond the outermost ring of the civilized world you drew a second circle, larger in radius and easier to defend, like the outer fortifications of a city. Here you built walls and established cities in diverse parts. The cities you filled with colonists; you introduced arts and crafts and established an orderly culture. . . . Your military organization makes all others childish. Your soldiers and officers you train to prevail not only over the enemy but over themselves. The soldier lives under discipline daily, and none ever deserts the post assigned him.

"You alone are, so to speak, natural rulers. Your predecessors were masters and slaves in turn; as rulers they were counterfeits, and reversed their positions like players in a ball game. . . . You have measured out the world, bridged rivers, cut roads through mountains, filled the wastes with posting stations, introduced orderly and refined modes of life. . . .

"Be all gods and their offspring invoked to grant that this empire and this city flourish forever and never cease until stones float upon the sea and trees forbear to sprout in the springtide. May the great Ruler and his sons be preserved to administer all things well."

6. The Severi

If the pretorians could choose an emperor so could other soldiers also. At the same time as the pretorians were selling the throne to Didius Julianus three frontier armies saluted their generals as emperors—Pescennius Niger in Syria, Clodius Albinus in Britain, and Septimius Severus in Pannonia. Severus was nearest, and marched on Rome "to avenge Pertinax." When he reached Italy the senate deposed and executed Julianus (A.D. 193) and ratified the nomination of Severus. Severus ordered the pretorians to meet him in parade dress unarmed.

[1]Severus surrounded them before they knew what was going to happen, reviled them bitterly for their violence to their emperor, took away their arms and horses, and banished them from Rome. . . . Then he entered the city. As far as the gates he came on horseback, in cavalry uniform; then he changed to civilian dress and went on foot. Cavalry and infantry accompanied him, fully armed. The spectacle was the most brilliant I have ever seen. The whole city was wreathed with flowers and laurel, decked with varicolored bunting, and ablaze with lights and incense. People with joyous faces, dressed all in white, shouted felicitations. Soldiers moved about in resplendent armor as in a holiday procession. And we senators walked in state. The crowd was on edge in their eagerness to see and hear him, as if he had somehow been transformed by fortune. Some even hoisted one another up to get a better view of him.

After such an entry he made the declarations good em-

[1]Dio Cassius, 75.1.

146

perors had made in the past, promising that he would never kill a senator. He took an oath upon it and moreover ordained that it be confirmed by a joint vote decreeing that the emperor and any who assisted him in such a deed, both themselves and their children, should be outlawed. But he himself was the first to violate this law, and put many senators to death.

[1]When he had established himself in power Severus erected a shrine to Pertinax and commanded that his name should be added to all prayers and oaths. He ordered that a golden statue of Pertinax be brought into the amphitheater in a chariot drawn by elephants and that three gilded thrones should be brought into other theaters in his honor. Although he had been long dead, his funeral was carried out as follows. In the Roman Forum a wooden platform was erected near the Rostra, and upon it an open structure of columns of ivory and gold. Into it was brought a bier of the same materials with a border of heads of land and sea animals, covered with draperies of purple and gilt. Upon the bier was placed a wax figure of Pertinax, decked in triumphal accouterments. A handsome boy swept flies away with a peacock fan, as if the figure were only sleeping. As the figure reposed there we senators with our wives, wearing mourning, stepped forward; the women sat in porticoes, and the men in the open air. After this there passed in procession first images of all the famous Romans of old, then choirs of boys and men chanting a dirge to Pertinax. After them came all the subject nations, represented by bronze statues in their native dress, and then followed the guilds of the city— lictors, scribes, heralds, and the like. Then came statues of other men who had been distinguished for some deed or invention or improvement. After them came cavalry and infantry in arms, race horses, and the funeral offerings that

[1]Dio Cassius, 75.4.

the emperor and we and our wives and the distinguished equestrians and communities and corporations in the city had sent. Next was an altar covered with gold and decorated with ivory and Indian gems. When the procession had passed, Severus mounted the Rostra and read a eulogy of Pertinax. We gave many shouts of approval, praising or lamenting Pertinax, during the address, and many more when he concluded. Finally, when the bier was about to be moved, we all wailed and wept. It was brought down from the platform by the chief priests and magistrates, those then serving and those elected for the next year, and they gave it to certain equestrians to carry. All the rest now walked before the bier, some beating their breasts, others piping a dirge on the flute: the emperor followed behind. In this order we reached the Campus Martius. There a pyre had been erected in the shape of a three-story tower, adorned with ivory and gold and statuary, and on its top was a gilded chariot that Pertinax used to drive. Into this pyre the funeral offerings were cast, and the bier was placed in it, and then Severus and the relatives kissed the effigy. The emperor then ascended a tribunal, and the senate, except the magistrates, sat on benches so that we might view the proceedings safely and conveniently. The magistrates and equestrians in full dress, and likewise the cavalry and infantry marched around the pyre in intricate evolutions, civilian and military. Then the consuls kindled the fire. At this point an eagle soared up out of it to show that Pertinax was deified.

Spectacular displays and periodic distributions of money and food were not Severus' only devices for winning a special esteem in Rome. Though he was of African birth and had a sister whose broken Latin embarrassed him, he declared himself the son of Marcus Aurelius, and assumed and gave his sons the name. He could not then leave the memory of his "brother" Commodus in disgrace, and so caused him to be apotheosized. His eight-year-old son (Caracalla) he called Antonius, and made him heir apparent by designating him Caesar. It was clearly his intention to establish a dynasty and clothe it with the halo of divinity. In the army emperor-worship replaced worship of the standards. His Syrian wife Julia Domna, who was something of a philosopher and a religious enthusiast, was doubtless influential in this direction. She received the title of Mater Augusti, was worshiped by the soldiers as Mater castrorum, and was later identified with Juno Caelestis. It was Julia who enlarged and reorganized the order of Vestals, and who promoted the cult of Apollonius of Tyana.

One of his rivals, Clodius Albinus, Severus lulled to inaction by designating him Caesar; against Pescennius Niger, who was preparing to march on Italy and already held Byzantium, he made war. His final victory over him was at Issus (A.D. 194), where Alexander had defeated Darius five hundred years before. In punitive campaigns against peoples who had supported Niger, Antioch and Byzantium in particular suffered. To diminish the capacity of future governors to revolt, he divided Syria into two provinces; later he did the same in Britain. In 196 he hurried back to Europe to settle with Albinus, who had assumed the title of Augustus and occupied Gaul.

[1]The contest between Severus and Albinus was settled at Lugdunum [A.D. 197]. Each side had 150,000 soldiers. . . . Severus won, but the strength of the Romans suffered severely, for the casualties on either side were numberless. Many even of the winning side deplored the disaster. . . . Albinus took refuge in a house near the Rhone, but when he saw that the place was surrounded he killed himself. I am saying not what Severus wrote but what actually happened.

[1]Dio Cassius, 76.6.

When Severus saw the body he looked and spoke his fill; the torso he ordered flung out, the head he sent to Rome to be impaled on a staff.

Directly after his defeat of Albinus, Severus marched east to suppress Parthian ambitions and implement his policy of extending the empire. The Parthian capitals of Seleucia and Ctesiphon were sacked (198), and Mesopotamia organized as a province. In 208 Britain was troubled by invasions from Caledonia, and Severus, accompanied by Julia Domna and their sons Caracalla and Geta, now both Augusti, carried his operations into Scotland. Hadrian's turf wall, which had been breached, he reinforced by a stout wall of stone. Before the north was pacified, however, he died, at his headquarters at York, A.D. 211.

Severus' reign marks a significant change in the character of the empire. His chief care was for the military establishment. He enlarged the army, enrolled barbarians in it, increased the soldiers' pay, and allowed them to marry. He built walls not only in Britain but also in Africa and from the Danube to the Rhine, and lines of fortresses along the Danube and in Asia. The treasury, which Commodus had left bankrupt, he filled by confiscations among the wealthy adherents of Albinus, by debasing the coinage, and by reorganizing and regularizing the fiscal structure. Taxes had grown so high that they were evaded; now municipal councils were made responsible for revenue. Local magistracies which had carried honor became so burdensome that prospective victims left their all and ran away into hiding. Benefactions which had been motivated by philanthropy, on the part of individuals or guilds, were now exacted as obligations. The bureaucracy was further enlarged and rigidified, and the postal service was taken over and improved. The poor and orphans were provided for by regular distributions of money, food, and medicines. Not in the army alone but in the administration generally non-Italians tended to replace Romans. At least two thirds of the senate was eastern or African. But under an emperor who realized that power rested upon army and treasury and a contented populace it was natural that the senate's authority, except as a mark of social prestige, should tend to disappear. Many of Severus' executions of senators seem to have had no other motive than to humiliate that body. Its only function, indeed, was to applaud the communications the emperor deigned to send it.

The actual center of administration was in the judicial council, which kept close watch over provincial governors. The city prefect had jurisdiction over cases within a radius of a hundred miles of Rome, and the pretorian prefect, in effect the second most powerful man in the empire, had jurisdiction over all the rest. This was the great age of the Roman jurists. Papinian, the ablest of them, was pretorian prefect under Severus, and his younger contemporaries Paul and Ulpian were almost as distinguished. For posterity the work of the jurists and the increased tempo of romanization as a consequence of the military establishments on the frontiers are the chief legacy of Severus.

On his deathbed Severus had admonished his sons to "live in peace with each other, enrich the soldiers, and scorn all other men." Their failure in regard to the first precept was the most notable. Like Commodus at the death of Marcus Aurelius, Caracalla (A.D. 211–217) and Geta left their father's military operations incomplete in order to hurry to Rome.

[1]Even on the road there was friction between them; they did not use the same inns or dine together. Each suspected every morsel and drop, fearing the other might overreach

[1]Herodian, 4.1.

him and suborn some servant to poison him. For this reason they traveled in haste, each thinking he would be more secure in Rome. The palace was very spacious, more extensive, indeed, than a city, and each could occupy separate quarters as he wished.

When they reached Rome the people, bearing laurels, and the senate presented an address. The princes, attired in purple, led the procession, and the consuls followed, carrying the urn with the remains of Severus. Those who had addressed the new emperors followed, doing obeisance to the urn. With this ceremonial escort the urn was deposited in the temple where the monuments of Marcus Aurelius and earlier emperors are displayed. Then they performed the sacrifices customary for royalty and retired to the palace. This they divided so that each had a separate residence, blocked all private corridors, and used only the public entrance of the palace, where each posted his own guards. They met only on the few occasions when they had to appear in public together. . . .

The brothers sought every possible means to dispose of one another, and bribed butlers and cooks to use poison. But this was not easy, for each dined with the utmost caution. At last Caracalla's lust for sole dominion made him impatient and he determined to use violent means, win or lose. Once when both were visiting their mother Caracalla stabbed his brother as he sought refuge in his mother's arms. Mortally wounded, Geta shed his blood over his mother's bosom. After perpetrating this murder Caracalla sprang up and ran through the palace shouting that he had barely escaped a mortal peril. The soldiers on guard in the palace he ordered to hurry him to the camp for protection, declaring that he was doomed if he remained in the palace. Unaware of what had happened, the soldiers believed him, and accompanied him as he ran. The people were astonished when they saw their emperor running through the streets late in the evening. When he reached the camp he prostrated himself at the temple where the standards and images of the army are worshiped, gave thanks, and offered sacrifices for his deliverance.

[1]Caracalla condemned large numbers for alleged sympathy with Geta, not only people who had written him or sent him gifts when he was Caesar or had become emperor, but others who had never had dealings with him. If anyone even wrote or spoke the name of Geta he was killed. The poets no longer used the name in their comedies. The possessions of people who had mentioned Geta in their wills were confiscated.

Among Caracalla's victims was the jurist Papinian. The new emperor was doubtless as brutal and profligate as our sources represent him, but his reign was not a cipher. In keeping with his father's practice and advice, he made special efforts to conciliate the army, and almost his entire reign he spent on the frontiers. In 213 he waged a moderately successful campaign against the Alamanni—the first appearance of the people who gave the French their name for Germans. In 214 he was fighting on the Danube and drilling his troops in the Macedonian phalanx. Alexander was his particular ideal, and he even hoped to realize Alexander's goal of fusing Iranians and Westerners into a single people. His grant of citizenship to all communities in the empire (the most notable event in his reign) was a major contribution to the ecumenical ideal. Here is a copy of his edict on the subject found in Egypt:

[2]"Edict of the Emperor Caesar Marcus Aurelius Antoninus Augustus (Caracalla). To divine power I refer the reasons and considerations whereby I should worthily show my gratitude to the gods for preserving me in safety in the

[1]Dio Cassius, 78.12.   [2]Giessen Papyrus (1912).

midst of great peril. I believe I can render proper service to their majesty in dignified and reverent worship if I bring as many myriads as owe me obedience to share in sacrifice to the gods. Accordingly I bestow Roman citizenship on all my subjects throughout the world, no one except *dediticii* being denied citizen rights. It is proper that my people should share not only the common burdens but also the joy of my victory. This ordinance shall extend the might of the Roman people since the distinction for which Romans have been honored has now been granted to others."

In part, at least, this gesture had the practical motive of making larger numbers liable to certain taxes. Not only military expenditures but an ambitious building program, including the enormous and elegant Baths, caused financial stringency which Caracalla met by increasing taxes on inheritances and manumissions and by further debasing the currency. In 215 Caracalla went to the east for a war against Parthia. After settling disturbances in Alexandria he invaded Media, and was assassinated at the instigation of Macrinus, at Carrhae, in A.D. 217.

Macrinus (A.D. 217–218) was the first of the emperors who was not a senator. He was an African, with pierced ear, whose competence had raised him to be pretorian prefect under Caracalla. He attempted various retrenchments, patching up a peace with the Parthians, abolishing oppressive taxes, and canceling increases of pay which Caracalla had granted the soldiers. This so antagonized them that they transferred their allegiance to the great-nephew of Julia Domna, who came to be known as Elagabalus.

[1]Julia Domna, wife of Severus and mother of Caracalla, had a sister named Maesa, a Phoenician woman from Emesus. During the reigns of Severus and Caracalla, while

[1]Herodian, 5.3.

her sister was alive, Maesa had lived in the imperial court, but after Julia's death and the murder of Caracalla Macrinus ordered her to return to her own country to live as a private citizen with all her possessions. These were very considerable, for she had been maintained at court over a long period. And so the elderly lady returned to her own home and lived there. She had two daughters, the elder called Soaemis and the younger Mammaea. Soaemis had a son called Bassianus [Elagabalus] and Mammaea one called Alexian [Alexander Severus]; the boys were brought up under the care of their mothers and grandmother. Bassianus was about fourteen years old and Alexian ten; both were priests of the Sun, who is greatly revered by the natives, who call him Elagabalus in their own language. They had built a large temple to him, lavishly decorated with gold and silver and precious stones. Not only natives but neighboring satraps and barbarian kings vied with one another in sending the god rich offerings annually. There was no image wrought to represent the god, as among Greeks and Romans, but only a large stone round at the bottom and rising to a point at the top, like a cone, and of black color. They declare that it fell from heaven, and say that certain protuberances and markings on it are a natural likeness of the sun.

Bassianus was priest to this god, and as the elder performed his service. He was most magnificently attired in the barbaric manner . . . and exceedingly handsome . . . so that he was universally admired, and not least by the Roman soldiers, not only for his beauty but for his connection with the imperial house. There was a large encampment in the vicinity, for the purpose of protecting Phoenicia; later this army was removed. Many of the soldiers who visited the city went to the temple to worship and took pleasure at the sight of the lad. Many of these were exiles, and familiars of Maesa. When the soldiers admired the boy Maesa told them (whether it was truth or invention) that he was actually the natural son of Caracalla, though he passed for another's. When she lived in the palace with her sister, Caracalla had frequently visited her daughters, who were young and handsome. The soldiers soon passed this story to their comrades and it was spread through the whole camp. Maesa, it was said, had whole mounds of money, and would readily distribute it to the soldiers if her family were restored to the throne. It was agreed that they would secretly open the camp gates to her at night, admit her and her family, and proclaim Bassianus [Elagabalus] son of Caracalla and emperor.

[1]Elagabalus came to Rome with high expectations on the part of army and senate, but he defiled himself with every species of licentiousness. The lust which his natural impotence could not satisfy he turned upon himself, and insisted on being called Bassiana, in the feminine, instead of Bassianus. He went through a marriage form with a Vestal, and he lopped off his genitals and dedicated himself to the Great Mother. His cousin, later called Alexander, he made a Caesar [at the instigation of Maesa, who foresaw Elagabalus' fall and wished to retain her extraordinary power through her other grandson.] Elagabalus was killed by rioting soldiers, who dragged his body through the city streets like a dog's and reviled him as a rabidly lustful bitch. When the opening of the sewer proved too small to receive the cadaver they dragged it to the Tiber and flung it in with a weight attached so that it should never rise. From this circumstance he was called Tiberius or The Dragged. He lived sixteen years.

[2][Elagabalus was succeeded by his cousin Severus Alexander (A.D. 222–235), who was then thirteen,] but the management of the empire was in the hands of his grand-

[1]Aurelius Victor, 2.3.   [2]Herodian, 6.1.

mother and mother, who sought to restore sanity and dignity. In the first place sixteen reputable, mature, and prudent senators were chosen to be a council of assessors to the emperor, and nothing was said or done without their approval and consent. This transformation of a capricious tyranny into an aristocratic form of government was pleasing to people, army, and especially to the senate. First they restored to their own appropriate temples and shrines the statues of the gods which Elagabalus had removed. Next, persons whom he had advanced to dignity and power unreasonably or for their outstanding licentiousness were deprived of their gains and reduced to their former station. As for official business and administration, civil matters were entrusted to reputable men expert in law, and military matters to men experienced and distinguished in regular military service. When the state had been so administered for some time, Maesa, now an old woman, died. She received high honors and, following the Roman custom, was deified.

But Mammaea alone could and did exercise close supervision over her son. She kept him from undesirable associations, made the distinguished jurist Ulpian pretorian prefect, and found him a suitable wife (in A.D. 225)—whom she subsequently caused him to divorce when she grew jealous of her influence.

[1]Severus Alexander's mode of life was this: First, in the early morning hours if it was permissible, that is, if he had not lain with his wife, he would perform his devotions at the household shrine, in which he kept figures of deified emperors, choosing only the best, and of holy personages, among whom were Apollonius of Tyana, and, according to a contemporary writer, Christ, Abraham, Orpheus, and others of that character, and also portraits of his ancestors. If this was not possible he would ride or fish or stroll or hunt,

[1]Historia Augusta, Severus Alexander, 29.

according to the nature of the place. Then, if the hour permitted, he would address himself most attentively to public business. Matters both civil and military were previously worked over by his friends—always upright and faithful men, never venal—and he would confirm their decision or make some alteration. . . . After public business, military or civil, he devoted himself to a Greek book, Plato's *Republic*. When he read Latin his favorites were Cicero *On Duties* and *On the State*. . . . The afternoon he gave to signing and reading letters. The secretaries of correspondence, petitions, and records would stand by, or if their health did not permit, sit. Scribes and bureau heads would read everything over to him, and he would make necessary additions with his own hand, but according to the best expert opinion on the matter.

Rome had a few years of tranquil and economical administration. Taxes and expenditures were reduced, though distributions and the building program were maintained. But the army was restive, and a new danger had arisen in the east. In A.D. 227 the Persian Ardaschir (Artaxerxes), founder of the Sassanid dynasty, revived Zoroastrianism as the national Persian religion, overthrew the Parthian dynasty of the Arsacids, and, as successor of Cyrus and Darius, claimed Rome's eastern provinces. In 231 the Persians drove the Roman troops out of Mesopotamia and penetrated Cappadocia and Syria. The situation was aggravated by a mutiny among the troops in the east, and to meet the danger new soldiers had to be recruited in Italy and the frontier defenses on the Danube weakened. Two of the three prongs of Severus Alexander's attack failed but the third was so successful that Mesopotamia was recovered. But his troubles were not over.

[1]Suddenly Alexander received disturbing letters which

[1]Herodian, 6.7.

caused him great anxiety. The procurators of Illyria reported that Germans had crossed the Rhine and Danube, had ravaged Roman territory, and had overrun the camps, cities, and villages on the banks of the river with large forces. The Illyrian peoples adjacent to Italy were in no slight danger. It was imperative that he come and bring the largest possible forces. These tidings shocked Alexander and depressed his Illyrian troops, who felt they had suffered a twofold calamity: their own defeat by the Persians and the destruction of their families by the Germans. They were angry and blamed Alexander for his negligence or cowardice in the east and his delay and hesitance in the north. Alexander and his friends with him were anxious for Italy itself, for the danger from Germans was much nearer than the danger from the east.

Leaving as small a force as he dared in the east, Severus Alexander moved his army to the Rhine and took up headquarters at Mainz. But, probably at his mother's suggestion, he hesitated to take vigorous measures and made attempts to buy the Germans off.

[1]The soldiers chafed at this futile delay. Alexander, they said, showed no spirit or zeal for the war, but was interested only in horse races and high living; he would better attack and punish the Germans for their effrontery. There was in the army a certain Maximinus who came from a village in the semi-barbarous interior of Thrace where he had been a shepherd in his youth.

[2]Once when the emperor Septimius Severus was celebrating his son's birthday with military contests Maximinus begged the emperor in his native tongue to allow him to wrestle with the trained soldiers for the prizes. Septimius marveled at his size—it is said that he was more than eight feet tall—and bade him wrestle with the camp followers:

[1]Herodian, 6.8.   [2]Jordanes, 84ff.

he did not wish his soldiers to be hurt by this prodigy. Maximinus thereupon easily threw sixteen men one after the other without resting between bouts. His victory admitted him into the army, and he served with the cavalry. Three days later the emperor observed him galloping about in the barbarian style, and ordered a tribune to restrain him and teach him the Roman discipline. Maximinus sensed that the emperor was speaking about him, and proceeded to run ahead of the emperor, who was mounted. The emperor trotted and wheeled and dodged until he was weary; then he said, "Will you wrestle now after your running, my little Thracian?" "As much as you like, Emperor," Maximinus answered. Severus sprang to the ground and ordered the freshest of his soldiers to wrestle with him. Again Maximinus threw seven very stout lads without taking time out to breathe. He received silver prizes and a gold necklace, and was enrolled in the bodyguard. Later he served with distinction under Caracalla, and was advanced through the grades to a centurionship. When Macrinus became emperor he refused to serve for three years, though he was now a tribune, and avoided Macrinus because he had won his rule through a crime. He entered upon his tribuneship under Elagabalus because he believed he was the son of Antoninus. Then he served with distinction against the Parthians, under Alexander son of Mammaea.

[1]Because of his military experience Alexander put Maximinus in charge of training all army recruits and preparing them for service. He performed his duty with the greatest diligence and won the soldiers' good will. He not only taught them what was to be done but was himself always the first to do it, so that they not only learned his lessons but imitated and emulated his energy. He also used gifts and various marks of distinction to win their affection. Thus

[1]Herodian, 6.8.

it came about that the recruits, who were largely from Pannonia, admired Maximinus' prowess and derided Alexander for being governed by his mother, for leaving all power and decision in the hands of a woman, and for being sluggish and cowardly in the conduct of war. They recalled to one another the disasters his tardiness had caused in the east, and pointed out that he had shown no courage or energy since he marched against the Germans. They were in any case ripe for revolution and impatient at the length of the current reign, for their awards were used up and there was no more profit: they could hope for gain if someone should attain power unexpectedly and shower attention upon them. Accordingly they decided to do away with Severus Alexander and hail Maximinus emperor; he was their comrade and tent mate, and his experience and courage were necessary for the war in hand. They assembled on the parade ground under arms, as if for their customary drill, and when Maximinus took his place at their head (whether privy to the plan or taken unawares) they threw the royal purple over him and hailed him emperor. At first he resisted and threw the purple off, but when the insistent soldiers drew their swords and threatened to kill him, he preferred the remoter to the present danger and accepted the honor.

7. "Thirty Tyrants"

And so Severus Alexander and his mother Mammaea were killed and the Thracian Maximinus became emperor (A.D. 235–238), the first barbarian, and the first soldier who rose from the ranks with no civilian career, to do so. Others followed in rapid succession, so that during the next fifty years there were no fewer than twenty-six recognized emperors, besides numerous usurpers, only one of whom died a natural death. The armies, recruited now almost entirely from the frontiers, had no interest in the empire or the provinces they garrisoned; their sole concern was to enrich themselves by plunder and the high pay and bonuses of the emperor they supported. And since the army's dissatisfaction was his immediate doom, the emperor must subordinate all other considerations to keeping the army happy and rich. The imperial system broke down, the pax Romana ended. Civil war was continuous and the frontier defenses on the Rhine, Danube, and Euphrates collapsed, and everywhere invasion swept in. From the North Sea Saxons raided the shores of Britain and Gaul. Franks on the lower Rhine, Alamanni on the upper Rhine, Marcomanni on the upper Danube, Goths and Heruli on the frontiers of Dacia and above the Black Sea were almost unopposed. Provincials could only rely upon local leaders; Gaul with Spain and Britain in the west, Syria with Arabia and Egypt in the east, went their own way, and the unity of the empire was temporarily lost. And towards the end of the half century pestilence entered the Roman world from the east and raged for fifteen years.

*Like most of his successors, Maximinus was effective
enough as a soldier. In 236 he dealt the Germans across the
Rhine such a blow that Gaul was secure for another twenty
years. He fought on the Danube until 238, when his
enormous financial demands, exacted with callous indifference to the general welfare, precipitated revolution. The
movement this time was from Africa.*

[1]The procurator of the Carthaginian region was brutal
and ruthless in his judgments and exactions out of a desire
to win the approval of Maximinus, who favored only those
he knew to be like-minded with himself. Even honest financial officials (a rare enough thing) unwillingly imitated the
others, for they knew Maximinus' rapacity and were afraid.
Among other violent exactions, the procurator in question
had condemned certain wealthy young men of good family
and attempted to confiscate all their ancestral fortunes at
once. The aggrieved young men agreed to pay the money
and asked for a respite of three days. They formed a conspiracy, including all who had suffered similar abuse or expected to, and they passed word to their young farm hands
to come with clubs and axes. These obeyed willingly, and
assembled in the city before dawn, with improvised weapons
under their clothing. There was a good crowd, for Libya is
populous and has many farmers. The young men ordered
their crowd of servants to follow them, but as if they were
part of the populace; they were to bring their weapons out
and set to only when they saw soldiers or citizens attacking
them for what they were about to do. They themselves with
daggers in their bosoms approached the procurator as if to
discuss the payment of their money. They fell upon him
while he suspected nothing and struck him dead. When his
soldiers drew sword to avenge the murder, the countrymen
set to with clubs and axes and easily routed their adver-

[1]Herodian, 7.4.

saries. The deed done, the desperate young men realized that their only salvation was to venture even greater daring, to make the proconsul of the province share their enterprise and raise general rebellion. They knew that the people desired such a move, for their hatred of Maximinus, but were restrained by fear. Accompanied by the crowd (it was now midday), they proceeded to the residence of the proconsul. His name was Gordian, he was eighty years old, and he had obtained the consulship by lot. He had held many governorships previously, and had proven his ability in important affairs. They thought he would welcome the imperial office as a culmination of his career, and the senate and Roman people, they thought, would welcome a man of noble birth who had ascended to emperorship by appropriate degrees.

After some hesitation Gordian accepted, and associated his son (Gordian II) with himself. The senate and the European provinces acknowledged him, but Capellianus, governor of Numidia, with a legionary army defeated the Gordians' volunteers; Gordian II was killed and Gordian I committed suicide. They had ruled less than a month. The senate had tried to assume direction of affairs; the army proved supreme. The senate appointed two of its number, Balbinus and Maximus, as emperors, with the thirteen-year-old Gordian III as Caesar. Maximinus marched to Rome, but stopped to besiege Aquileia, and he and his son were murdered by his soldiers, who had been kept on short rations. Soon the two new emperors were murdered by the pretorians, who proclaimed Gordian III emperor (A.D. 238–244). Government was virtually in the hands of Timesitheus, Gordian's pretorian prefect and father-in-law, who had risen from one office to another and whose impersonal efficiency had survived changes in the imperial office. In 242 the Danubian frontier was re-established and in 243 a campaign was undertaken against Sapor I of Persia, who had

*invaded Syria. The Romans saved Antioch, recovered
Carrhae and Nisibis, and were planning an advance on
Ctesiphon when Timesitheus died.*

[1]Some say that Timesitheus' death was due to disease,
many that it was plotted by Philip the Arab, who succeeded
him as pretorian prefect. Timesitheus made the Roman
state his heir, and his property was added to the city revenues. . . . Philip was base-born but arrogant, and could
not be satisfied with his sudden and enormous rise but immediately used the military to compass the downfall of
Gordian, who treated him as a father. Timesitheus had
stored up such quantities of supplies at every point that
Roman administration could not be affected by shortages.
Philip contrived first to have the grain ships diverted and
then for the soldiers to be moved to places where they
could not be provisioned. Thus he provoked the soldiers
against Gordian, for they did not realize that the young man
was the victim of Philip's cunning. Furthermore Philip
spread talk among the soldiers to the effect that Gordian
was a stripling incapable of ruling and that it would be better to have someone who understood administration and
could govern the army. He then bribed their leaders, to the
point that there was an open demand for Philip to be emperor. Gordian's friends at first resisted vigorously, but when
the soldiers were overcome by hunger Philip received emperorship and the soldiers ordered that Philip should act
as a guardian over Gordian and have equal authority with
him. . . . When Gordian saw that he was rejected he
asked that their power be at least equal, but failed of his request. Then he asked that he be made a Caesar, in vain.
He asked to be Philip's prefect, and this too was denied.
His last request was that Philip make him a general and let
him live. . . . Reflecting that the soldiers might one day

[1]*Historia Augusta, Gordians,* 28.

change and restore rule to Gordian if he should ask for it, since their present annoyance was due to hunger, he ordered him to be carried out of their sight, protesting and crying out, and to be stripped and killed [A.D. 244].

Philip (A.D. 244–249) patched up a peace with Persia, made his son Caesar, and went to Rome, where the senate confirmed his position. In 247 he defeated the Carpi at the Danube, and on April 21, 248, gave a magnificent celebration of Rome's thousandth birthday. But though Philip was conscientious and maintained cordial relations with the senate, the problems of army and treasury were insuperable. The Goths invaded Moesia, and in the east as well as in the Balkans generals were proclaimed emperors. To maintain the military, taxation and compulsory service became more oppressive, and the civil population was ground down by the tyranny of a militarized bureaucracy. When Decius was proclaimed emperor by his troops, Philip and his son marched against him and were killed in a battle at Verona (A.D. 249). Later (and very dubious) tradition made Philip the first Christian emperor.

[1]It is recorded that Philip was a Christian and that on the day of the last paschal vigil he wished to share the prayers at the church with the multitude. . . . His action gave evidence of a genuine and pious disposition towards the fear of God. . . . He was succeeded by Decius [A.D. 249–251], who, because of his enmity towards Philip, raised a persecution against the churches.

Decius' persecutions (there were very few actual executions) were part of a consistent plan to restore unity in the empire. Rome was tolerant to foreign creeds provided proper reverence was shown to the religion of the state, which was essentially political in character. But Christians could not

[1]Eusebius, *Ecclesiastical History*, 6.34.

acknowledge paganism in any form, and their proselytizing activities and gospel of international peace were at variance with a program of reviving the unity and imperial greatness of Rome. In keeping with this program, Decius repaired roads and fortifications on the frontiers, restored discipline to the army, and created a new office somewhat like the old censorship, to which he appointed the future Emperor Valerian, to supervise finances and the state religion. In 250 two armies of Goths invaded Moesia, and plundered and massacred its people. Decius drove them off, but when he tried to cut their retreat off he and his son were trapped and killed through the treachery of his lieutenant Trebonianus Gallus (A.D. 251). The Christians were naturally relieved at Decius' death.

[1]After a long interval that execrable beast Decius arose and harassed the church: who but a wicked man would persecute justice? It was as if he had been advanced to the imperial height for the purpose of raging against God, so that he should straightway fall. When he marched against the Carpi, who held Dacia and Moesia at the time, he was at once surrounded by the barbarians and destroyed with a large part of his army. He could not even be buried. Stripped naked, he provided food for beasts and birds, as is proper for an enemy of God.

Gallus, whom the soldiers proclaimed emperor, was so eager to have his title confirmed at Rome that he not only let slip an opportunity to crush the Goths but permitted them to return home with their booty and Roman prisoners, and agreed to pay them an annual tribute. To give color to his story that the Decii had fallen in battle Gallus made Decius' younger son Hostilianus, and later also his own son Volusianus, Augustus, so that Rome had three Augusti

[1]Lactantius, On the Deaths of the Persecutors, 4.

simultaneously, until, within a few months, Hostilianus died of the plague.

The reign of Gallus and his son Volusianus (A.D. 251–253) was an unrelieved disaster. Moesia, Thrace, and Asia Minor suffered devastating invasions of Goths, pestilence devastated whole cities, and Gallus could only revive the persecution of Christians to divert the populace. When Aemilianus, governor of Moesia, won some success against the Goths, his soldiers proclaimed him emperor, and he marched on Italy. Gallus' soldiers murdered him and his son, and swore allegiance to Aemilianus. Him they killed on the approach of Valerian, whom Gallus had summoned to his assistance from the Rhine; Valerian was proclaimed emperor (A.D. 253–260) and made his son Gallienus (A.D. 253–268) partner in rule. In 256 he went east to repel a Persian invasion and left Gallienus in charge of the west. Valerian's efforts were complicated by a Gothic invasion of Asia Minor and by pestilence among his soldiers. King Sapor captured him by a ruse (258), and he died in captivity. Simultaneously in the west Goths penetrated to Macedonia and Greece and Alamanni to the Po Valley. When Gallienus hurried to Milan, where he defeated them, the Franks crossed the Rhine and poured over Gaul and Spain. Roman possessions on the right bank of the Rhine were lost forever. At the same time an uprising by a native Berber chieftain in Numidia was put down with difficulty. Gallienus was able to suppress two usurpers in Pannonia, but in Gaul he was unable to depose the governor Latinius Postumus, who assumed the imperial title over Britain and Spain as well (A.D. 258). Postumus established his own senate and struck his own coinage. His defection weakened the central authority, but his defense of the Rhine frontier saved the west.

In the east the oasis city of Palmyra, between Damascus

and the Euphrates, which had been a Roman dependency, rose to head a virtually independent empire. When Valerian was captured and the Roman power in the east collapsed, Gallienus made Odaenathus, a Palmyrene prince who held senatorial rank, Commander of the East. Odaenathus cleared Mesopotamia and Syria of the Persians and, though he acknowledged Roman suzerainty, ruled as an independent king. When he was assassinated, in 266, his wife Zenobia ruled.

[1]This proud woman occupied a regal position in the reign of Gallienus and afterwards when Claudius was occupied with the Gothic War; in the end she was barely beaten by Aurelian, led in triumph, and subjected to Roman law. There is extant a letter of Aurelian's which is a testimonial to this captive woman. Some had been critical of so brave a man triumphing over a woman as if she were a general, and he defended himself before the senate and Roman people by the following letter of justification: "I hear, gentlemen, that objection is taken to my triumphing over Zenobia as being unmanly. The very people who criticize would praise me if they knew the sort of woman she is, how wise in counsels, how steadfast in plans, how firm towards the soldiers, how generous at need, how severe when discipline demands. I can say that it is due to her that Odaenathus defeated the Persians, pursued Sapor, and reached Ctesiphon. I can add that this woman so overawed the east and Egypt that neither Arabs nor Saracens nor Armenians stirred. Nor would I have spared her life had I not known that she served the Roman state greatly by maintaining the rule of the east for herself or her children." . . .

Her continence was said to be such that she would not know even her own husband except for conceiving. When she had once lain with him she would refrain till her period

[1]*Historia Augusta, Thirty Tyrants*, 30.

to see if she were pregnant; if not, she would again afford him an opportunity of begetting. She lived in regal pomp. It was more in the Persian fashion that she received adoration, and in the fashion of the Persian kings that she banqueted. But it was in the fashion of Roman emperors that she marched to assemblies, helmeted, with a purple sash with jewels hanging at its fringes and fastened at the middle with a cochlis jewel instead of a woman's brooch, and frequently with her arms bare. Her complexion was dark and tanned, her eyes black and preternaturally vivid, her spirit was godlike, her charm unbelievable. Her teeth were so white many thought she had pearls for teeth. Her voice was clear and deep. Her sternness was like a tyrant's when need demanded, her clemency like a good emperor's when justice was in question.

In the chaos of Gallienus' reign it was a blessing rather than otherwise that Gaul and the east were protected by usurpers. More vexatious and more permanently damaging were the Goths, who had seized the harbors on the north coast of the Black Sea. In 262 they passed the Bosporus and Hellespont and raided the Aegean shore; in 267 they sacked the chief cities of Greece, including Athens. During his reign the authority of Gallienus was challenged by some twenty usurpers in various provinces, and in 268 he was killed and replaced by Claudius (A.D. 268-270), whose victory over the Goths, who had again overrun the Balkans, earned him the title of Gothicus. A sense of the political atmosphere in Rome is revealed by the acclamations said (though probably falsely) to have been shouted in his honor by the assembled senators:

[1]"Claudius Augustus, may the gods preserve you! (said sixty times); Claudius Augustus, you or your like we have always desired for emperor (said forty times); Claudius

[1]Historia Augusta, Claudius, 3.4.

Augustus, the state needed you (said forty times); Claudius Augustus, you are brother, you are father, you are friend, you are a good senator, you are a true prince (said eighty times); Claudius Augustus, deliver us from [the usurper] Aureolus (said five times); Claudius Augustus, deliver us from the Palmyrenes (said five times); Claudius Augustus, free us from Zenobia and Vitruria (said seven times); Claudius Augustus, [Emperor of Gaul] Tetricus has accomplished nothing (said seven times)."

[1]After Claudius' death Aurelian [A.D. 270–275] succeeded to the throne. He was born in Dacia and an excellent general, but had a sharp temper and was sometimes cruel. He fought the Goths with energy and defeated them, and his military successes extended the empire to its former limits. He overthrew Tetricus in Gaul . . . and took Zenobia prisoner in an engagement near Antioch. She had killed her husband Odaenathus and dominated the east. . . .

In Aurelian's reign the moneyers of the mint raised a rebellion in the city; they adulterated the coinage and killed the commissioner of the treasury. Aurelian suppressed them with extreme rigor; several senators he executed. He was a ruthless man, but such as the times required for an emperor. He was always strict, and condemned even his own nephew. But he reformed military discipline and loose morality. He surrounded Rome with strong walls [which stand to this day, evidence that the pax Romana was a thing of the past]. He built a temple to the sun, and placed quantities of gold and precious stones in it. The province of Dacia, which Trajan had formed beyond the Danube, he gave up; it could not be retained after the depopulation of Illyricum and Moesia. Dacia had been on the left of the Danube as it runs to the sea; now Aurelian gave the name

[1]Eutropius, 9.13.

of Dacia to the land between the two Moesiae on the right
of the Danube, and he settled there the Roman citizens
whom he removed from the towns and countryside of the
old Dacia.

Aurelian's well-earned triumph of A.D. 273 was a magnificent show:

[1]There were three royal chariots. One, Odaenathus', was
elaborately wrought of silver, gold, and jewels; another, of
similar workmanship, was given Aurelian by the king of the
Persians; the third Zenobia had made for herself, expecting
to visit Rome in it, nor was she wrong, but she entered the
city with it vanquished and triumphed over. There was
another chariot with a team of four stags, said to belong to
the king of the Goths. Many have recorded that Aurelian
rode up to the Capitol in this, there to slaughter the stags
and offer them with the chariot in fulfillment of a vow to
Jupiter Optimus Maximus. In the procession were 20 elephants, 200 tamed animals of different sorts from Libya and
Palestine (these Aurelian presented at once to individuals,
to spare the state the expense of their upkeep), 4 tigers,
giraffes, elks, and other such animals, 800 pairs of gladiators,
and captives from the barbarian tribes. . . . Among the
captives was Tetricus, dressed in a scarlet cloak, yellow
tunic, and Gallic breeches, accompanied by his son, whom
he had proclaimed emperor in Gaul. There was also
Zenobia, decked with jewels and with golden chains which
others carried.

[2]Zenobia's life was granted her by Aurelian, and thereafter she is said to have lived with her children in the
style of a Roman lady on an estate given her at Tibur. It is
still called Zenobia, and is not far from Hadrian's villa and
the place called Concha.

[1]Historia Augusta, Aurelian, 33.
[2]Historia Augusta, Thirty Tyrants, 30.

Tetricus too was not only spared but given a high position as supervisor of morals in Lucania. The new wealth from the east enabled Aurelian to reform the coinage and restore financial confidence, and to regularize and increase the distribution of food and other social services. If the state was stronger, it strengthened its control over the lives of its individual members. Aurelian canceled all arrears to the treasury, burned the registers of these debts in the Forum of Trajan, and suppressed the informers who blackmailed debtors on the strength of them. He showed consideration for the senate and rewarded equestrians who had served the state well by advancing them to that rank. Whether because of the third-century tendency towards monotheism, or because he sought a cult which might unify the whole empire, Aurelian worshiped the sun, but unlike Elagabalus he never identified himself with the god he worshiped. Possibly in order to emphasize the pre-eminence of Rome in the empire he adjudicated a quarrel between Christian bishops over the see of Antioch by referring the question to the Christian authorities in Rome.

[1]When Paul fell from orthodoxy in the faith and from the episcopate, Domnus succeeded to the ministry of the church at Antioch. But Paul insisted on not yielding the church building, and the emperor Aurelian, who was appealed to, rendered an extremely just decision in the matter. He ordered that the building be assigned to those whom the bishops in Rome and Italy should designate. Thus Paul was driven from the church with utmost indignity by the world ruler. Such was Aurelian's disposition towards us at that time, but later in his reign he changed his mind and was moved by certain counsels to stir up persecution against us. There was much talk about this on all sides. But as he was on the point, one might say, of signing the decrees

[1]Eusebius, *Ecclesiastical History*, 7.30.18.

against us, divine justice all but fettered his arms to prevent him.

[1]In the end Aurelian's own servants, counterfeiting his hand, wrote a list of officers Aurelian intended to kill and showed it to the men whose names they had put down, who were all friends of Aurelian. They killed him on the road midway between Constantinople and Heraclea [A.D. 275]. At this time there was a kind of interregnum.

Perhaps to dissociate themselves from the murder of one of the best of the Roman emperors and to await the decision of Probus, Aurelian's best and most loyal general, then in Egypt, the army refused to name a successor and petitioned the senate to do so. The senate named Tacitus (A.D. 275–276), then seventy-five years old. Tacitus was murdered, and his half brother and pretorian prefect Florian assumed the purple. But the army of the east proclaimed Probus emperor, and when Florian's soldiers refused to fight for him he committed suicide. Probus (A.D. 276–282) succeeded in repelling new Germanic invasions, subduing the rebellious and piratical Isaurians in Asia Minor, and suppressing a revolt in Egypt, but his soldiers chafed at his discipline, murdered him, and made Carus, another good general, emperor. Carus fought a successful campaign against the Persians and captured Ctesiphon, but he was murdered on the return march (A.D. 282). Carus had made his elder son Carinus his co-ruler, in charge of the west; his younger son, Numerianus, took charge of the army. Numerianus was assassinated by the pretorian prefect Aper, who expected to succeed, but the army chose Diocletian instead (284). Carinus moved against Diocletian from the west, and in the course of a battle between the two in Moesia Carinus was murdered by his own officers (285). With Diocletian a new epoch of history begins.

[1]Aurelius Victor, 35.

8. Diocletian and the Constantines

No individual so revolutionized the empire as did Diocletian (A.D. 285–305). Though he rose, like the other Illyrian emperors, through military competence, his highest abilities were in government and organization. No previous reformer had been so thoroughgoing, and none more disinterested, as his abdication on the date he appointed shows. The first Caesar had envisaged absolutism, the second had disguised it, but in the intervening centuries the disguise, sometimes very thin indeed, only served to rob absolutism of its efficiency. The peace of the world demanded that absolutism become open, and Diocletian showed true statesmanship in shaping the empire according to the realities.

During the preceding half century the empire had been repeatedly fragmented by successful and ambitious generals. No potentially insubordinate general must therefore be allowed such dangerous successes, and so Diocletian himself kept near the important frontiers in the east. But the west too needed watching, and so he chose as his colleague for the west another Illyrian soldier, Maximian. Himself he called Jovius and Maximian Herculius. Diocletian's principal seat was Nicomedia, Maximian's Milan. Rome retained its prestige, and was fed and entertained at the empire's expense, but it was no longer the seat of empire; the senate was now in effect a municipal council. But two emperors were not enough, and a succession had to be provided for. On 1 March 293, therefore, Diocletian named

Maximianus (not Maximian's son Maxentius) Caesar, and Maximian named the pretorian prefect Constantius. The Augusti, it was ordained, were to rule for twenty years and then step down in favor of the Caesars.

Maximian's first task was to suppress a widespread paramilitary movement among Gallic peasants who called themselves Bagaudae. It is to this achievement that Maximian's panegyrist here refers:

[1]"In undertaking the tasks proffered by your excellent brother your energy matched his prudence. It was not merely that you put a helpful hand to the tiller when a favoring breeze from the stern drove the ship of state forward: when, after the ruin of preceding ages, the restoration of the state required divine aid, and not one man's only, side by side with the prince you supported the tottering Roman name. Your assistance was like your namesake Hercules' to his namesake Jove. When Jove was struggling in the war of the giants Hercules' help proved that he could give the gods heaven as well as receive it from them. The evil that afflicted this country was like that of the misshapen monsters, and you, Caesar, suppressed it by your vigor—or shall I say allayed it by your clemency? Ignorant rustics aspired to soldierly ways; plow hand aped infantryman, shepherd cavalryman, the farmer imitated the barbarian enemy and wasted his own land. But I observe—such is your piety—that you prefer to forget that victory rather than glory in it."

Another panegyrist, speaking before Constantine at Autun in A.D. 311, mentions the desolation the Bagaudae had wrought in Bourgogne:

[2]"Land which has never repaid cultivation is necessarily abandoned, and so it is when impoverished farmers are so

[1]Panegyrici Latini (Mamertinus), 2.4.
[2]Panegyrici Latini, 8.4.

weighed down by debt that they are not free to channel water or clear brush; and so soil that was once tolerable is sunk in marshes or overrun with brambles. But even the famous region [of Beaune and Chalon-sur-Saône] is smitten with sterility. Its lowest portion has some vines, but to the rear all the rest is forest and inaccessible rocks, the haunts of wild beasts. The plain at the foot of the hills stretching to the Saône was at one time, I hear, a flourishing place. Constant care in each farm kept the channels clear to drain the flow of the springs. Now it is abandoned and the channels are choked: the rich bottom land has been turned into a swamp. Even the vines which the ignorant admire so are grown too old to respond to cultivation. . . . Why should I speak of other localities in that area? You have confessed that they brought tears to your eyes. You saw no cultivated, cleared, flourishing land, no easy roads, no navigable rivers washing the very gates of towns, but immediately after the fork of the road to Belgium everything was desolate, uncared for, rank, mute, and dismal. Even the military roads were so rough and hilly and broken as not to admit half-loaded or even empty carts."

After crushing the Bagaudae Maximian repelled attacks of Franks, Alamanni, and Burgundians from across the Rhine, but was unable to subdue Carausius, who held Britain and the Gallic coast and proclaimed himself Augustus. But when there were four able and authorized generals to deal with frontier wars or attempted usurpations, disturbances which would have intensified chaos in the preceding century were dealt with energetically and promptly. Constantius recovered Britain, Maximian suppressed an uprising of the Quinquegentiani in Africa, Diocletian crushed a usurper named Achilles in Egypt, Galerius repelled invasions of Iazyges and Carpi on the Danube and defended Armenia from a Persian invasion. Border defenses were strengthened and garrisoned with militia called limitanei, and a powerful mobile force called comitatenses was kept ready for emergencies. To prevent concentration of power in a single official, military and civil authority in the provinces were divided. Provinces themselves were now subdivided so that their number exceeded a hundred; they were grouped in thirteen dioceses, administered by vicarii subordinate to the pretorian prefects.

The fiscal situation Diocletian sought to remedy by imposing uniform taxation, which was to be equably if strictly collected. To the coinage, which was debased to the point where lead was merely coated with silver, he tried to give a real value by increasing content of precious metal. When inflation persisted nevertheless, he issued his famous edict on prices, of which the following is the preamble:

[1]"Next to the immortal gods, recalling our successful wars, we must be grateful to the fortune of our state for a world that is tranquil and serenely quiet and for the blessings of peace achieved with heavy toil. Public decency and the dignity and majesty of Rome demand that that fortune be organized efficiently and managed successfully. By the kindly favor of the gods we have repressed the former ravages of the barbarians by destroying them, and we must protect the peace established for eternity by defenses which justice can claim. Avarice boundless and frenzied, with no consideration for humankind, multiplies its spreading grasp like wildfire, not by years or months or days but every hour and minute. If self-restraint could curb its excesses or if the general welfare could tolerate the rank license which wickedly lacerates it daily, there might be place for turning a blind eye and keeping silent till public suffering should temper the abominable and pitiable cruelty. But since the unrestrained madness of lust will take no thought for the

[1]Edictum Diocletiani de Pretiis Venalibus, ed. Blümner.

common welfare, since only necessity, not their own wish, can check the seething and torrential avarice of unscrupulous exploiters whose creed it is to prey upon the fortunes of all, and since the impoverished victims have been forced to an awareness of their wretched state—in view of this situation we who are protectors of humankind have resolved that justice should intervene as arbiter so that the remedies we provide may effect the general improvement which mankind has long hoped for but could never itself attain. As everyone must realize from the facts, it is almost too late for our measures. We made plans and delayed their execution in the natural hope that the apprehension of their offenses might induce men to reform, for it seemed better that their own sensibilities should cleanse the stains of ruthless spoliation from their minds. But they plunged deeper into malefaction and in their blindness turned to crimes against the state; their savage cruelty was actionable as well as inhuman. The remedies which the situation has long demanded we therefore hasten to apply, assured that our intervention cannot be criticized as untimely or unnecessary or trivial. Our long silence has been a lesson in restraint; those unscrupulous men have been unwilling to profit by it.

"Is anyone so dull and unfeeling as not to know, not to have seen, that the high prices in our markets, on which the daily life of our cities depends, are not checked by abundance or bumper crops? So abandoned is the passion for gain that men in the business actually try to control wind and weather by the movement of the stars and wickedly abhor the rains which make fields fertile, for the abundance which favorable weather brings they calculate as a loss. . . . Men with enough wealth to satisfy whole nations try to capture smaller fortunes and strive after ruinous percentages; concern for humanity in general persuades us to set a limit to the avarice of such men. Now we must detail the facts whose urgency has finally overcome our tolerance."

Diocletian proceeds to show instances of profiteering, especially to the disadvantage of soldiers and veterans, and to enact capital punishment for vendors who charge more than the maximum prices for goods or services set down in a long list subjoined, or who refuse to sell goods when they are available. But the measure failed of its purpose and was disregarded except as material for vilifying its author. Like Rome's first emperor, Diocletian seems to have considered religion a means for unifying the empire, as his use of the names Jovius and Herculius suggests. It was inevitable that he should find the Christians a stumbling block, and he took ruthless measures to suppress them as a dissident element in the empire. In the Christian writers Diocletian is a monster of wickedness.

[1]Diocletian, that inventor of crime and contriver of wickedness, ruined everything and did not spare God Himself. Partly through avarice and partly through timidity he overturned the Roman empire. He chose three men to share his government, and while the empire was quartered armies were multiplied. Each of the four rulers desired to keep a larger army than any single emperor had done in the past. There were fewer people to pay than there were to receive. Farmers were impoverished by huge exactions, farms were abandoned, tilth degenerated to woodland. To saturate every corner with terror the provinces were divided into fragments, each of which and almost every town had a host of officials great and small to oppress it. There were hierarchies of bailiffs and deputies of the administrators. Very few civil cases came before them, but people were condemned every day and their property confiscated. There were countless taxes on commodities, repeated over and

[1]Lactantius, On the Deaths of the Persecutors, 7.

over and running continuously, and imposts were unendurable.

Revenue for maintaining the army might have been tolerable, but Diocletian's avarice was so insatiable that he would never allow the balance in his treasury to fall; to keep his hoard inviolate and undiminished he constantly accumulated special levies and free contributions. When his multifarious extortions had made everything very dear he tried to limit prices by ordinance. Then blood was spilt for the merest trifles. People were afraid to offer anything for sale, and prices were dearer than ever. When the ordinance had ruined many people it could only be abrogated. A boundless passion for building aggravated matters. This involved huge exactions from the provinces to pay laborers and craftsmen and supply carts and other necessities for construction work. Here a basilica, there a circus, here a mint and there a factory for war matériel; in one place a residence for his empress, in another for his daughter. Soon a large part of the city was depopulated; people moved, with wives and children, as from a town taken by an enemy. When these buildings were finished, to the ruin of whole provinces, Diocletian would complain that they were not right and change the design. Then they had to be pulled down or altered, perhaps only to be pulled down later. Such were the foolish measures he took to make Nicomedia rival the magnificence of Rome. How many people perished because of their property or riches I will not say; such cases were frequent, so frequent, indeed, as to seem almost lawful. It was habitual with Diocletian, whenever he saw a flourishing farm or an elegant house, to prepare a false indictment involving capital punishment against the owner. It seemed as if he was compelled to compound robbery with murder.

Christian indignation is easy to understand. In 303 Diocletian issued an edict depriving Christians of citizenship (and hence of eligibility to office), forbidding the emancipation of Christian slaves, and ordering the demolition of churches. After fires in the palace at Nicomedia and an uprising in Syria, which were blamed on the Christians, Diocletian issued a second edict, ordering the imprisonment of the clergy, and a third, compelling them to sacrifice to the gods of the state. In 304 this latter requirement was applied to all Christians. Constantius in Gaul virtually disregarded the edicts; Maximian and Galerius were active persecutors. Christian sources attribute the persecution to Galerius' instigation. On 1 May 305 Diocletian and Maximian abdicated their authority in accordance with their agreement, Diocletian in Nicomedia and Maximian in Milan, the former with great relief, the latter with great reluctance.

[1]When Diocletian and Maximian retired from governing Constantius and Galerius became Augusti. The Roman world was divided so that Constantius held Gaul, Italy, and Africa, and Galerius Illyria, Asia, and the east. Their two Caesars were Valerius Severus and Maximinus Daia. Constantius was content with his dignity as emperor, and declined the government of Africa. He was a good and kindly man who strove to improve the fortunes of provinces and individuals and was indifferent to enriching the treasury; he used to say that it was better for the national wealth to be in the hands of individuals than to be stored away in a prison. . . . The Gauls loved and revered him because under his administration they had escaped the suspicious prudence of Diocletian and the headstrong violence of Maximian. Constantius died in Britain at York in the thirteenth year of his reign [A.D. 306]. . . .

After Constantius' death Constantine, his son by a wife of obscure birth, was made emperor in Britain and proved a

[1]Eutropius, 10.1.

most desirable ruler. At Rome meanwhile the pretorian guards rose up and proclaimed as emperor Maxentius son of Maximian Herculius, who lived in the state lodging house outside the city. At news of this action Maximian hoped to recover the imperial dignity which he had reluctantly resigned. He hurried to Rome from Lucania (where he had retired to spend his old age in a delightful spot) and wrote Diocletian urging him to resume the authority he had laid down; these letters Diocletian ignored. Galerius dispatched Severus to Rome to suppress Maxentius and the pretorians, but his army deserted him as he was besieging the city. He fled and was killed at Ravenna, and Maxentius was thus established in power. When his father Maximian later attempted to divest Maxentius of this power the soldiers reviled and disobeyed him. Maximian then set out for Gaul, making it appear that he was going to join his son-in-law Constantine because his son had driven him away, but in fact intending to cut Constantine off if he could find an opportunity. Soldiers and provincials alike admired Constantine; he had defeated Franks and Alamanni with great slaughter and had thrown their captured kings to wild beasts in a magnificent spectacle. Fausta informed her husband Constantine of her father's plot, and Maximian was overtaken at Massilia, from which he meant to join his son. His death [A.D. 310] was deserved, for he was most cruel, faithless, perverse, and without consideration for others.

In 311 Galerius interpreted a mortal illness as the punishment of the Christian God for his persecutions, and rescinded his anti-Christian decrees. There were now four Augusti (and no Caesars) distributed as follows: Constantine held Britain, Gaul, and Raetia; his brother-in-law Licinius the Illyrian and Balkan provinces; Maxentius Spain, Italy, and Africa; and Maximinus Daia the lands east of the Bosporus, including Egypt. By 324 Constantine had eliminated the others and become sole emperor. First Maxentius, who was supported by Maximinus Daia, sought to add Raetia to his domain. Constantine, supported by Licinius, marched into Italy and defeated Maxentius, who was killed in a battle near the Milvian bridge (A.D. 312). It was on this occasion that Constantine saw his famous vision of the cross, on the pattern of which he designed the labarum.

[1]Constantine called upon God in prayer, begging and beseeching that He would reveal Himself and stretch His right hand out for the enterprise in hand. As the emperor offered his prayer and ardent petition a most extraordinary sign appeared. If anyone else reported it it would not be easy to believe, but when the victorious emperor himself confirmed it on oath in writhing to the author of this narrative many years later when I was judged worthy of his acquaintance and conversation, who would hesitate to credit the story? Indeed, subsequent events demonstrated the truth of the matter. A little after noon, as the sun began to decline, he declared that he saw with his own eyes in the sky beneath the sun a trophy in the shape of a cross made of light with the inscription "By this conquer." He was astounded by the spectacle, as were the soldiers who accompanied him on his march and saw the miraculous phenomenon. At first he was at a loss to know what the apparition meant, and when night fell he was still reflecting and puzzling over the matter. But when he fell asleep God's Christ appeared to him with the sign which he had seen in the sky and instructed him to fashion a likeness of the sign and to use it as a protection in the encounters of war.

At dawn he arose and told them the secret. Then he summoned craftsmen in gold and precious stones and sat in their midst to explain the form of the sign and ordered

[1]Eusebius, Life of Constantine, 1.28.

them to reproduce it in the precious materials. Its figure was as follows. There was a tall spear, covered with gold, which had a transverse bar to make a cross. On the top of the spear was fixed a crown woven of gold and precious stones, on which the name of the Saviour was symbolized by its initial letters, XP.

In 313 Constantine and Licinius met at Milan to celebrate the marriage of the latter to the former's sister. At this meeting was drawn up the annulment of the anti-Christian measures which has come to be known as the Edict of Milan:

[1]"When, happily, I Constantine Augustus, and I Licinius Augustus, foregathered at Milan and dealt with all matters which pertain to public convenience and security, among other matters which we saw would profit the majority we came to believe that regulations concerning reverence to divinity merited prime attention, to the end that we should grant to Christians and all others the free possibility of following the religion which each man prefers, so that the divinity in the celestial seat should be benign and propitious to us and to all who are under our government. Accordingly we believed that in keeping with wholesome and correct reasoning we should adopt the following principle: no one at all must be denied the possibility of devoting himself to the observances of the Christians or to whatever religion he feels suitable for himself, so that the supreme deity whose religion we follow with free minds might vouchsafe His favor and benevolence to all. Your reverence must then know that it is our pleasure that all the conditions which we transmitted to your office in writing concerning the subject of Christians are altogether removed. Now each and every person who wishes to observe the religion of the

[1]Lactantius, *On the Deaths of the Persecutors*, 48.2.

Christians may proceed to do so without any disturbance or molestation. And we believed that, because of your solicitude, this matter must be made known to you in the fullest terms, so that you may be aware that we have granted the Christians free and unconditioned liberty of worship according to their religion. And when you perceive our indulgence to the Christians your reverence will understand that the same open and free exercise of their religion is granted to others also. It is our pleasure that in accordance with the serenity of our age each man shall have free opportunity to worship as he chooses, so that we may not detract from any man's dignity nor from any religion. Moreover we have taken the following decision in the case of Christians: the places at which they had been accustomed to foregather, which were included in the instructions transmitted to your office in writing, which have been purchased either from the treasury or from individuals, those places must be restored to the Christians without money or other consideration; this requirement is not to be evaded or temporized with. Any who have received such places as a gift must return them forthwith. If those who purchased these places or received them as a gift think some compensation is due them from our benevolence they shall apply to our surrogate, who will look out for their interests through our clemency. All this property is to be handed over to the body of Christians through your intercession and without delay. And since the Christians are known to have possessed not only the places in which they meet but other places also which belonged not to individuals but to their body in general, that is their churches, we include all such places in the regulation aforementioned. You will order them to be restored to these same Christians, that is to their society or conventicles, without evasion or controversy. Again the proviso mentioned above will be preserved, that persons who do restore them without price may hope for indemnity from our benevolence. In all these matters you are to show great diligence in behalf of the Christians so that our instructions may be carried out speedily and thereby public tranquillity be promoted through our clemency. Thus shall it come about that the divine favor which we have experienced in matters most important shall persevere through all time for our success and the public happiness. And in order that the form of this our sanction and benevolence shall reach the notice of all men, it will be appropriate for you to publish these writings everywhere and bring them to the attention of all men, so that the sanction of this our benevolence shall not remain unknown.

For Licinius the publication of the edict of toleration was a factor in his design to overreach Maximinus Daia, with whom it was evident he would have to contest the dominion of the east. When, shortly after the promulgation of the edict, Constantine was called away to suppress a Frankish rebellion, Maximinus seized the opportunity to cross the Bosporus. Licinius encountered and defeated him near Adrianople. Maximinus, who escaped, sought to conciliate the Christians and Constantine by issuing his own edict of toleration, but before the end of 313 he died, and Licinius and Constantine were left as joint rulers of the empire. This arrangement continued for ten years, but the friction of competing ambitions made it clear that one must get the upper hand. One aspect of the differences between the men was their treatment of Christians: Constantine courted their support by granting them special privileges, Licinius was hostile to them and restricted their privileges. In 322 Constantine trespassed on Licinius' domain to repel a Gothic invasion, which their agreement permitted him to do, and Licinius treated the trespass as an act of war. Constantine

defeated Licinius' army at Adrianople, and his son Crispus
Licinius' fleet at the Hellespont. Licinius withdrew to Nico-
media, where Constantine besieged him.

[1]Knowing that his forces were inadequate, Licinius
despaired of fighting. He came out of the city to Constantine as a suppliant, offered him his purple and hailed
him lord and king, and begged forgiveness for bygones. He
felt sure that he would be allowed to live, for his wife had
received her brother Constantine's solemn oath to that
effect. Constantine delivered Martinianus [Licinius' Caesar]
to his guards for execution and sent Licinius to Thessalonica, allegedly for his safety; but after a short time he
violated his oath, as was habitual with him, and hanged
him.

Now that the whole empire devolved upon Constantine,
he no longer concealed his malignity but allowed it free
scope to act at will. He still practiced the ancestral rites, not
out of reverence but out of expediency. Hence he hearkened
to soothsayers, for he found that they had prophesied truly
concerning all his successes. When he came to Rome,
swollen with pride, he thought proper to begin his impiety
at his very hearth. Disregarding all ties of nature, he killed
his own son Crispus, who held the dignity of a Caesar, because he was suspected of consorting with his stepmother
Fausta. When Constantine's mother Helen was indignant
at such a calamity and distressed at the death of the young
man, as if to console her Constantine remedied one evil
with a greater. He ordered the bath to be heated to a very
high temperature, placed Fausta in it, and brought her out
dead. Conscious of these crimes and of his violation of
oaths, he went to the priests to seek purgation of these
offenses. When they replied that no traditional mode of
purgation could suffice for such enormities, a certain Egyp-

[1]Zosimus, 2.28.

tian who came to Rome from Spain and had become a
familiar of the court ladies conversed with Constantine and
assured him that the doctrine of the Christians could
abolish all guilt, that this faith could receive sinful persons
and immediately free them from every fault. Constantine
readily accepted this argument, and dismissed his ancestral
usages; when he received what the Egyptian gave him, he
began his impiety by suspecting the art of divination.
Though the many successes which this art had foretold had
actually come to pass, he feared lest the future should
similarly be foretold to other inquirers, and this apprehension caused him to abolish the practice. When the festival
upon which the army traditionally ascends the Capitoline
came round, he reviled the ascent shamefully and withdrew from the sacred observance, and so incurred the hatred
of senate and people.

Constantine could not endure the universal execrations,
as it were, and sought for a city to rival Rome in which to
establish his palace. When he came to the region of the
Troad near the site of ancient Troy and found a spot suitable for building a city, he laid his foundations and raised
walls to a considerable height; they can be seen even now
as one sails towards the Hellespont. But he changed his
mind and left this work incompleted, and moved to Byzantium. He admired its site and resolved to enlarge it greatly
and make it suitable for a king's residence. The city lies
upon a hill, occupying part of the isthmus formed by the
Horn and the Propontis. Formerly it had a gate at the end
of the portico which the emperor Severus built when he
laid aside his wrath against the Byzantines for receiving his
enemy Niger into their city. The wall descended the hill on
the west to the temple of Venus and the sea opposite
Chrysopolis. On the north the wall descends to the harbor
called Naval Docks and beyond it to the sea directly oppo-

site the mouth which leads to the Euxine. This narrow space runs for about three hundred stades. This was the extent of the ancient city. Constantine built a circular market place where the gate formerly was, and enclosed it with a two-story portico. He made two large arches of marble of Proconnesus facing each other which afforded entrance to Severus' portico and egress to the old city. Wishing to enlarge the city greatly, he built a new wall fifteen stades beyond the old, embracing the whole isthmus from sea to sea. When he had thus enlarged the city he built a palace not much smaller than that at Rome. He constructed a very elaborate hippodrome, in part of which he placed a shrine of Castor and Pollux; their statues can still be seen standing on the colonnade of the hippodrome. In part of the hippodrome also he placed the tripod of Delphian Apollo [still in Constantinople] with Apollo's statue on it. Byzantium has a very large market place with quadruple porticoes. At the end of one of these, reached by a long stairway, he built two temples and placed statues in them. One held the statue of Rhea, mother of the gods, which Jason's comrades on his voyage had set up on Mount Didymus, which overhangs the city of Cyzicus. They say that he mutilated this statue out of disrespect to religion; the lions on either side he removed, and he changed the posture of the hands. Originally they seemed to be holding the lions; now he put them in an attitude of prayer, observing and overseeing the city. In the other temple he placed a statue of Fortuna Romana. He also built houses for certain senators who followed him from Rome.

The dedication of the new city on 11 May 330 gave formal recognition to a fact which had been sensed by intelligent observers from Mark Antony onwards—the capital of the empire must be situated at the crossroads of the world. The new Rome reproduced the organizations and institutions of the old—a senate, public festivals, and free bread for the populace, for which grain from Egypt was now diverted from the old Rome. The fact that Constantinople continued to be the capital of western civilization until 1453 testifies to Constantine's wise choice of location. But old Rome continued eternal, and the pride of its nobles was never abated.

If Constantinople is one great achievement which preserved its founder's memory, a greater is his recognition of Christianity as the state religion. What Constantine's inward attitude to Christianity was is difficult to determine. Writers ancient and modern differ so diametrically, it is hard to realize that they are dealing with the same man. We move from the hostility of the pagans, of which the passage cited from Zosimus above is a mild example, to the adulation of a Eusebius:

[1]When I gaze in spirit upon this thrice-blessed soul, united with God, free of all mortal dross, in robes gleaming like lightning and in ever radiant diadem, speech and reason stand mute.

Eusebius' Life clearly falsifies history, if only by making a virile and competent emperor a sanctimonious prig. On the other hand it is futile to cite Constantine's numerous murders and perjuries, even his bearing such pagan titles as Pontifex Maximus, to prove that he was not a Christian; most Christian princes of later ages have been guilty of similar inconsistencies. What may be said is that, whatever religious beliefs he may have had, it was political wisdom to join rather than fight the Church. Christianity had proved a sounder banner for unifying the empire than the state religion of Rome, and its episcopal organization observed and exacted fuller discipline than the organs of the state. The Nicene Council shows that Constantine hoped to control

[1]Eusebius, Life of Constantine, 1.2.

the Church; within the century the Church asserted its claim to control the emperor.

But aside from his services to Christianity Constantine merited the title Great. He was a good general and gave the empire a respite from invasion and civil war and an efficient and vigorous administration. His governmental reforms complemented those of Diocletian, so that it is in fact impossible to distribute measures between the two. His rule was a despotism, resting on the power of the army and the bureaucracy. Both were increasingly filled with non-Roman elements. To maintain them the civil population was ground down with exactions of money and personal services. For the great majority personal freedom was gone, and with it hope and courage. On the feast of Pentecost in A.D. 337, while preparing an expedition against Persia, Constantine received baptism and died in Nicomedia.

Constantine too had realized that the empire needed more than one ruler, but unlike Diocletian resolved to choose his successors among his own family. In 335 he had arranged that the empire should be divided among his sons, Constantine II, Constans, and Constantius, and his nephew Delmatius. But on Constantine's death the troops killed Delmatius and the other collateral relatives of Constantine except his nephews Gallus and Julian. From A.D. 337 to 340 Constantine II ruled Spain, Gaul, and Britain, Constantius Thrace and the east, and Constans Africa, Italy, and Illyricum. In 340 Constantine II encroached on the territory of Constans and was killed in battle; Constans annexed his domain.

From A.D. 340 to 350 Constantius and Constans ruled jointly, the former engaged in perpetual warfare with Sapor II of Persia over Mesopotamia and Armenia, the latter maintaining peace in the west. But in 350 his officers deposed

Constans in favor of a Frankish officer named Magnentius, and in Illyricum the soldiers proclaimed their commander Vetranio emperor. These usurpers Constantius disposed of, and ruled as sole Augustus until 360. In 351 Constantius made his cousin Gallus Caesar and put him in charge of the east, but Gallus was soon suspected of treasonable ambitions and was put to death in 354. But Gaul was again being subjected to invasions from across the Rhine and the need of an associate was brought home to Constantius.

[1]When the great dangers confronting the empire left Constantius at a loss his wife Eusebia, a highly educated woman and wise beyond her sex, suggested that he place as Caesar in charge of the nations beyond the Alps Julian, the brother of Gallus and the nephew of that Constantine who had been Caesar under Diocletian. Since the queen was aware that Constantius was inclined to suspect his relatives, she cajoled her husband as follows: "Julian is a quite simple young man who has spent all his life in study and is altogether without practical experience; for our purposes he will serve better than any other. If he proves successful his achievements will be ascribed to the emperor; if he fails and is killed there will be no one left of royal blood to be called to rule." Constantius was prevailed upon and summoned Julian from Athens, where he had been attending the philosophers and surpassing his teachers in every subject. When he arrived in Italy Constantius made him Caesar, betrothed his sister Helen to him, and sent him to the peoples across the Alps. And since Constantius was naturally distrustful and could not be sure that Julian would be loyal and true to him, he sent Marcellus and Sallust along and assigned the direction of affairs to them, not to Caesar. When he had made these arrangements concerning Julian, Constantius himself marched to Pannonia and

[1]Zosimus, 3.3.

Moesia, and when he had quieted the Quadi and Sarmatians he proceeded to the east where Persian incursions drew him to war. Julian crossed the Alps and arrived among the Gallic peoples assigned to him. When the barbarians persisted in their raids with undiminished license, Eusebia persuaded Constantius, using the same arguments, to entrust the direction of affairs in that area to Julian.

Julian's achievements during the remainder of his life have been dealt with at great length by historians and poets, but none of them has approximated his true greatness. Anyone who wishes may attain a full understanding by reading his discourses and letters, from which he can comprehend Julian's achievements the world over. But since it is not proper for me to interrupt my history I shall only mention details briefly at the appropriate junctures, especially such as seem to have been overlooked by other writers.

Though young and inexperienced, Julian won brilliant successes over the Franks and Alamanni; Zosimus compares his victories to those of Alexander the Great. In 360 the suspicious Constantius demanded that Julian, then in Paris, send him troops for his eastern campaigns. Instead Julian's troops raised him to the purple, and he marched east. From Naissus in Illyria Julian sent manifestos to various cities justifying his course. Here is part of his letter to the Athenians:

[1]"On my father's side my descent is the same as Constantius', as everyone knows; our fathers were brothers, sons of the same father. Close kin as we were, this is how that most humane emperor treated us: six cousins, mine and his, my father his uncle, another paternal uncle of us both, and my eldest brother he killed without a trial. Me and my brother Gallus he wanted to kill but finally sentenced to exile. Gallus he deprived of his title of Caesar and mur-

[1]Julian, *Letter to the Athenians*, 270d.

dered. . . . It was to gratify a eunuch, his chamberlain and chief cook, that Constantius gave over to his enemies to be killed a Caesar, his cousin, his sister's husband, his niece's father, the brother of his own first wife, who was bound to him by so many sacred family ties. Me he reluctantly let go, after dragging me here and there for seven whole months and keeping me under guard. If some god had not willed to save me and made the excellent and kind Eusebia well disposed towards me I could never have escaped from his hands. . . .

"Constantius gave me 360 soldiers, and in the middle of winter [355] sent me to Gaul, which was then in commotion, not as a commander of the garrisons there but as a subordinate of their generals. They had been sent letters with express orders that they were to watch me as strictly as the enemy, for fear I should cause revolt. . . . It would take too long to enumerate and record in detail the things I accomplished in four years. In sum, I crossed the Rhine three times while I was Caesar; I secured the return of 20,000 captives of the barbarians across the Rhine; in two battles and one siege I took 10,000 captives, not useless people but men in their prime; I sent Constantius four levies of excellent infantry, three that were inferior, and two outstanding squadrons of cavalry. At that time I recovered almost forty cities; now, with the help of the gods, I have recovered all of them. I call upon Zeus and all the gods who protect cities and our race to bear witness to my behavior and my loyalty to Constantius. . . .

"Constantius sent me orders for the withdrawal of all the efficient troops from Gaul; he assigned the task to Lupicinus and Gintonius and ordered me to hinder them in no way. . . . Among the troops and civilians there was great excitement, and an anonymous letter was circulated at Paris full of accusations against Constantius and lamentations over his betrayal of Paul. . . . Zeus, Helios, Ares, Athena, and all the other gods must know that no suspicion of the soldiers' intentions entered my mind. At sunset I was informed. The palace was immediately surrounded and everyone was shouting; I was still considering what to do and feeling very uncertain. My wife was still alive, and I had gone to the upper room near hers to rest alone. From there, through an opening in the wall, I prostrated myself to Zeus. When the shouting grew louder and the whole palace was in a tumult I prayed the god to give me a sign; he bade me yield and not oppose the wishes of the army. Nevertheless, despite the sign, I did not yield readily but resisted all I could and would not accept the salutation or crown. But I could not, being one, prevail over so many, and the gods whose will this was spurred the soldiers on and softened my resolution. About the third hour, when some soldier or other gave me the robe, I put it on and returned to the palace, my heart within me groaning, as the gods know."

But Julian was spared the inevitable battle with Constantius, who died (A.D. 360) as he was starting his campaign. Despite Julian's criticism Constantius had been a conscientious and effective ruler. Suspicion and cruelty were inevitable in the character of the imperial office, which necessitated a large network of secret agents and informers. About the beginning of the second century A.D. secret intelligence was made the responsibility of the frumentarii, whose original function was to oversee the grain supply for the troops. Diocletian changed their designation to agentes in rebus and placed them under the direction of the magister officiorum. Under an emperor like Constantius these agentes were very active.

[1]In Aquitania an old experienced hand who was invited

[1]Ammianus Marcellinus, 16.8.8.

to one of the fashionable and elegant banquets which are so frequent in that region noticed that the purple stripes of the couch covers were so wide that the attendants could fold them to make them appear a continuous purple and that the table was covered with a similar cloth. He turned the lapel of his cape to show the imperial emblem, and thus brought ruin to a rich house. Similar malice was shown by a secret agent in Spain, who was similarly invited to dinner. When the servants brought in the evening lights he heard them give the customary cry, "May we conquer (the darkness)"; he gave the expression a serious meaning and so cruelly destroyed a noble house. Actions of this sort multiplied because Constantius was timid, and so fearful for his life that he always expected an attack.

Constantine's Christian policy Constantius carried forward by outlawing paganism more vigorously, as appears in the following decree (A.D. ?346):

[1]It is our pleasure that in all places and in all cities the temples shall be immediately closed and access to them forbidden so that no abandoned men shall have the power of transgressing. It is likewise our will that all men abstain from sacrificing. If anyone shall be guilty of such an act he shall be struck down with the avenging sword. We decree also that the property of a man thus executed be confiscated to the treasury. The governors of provinces shall receive similar treatment if they fail to punish such crimes.

Constantius too sought to retain the predominance of the state, and within the Church the predominance of Rome, though he himself was almost a total stranger to the ancient capital.

[2]Leontius, governor of the eternal city, gave many proofs of being an excellent judge; he was very prompt in hearing

[1]*Theodosian Code*, 16.10.4.
[2]Ammianus Marcellinus, 15.7.1.

cases, very just in his decisions, and naturally kindly, though for the sake of maintaining authority he seemed to some severe and prone to condemn. . . . Under his administration, Liberius, a priest of the Christian religion, was ordered by Constantius to appear before the privy council [at Milan] on the charge of opposing the emperor's commands and the decrees of a majority of his own colleagues in a matter which I shall skim over briefly. Athanasius, then bishop of Alexandria, exalted himself beyond his calling and tried, as persistent rumors revealed, to manipulate matters alien to his office. A convocation of his co-religionists (they call it a synod) removed him from his religious post. It was said that he had sometimes prophesied the future on the basis of sooth-telling lots and the portents of augural birds, in which matters he was expert, and moreover that he had dabbled in other practices abhorrent to the principles of the religion over which he presided. Liberius was instructed by the emperor to depose Athanasius from his priestly position by an official writ, but though he held the same view of Athanasius he persisted in objecting, repeatedly exclaiming that it was a great iniquity to condemn a man unseen and unheard. This, of course, was overt recalcitrance to the emperor's will. Although Constantius, who was always hostile to Athanasius, knew that his desire had been carried out, he was nevertheless extremely eager to have it ratified also by the higher authority of the bishop of the eternal city. When he could not obtain this, he succeeded in deporting Liberius, but only with great difficulty and in the middle of the night, for fear of the populace, who were ardent adherents of Liberius.

[1]After the death of Constantius, Julian became emperor, and made war upon the Parthians with a very large force; [1]Eutropius, 10.16.

I too participated in this expedition. A number of Persian towns and fortresses he induced to surrender or took by assault, and when he had overrun Assyria he encamped for a time at Ctesiphon. On his victorious return he rashly joined in a hot skirmish and fell by the enemy's hand, on 26 June in the seventh year of his reign and the thirty-second of his age, and was enrolled among the gods. [At his death Julian is reported, probably apocryphally, to have said, "Thou hast conquered, Galilaean."] He was a remarkable man, and would have been an excellent ruler if the fates had allowed. He was an excellent scholar in all branches of learning, but far better read in Greek than in Latin. He possessed ready eloquence and a tenacious memory. In many ways he was more like a philosopher than a prince. He was liberal to his friends, but not as discriminating as a great emperor should be; some of his friends were a disgrace to him. He was very considerate of the provincials, and reduced their taxes as far as possible. He was indulgent to all men, and not anxious for the treasury; but he did love glory and would do anything to attain it. He was a persecutor of the Christian religion, but so that he abstained from shedding blood.

It is as a persecutor of the Christians that Julian's memory has come down. He had been brought up a Christian but rebelled (hence his title "the Apostate") when Christians massacred his family.

[1]When the time came that he could do as he wished he revealed the secrets of his heart and by open and explicit decrees ordered that the temples be opened, sacrifices brought to the altars, and the cult of the gods restored. To strengthen the effect of these ordinances he summoned the dissident Christian bishops who were at variance with their

[1]Ammianus Marcellinus, 22.5.1.

people and civilly instructed them to allay their discords: each should fearlessly serve his own beliefs and none must forbid him. He persisted in this course so that their freedom should increase their dissensions and he would no longer have a single-minded people to fear. Experience had taught him that most Christians behave more savagely to one another than wild beasts do to mankind.

Actually Julian's persecutions merely took the form of restoring the rights of Christian heretics who had been banished, depriving Christians of special privileges, and attempting to improve the organization and morale of the pagan priesthood. In an extant discourse he admonishes pagan priests to live up to the high moral responsibilities of their office and furnish a model for conduct.

[1]"Let no priest enter a theater or have an actor or charioteer for his friend; let no dancer or mime approach his door. As for the sacred games I permit anyone who wishes to attend, but only those in which women are forbidden not only to compete but even to be spectators. As regards the beast hunts performed inside theaters in the cities, it is needless to speak; not only priests but sons of priests must avoid them. . . .

"A man may be appointed a priest if he loves God and his fellow man. He proves his love of God by leading all his people to piety towards the gods; he proves his love of mankind if out of his little he shares with the needy and gives willingly, trying to benefit as many as he can. This point must be observed especially, and serve to effect a cure. When it came about that the poor were neglected and overlooked by the priests, I think, the impious Galilaeans observed the fact and devoted themselves to philanthropy. Through their good services they have prevailed with their evil deeds. It is like people who deceive children with cakes.

[1]Julian, *Letter to a Priest*, 304d.

By throwing it to them two or three times they persuade them to follow, and when they are far from their own people they put them on shipboard and sell them. The impression of sweetness makes all the rest of their life bitter. In the same way the Galilaeans begin with their so-called love feast or hospitality or service of tables (they have many forms and many names), and then they lead many people to godlessness."

Of Julian's anti-Christian measures the one that seems pettiest, and is at the same time characteristic of his convictions, is that prohibiting Christian teachers to use the pagan classics in their schools. Julian himself was the first Caesar after Julius to attain eminence as a writer. The extant body of his work includes orations, satires, and letters. As we should expect, estimates of Julian show the widest possible discrepancy, according as they emanate from pagan or Christian sources; the most lavish of praise is Libanius, who had been Julian's teacher in Athens, and the most damning Gregory of Nazianz, who had been his fellow student there. Perhaps the just approach is that of the Christian poet Prudentius:

[1]"As a leader of armies he was the bravest, as an establisher of law the most celebrated; his country he served well in word and act, but the religion we must observe he did not serve, for he loved gods by the hundred thousand. Faithless was he to God, but to mankind faithful."

With the death of Julian the dynasty of Constantine ends.

[1]Prudentius, Apotheosis, 450ff.

9. The End of the United Empire

[1]After Julian's death the soldiers elected Jovian, who had been one of his bodyguard, to rule. His father's reputation was better known to the soldiers than Jovian's own. Affairs were in confusion and the army suffering from shortages of provisions. Jovian was defeated in engagements with the Persians, and made a necessary but ignominious peace with Sapor. He was obliged to cede a part of the Roman empire to the enemy and retrench its boundaries. During the 1118 years since the empire had been founded such a disgrace was unexampled. Our legions had indeed been forced to pass under the yoke at Caudium, at Numantia, and in Numidia, but on those occasions no Roman territory was surrendered. Jovian's capitulation would not have been so reprehensible if he had determined to throw the constraints of the treaty off as soon as he could, as was done by the Romans in the cases I have mentioned; war upon the Samnites, the Numantines, and the Numidians was resumed at once, and the peace was never ratified. But while Jovian was in the east he dreaded a rival for the imperial dignity and took too little thought of glory. When he returned from the east and was proceeding towards Illyricum he died, in the seventh month of his reign and the thirty-third year of his age [A.D. 364].

Next the soldiers chose as emperor a Pannonian officer, Valentinian (A.D. 364–375), who immediately associated his younger brother Valens (364–378) with himself as Augus-

[1]Eutropius, 10.17.

202

tus. Valens defended the lower Danube and the east, Valentinian the Rhine, and his general Theodosius fought the Moors in Africa and the Scots, Picts, and Saxons in Britain. In Europe in particular the barbarian inroads were increasing in volume and tempo, and Valentinian showed unflagging energy in resisting them. He also made efforts to protect his subjects from official oppression, but here he was frequently hampered by the intrigues of his own officers. All our ancient writers speak of Valentinian's furious temper.

[1]When envoys from the Quadi were making him long-winded excuses Valentinian grew so furious that he was almost beside himself. The blood rushed to his mouth and obstructed the passage of speech. He died after spending nine months less a few days in Illyria, in the twelfth year of his rule.

In 367 Valentinian had made his eldest son Gratian, then eight years old, a third Augustus (367–383). Along with Gratian the army now acclaimed his four-year-old brother Valentinian II emperor. Valens had been almost continuously involved in a struggle with the Persians for Armenia and in defending the lower Danube from Gothic invasions. Peace was established with the Goths in 369, but the period of the great migrations was beginning and the Mongol Huns had appeared at the north of the Black Sea.

[2]The Huns, scarcely known from ancient sources, live beyond the Maeotic Marsh near the icy ocean and surpass every measure of savagery. From earliest infancy their cheeks are deeply furrowed with steel, so that the deep scars retard the growth of hair when it comes to sprout, and they grow old unbearded and with no attractiveness, like eunuchs. They all have compact and sturdy limbs and thick necks and are so monstrously ugly and misshapen that you might

[1]Zosimus, 4.17.   [2]Ammianus Marcellinus, 31.2.1.

suppose they were two-legged animals or the roughhewn stumps on the parapets of bridges. But though their shape is human it is disagreeable, and their mode of life is savage. They need no fire or prepared food but live on wild roots and the flesh of any kind of animal, eaten half raw; they warm it a little by putting it between their thighs and the backs of their horses. They are never sheltered in houses, but avoid them like tombs which are set apart from ordinary use. Not even a hut thatched with reeds can be found among them. They roam through mountains and forests and are inured to frost, hunger, and thirst from infancy. They will not enter a house, away from their haunts, except under extreme necessity; they never feel safe under a roof. Their dress is linen or skins of field mice stitched together, and they have no change of clothing, indoors or out. Once they have put their necks in a dun tunic they never take it off or change it until rottenness has crumbled it to rags. They cover their heads with round caps and their hairy legs with goatskins. Their shoes are not fitted to any shape and prevent their walking with a free stride. Hence they are little adapted to fighting on foot, but they are almost glued to their horses, which are ugly but tough; sometimes they sit them like women, and carry on their usual tasks. Day or night these people are all on horseback, buying and selling, eating and drinking, sleeping so deeply, bowed over the narrow neck of the animal, as to go through a variety of dreams. When deliberation on any serious matter is called for, they meet for consultation on horseback. No royal discipline directs them, but they find the disorderly leadership of their chiefs sufficient and crash through every obstacle. When provoked they fight, entering battle in wedges and uttering various savage yells. As they are agile and quick they purposely scatter in an irregular line and deal terrible slaughter as they dart about; because of their extraordinary mobility they are never known to attack a rampart or pillage an enemy camp. You would easily rate them the toughest of all warriors, because their missiles are tipped with sharp bone instead of points, fixed to the shafts with remarkable skill; then they gallop up and fight without regard for themselves. While their enemy guard against thrusts, they noose them with twisted strips of cloth and so prevent them from walking or riding. No one ever plows or touches a plowshare. None has a fixed dwelling; without home or law or stable livelihood, they roam about like refugees with the wagons in which they live. There their wives make their loathsome garments, cohabit with their husbands, give birth, rear their children to puberty. None of them can tell you his origin, for he was conceived in one place, born far from there, and brought up still farther away. In truces they are faithless and fickle, susceptible to every breeze of new hope, centered wholly on the momentary passion. Like unreasoning beasts, they are utterly ignorant of right and wrong. Their speech is ambivalent and enigmatic, and they are bound by no reverence for religion or superstition. They burn with lust for gold. They are so changeable and irascible that sometimes they quarrel with their allies and make friends again on the same day with no external persuasion.

[1]The invasions of the Huns reduced the Goths to such a state that their survivors abandoned their dwellings for the Huns to occupy and themselves fled down to the Danube and as suppliants petitioned the emperor Valens to receive them, promising that they would serve him as loyal and stout allies. The commander of the garrisons in the Danubian cities referred the matter to Valens.

[2]The emperor's practiced flatterers felicitated him on the good fortune which unexpectedly brought so many recruits from the ends of the earth. With his own and the foreign

[1]Zosimus, 4.20.　　　　[2]Ammianus Marcellinus, 31.4.4.

forces combined, they suggested, he would have an invincible army; furthermore the treasury would receive a great increment from exemptions from the annual conscriptions in the provinces. With these expectations various agents were sent to transport that truculent people; the operation was carried out most diligently, so that no future destroyer of the Roman state, even hopeless invalids, should be left behind. . . . At this time, when our barriers were unbarred and hordes of barbarians were spraying forth like sparks from Aetna, when a critical juncture demanded military organizers of proven achievement, then, as if by the design of an adverse deity, a group of tainted men was put in charge of the military. Their leaders, equally reckless, were Lupicinus, commander of Thrace, and Maximus, a ruinous general. Their treacherous greed was the source of all our woes. Passing over other offenses which these two, or others with their permission, committed out of the basest motives against the foreign newcomers who were as yet blameless, I shall mention one melancholy and unexampled crime which no leniency could absolve even if they were themselves the judges. When the refugee barbarians were pinched for food these odious generals contrived a foul traffic: they collected all the dogs their rapacity could discover, and exchanged them each for one slave, including even the sons of chieftains. . . .

The Theruingi [West Goths] had long since received permission to cross but were still kept wandering near the riverbanks because the wicked role the generals were playing deprived them of necessaries and purposely detained them for the unspeakable traffic. When they realized this they muttered that they were being forced to disloyalty to relieve their pressing need, and for fear of their defection Lupicinus used soldiers to make them move on [into the interior]. When the Greuthungi [East Goths] saw that our

soldiers were occupied elsewhere and that the patrol boats
which prevented their crossing were inactive, they seized
the opportunity to cross in crude rafts and encamped at a
great distance from Fritigern [a leader of the Theruingi].

News of these events [including a bloody attack upon
Lupicinus' army by the Goths, who were exasperated by
his treacherous murder of some of their leaders] was carried
far and wide. The Gothic chieftains Sueridas and Colias,
who had long ago been received and assigned to winter
quarters at Hadrianopolis, were mainly concerned with their
own safety and looked upon these events with indifference.
When they received orders of the emperor to cross to Hel-
lespontus they requested, with no show of intransigence,
travel money and food and a respite of two days. This irritated the city magistrate, who was annoyed with the Goths
because his country estate had been plundered; he brought
out the dregs of the populace and the workers in the muni-
tions factory, of which there are a large number in Hadrianopolis, armed them, sounded the war trumpet, and threatened extreme measures against all the Goths. The Goths
were shocked at this unexpected hostility and frightened by
the excited and ill-considered attack of the citizens, but
they stood stock-still; finally, however, they were exacerbated
by curses and abuse and the blows of occasional missiles and
broke into open rebellion. Many of the citizens whom their
petulance had carried too far they killed, and the rest they
routed, wounding them with various weapons. The Goths
armed themselves in Roman fashion from the stripped
corpses, joined with Fritigern, when they saw he was nearby,
and put the city under severe siege. . . . Daily numbers
of their countrymen, who had been sold by the traders or
exchanged by their famished people at their first crossing
for a drink of bad wine or a crust of wretched bread, flocked
to join them. Some who were expert in following veins of

gold could no longer endure their heavy oppression; these were gladly welcomed and were very useful, in wandering through strange localities, for pointing out hidden stores of grain and secret refuges and caches. With such guides nothing accessible was left untouched. Everything was ablaze with slaughter and conflagration, without distinction of age or sex. Sucklings were snatched from their mothers' breasts and butchered, matrons whose husbands were killed before their eyes were carried off, boys of every age were dragged away over their parents' bodies. Old men who cried they were done with life after the loss of their possessions and their handsome wives were led into exile with arms twisted behind their backs, weeping over the ashes of their ancestral homes.

Local commanders proved incapable of dealing with the peril, and Valens was summoned from Antioch and Gratian from the Rhine. Upon learning of Gratian's departure the Alamanni made a serious incursion into Gaul, and Gratian was compelled to turn back. After defeating the Alamanni he hastened to support his uncle, but Valens was drawn into action before Gratian arrived. At the battle of Adrianople (A.D. 378) the Roman army was virtually annihilated and Valens himself killed. Ammianus, who closes his history with a vivid account of this battle, notes that it was the greatest disaster to Roman arms since Cannae, but finds comfort in the traditional resilience of Rome, particularly in the recovery after barbarian invasions under Marcus Aurelius. But the situation was changed. Not only were the new invaders more numerous and formidable, but the will to resist was weakened. Within the empire life had grown so constricted and hopeless that revolutionary change could be regarded, if not with hope, at least with indifference.

The Goths had overrun all the Balkans, and to deal with the crisis Gratian raised to the purple Theodosius I (A.D.

*378–395), son of Valentinian's distinguished general of the
same name, who had gone into eclipse at his father's death.
Theodosius' first task was to pacify the Goths, which he did
partly by exploiting dissensions among them and partly by
making concessions. Part of his technique was to impress a
Gothic leader like Athaneric by entertaining him in Constantinople.*

[1]When Athaneric entered the royal city he marveled and
said, "I now see what I have often heard but never believed,
the glory of this stupendous city." He turned his eyes this
way and that, viewing with admiration the plan of the city,
its concourse of shipping, its magnificent buildings, its peoples of diverse races, as if the waves had sprinkled them into
a single pool from various directions, the orderly soldiery.
"Truly," said he, "the emperor is a god on earth, and whoever raises a hand against him makes himself guilty of his
own blood."

*Theodosius' arrangement with the Goths (A.D. 382) was
that they were to receive lands south of the Danube and
continue as an independent people under native rulers. They
were to receive fixed subsidies from Rome and in return
supply contingents for the Roman armies.*

[2]While this was the situation in Thrace, Gratian was
beset by difficulties hard to overcome. Yielding to courtiers, whose habit it is to corrupt the manners of princes, he
received a number of Alan deserters, enrolled them in his
corps, marked them out with lavish gifts, and esteemed
them so highly as to entrust matters of the highest moment
to them while he took no account of the troops. This produced hatred for their emperor on the part of the soldiers,
which increased to the point of making them susceptible to
revolution, particularly those garrisoned in the British Isles,
who are outstanding for intransigence and contumacy. To

[1]Jordanes, 28.   [2]Zosimus, 4.35.

this they were instigated by Maximus, a Spaniard by birth who had served with Theodosius in Britain. Maximus found it intolerable that Theodosius had been deemed worthy of kingship whereas he himself had not been so advanced, and therefore goaded the soldiers to hate their ruler. They revolted readily and hailed Maximus emperor, clothing him with the purple and diadem, and promptly crossed the channel to the mouth of the Rhine. The armies in Germany and adjacent regions very willingly approved the appointment, and Gratian prepared to fight, still having a good part of the army on his side. When the forces came together there was skirmishing for five days, and then Gratian observed that first all the Moorish cavalry and then the remaining troops deserted to Maximus and hailed him Augustus. In despair Gratian took 300 horsemen and fled headlong towards the Alps. When he found no garrison there he went to Raetia, Noricum, Pannonia, and upper Moesia. Maximus was not indifferent to Gratian's escape and dispatched his cavalry commander Andragathius, who came from the Euxine but was very loyal to him, with a strong force to pursue Gratian. Andragathius pursued without halt and overtook Gratian as he was about to cross the bridge of Singidunum. He killed him and thus made Maximus' rule secure [A.D. 383].

It is not irrelevant to mention the following. . . . Numa and the succeeding kings of Rome, and subsequently Octavian and all who succeeded to the empire, bore the title Pontifex Maximus. As soon as anyone attained emperorship the sacerdotal robe was offered him by the priests and he was immediately enrolled as Pontifex Maximus. All previous emperors showed great satisfaction in receiving the honor and bearing the title, even Constantine when he became emperor, though he turned from the true path of religion and chose the Christian faith, and after him the others in order, including Valentinian and Valens. But when the pontiffs, following custom, offered Gratian the robe he rejected it, regarding that dress improper for a Christian.

The quality as well as the course of the conflict of religions can be illustrated by the fate of the altar of Victory, in fact little more than a symbol of empire, which had always had its place in the Roman senate house. The altar was removed by Constantine in 357, restored by Julian, and again removed by Gratian in 382. St. Ambrose procured that the pagan senators who petitioned for its restoration were denied an audience. They petitioned again to Valentinian II in 384, their spokesman being the learned and urbane city prefect, Symmachus. Here is part of his appeal:

[1]"My task it is to exercise vigilance on behalf of your clemency. Must it not redound to the glory of our age that we defend our ancestral institutions and the laws and fortunes of our country? That glory is greater because of your awareness that our forefathers' usages must not be transgressed. We request the restoration of the state religion which has so long served our country. To be sure, there have been emperors of either persuasion: some have practiced the rites of our ancestors, the more recent have not abolished them. If you do not take the earlier emperors as an example, follow the tolerance of the later. Who is so friendly to the barbarians that he does not desire an altar of Victory? We take precautions for the future and avoid unfavorable portents. The name [nomen] at least should retain the honor which is denied to its divinity [numen]. . . . Grant, we beseech you, that what we received as children we may as elders transmit to our posterity. Attachment to old ways is very strong."

It was not for the religion so much as for the traditional cultural values of which it was symbol and guardian that

[1]Symmachus, Relatio, 3.

Symmachus appealed. Again it was the energetic intervention of Ambrose that averted a pagan victory. Here is the opening of the first of his three letters on the subject:

[1]"Just as all men under Roman dominion are your soldiers, earth's general and emperor, so you are the soldier of almighty God and His holy religion. There can be no total safety unless everyone worships the true God, that is, the God of the Christians, by Whom all things are ruled. He alone is the true God, Who is worshiped from the depths of the heart, for 'the gods of the nations are demons,' as Scripture says. A man who is truly God's soldier, who is devoted to His worship, will not turn a blind eye or connive but pay the full measure of faith and devotion. If he does not, yet must he show no complaisance to idolators and profane ceremonials. No one can deceive God, to Whom all the secrets of the heart are manifest. Since you, therefore, Most Christian Emperor, must show faith in the true God, and the zeal, caution, and devotion that appertain to faith, I wonder how certain men can have expected that you should by your edict restore the altars of the gentile gods and supply the requirements of profane sacrifices."

During the rebellion of Arbogast and Eugenius in 393 the altar was restored, but it was removed forever by Theodosius in the year following. So effective had Symmachus' eloquence proved, however, that the Christian poet Prudentius felt constrained to offer a rejoinder twenty years later.

[2]That eloquent man persists in asserting that in the search for one God the road is manifold and the paths various. Wayfarers approach from diverse and disparate directions, each by his own winding path, but in the end the paths converge and coalesce. Sky and earth, winds, sea, and clouds,

[1]Ambrose, *Epistle*, 17.
[2]Prudentius, *Against the Address of Symmachus*, 2.774ff.

he says, are given to all in common, both to us who worship thee, Christ, and to those who offer noisome entrails to graven stones. I do not deny that enjoyment of air, stars, sea, land, rain, is common to all living beings, nor indeed that the unjust and the just live under a single sky, the pious and impious breathe the same air, the chaste and the wanton, the harlot and the matron, nor that the animating breath in the priest's mouth is the same as in the gladiator's. . . . Life is common to all, but merit is not. . . . Yet Roman and barbarian differ as quadruped from biped, as the mute from the articulate; no less different are those who dutifully obey the precepts of God from those who worship stupid cults and their errors.

The Church Fathers of the fourth century were equally outspoken on luxury and low moral tone, but here the pagan Ammianus is almost as critical.

[1]The few houses that were formerly distinguished for the cultivation of serious pursuits now overflow with the pastimes of inert sloth and resound with singing and piping and harping. In place of the philosopher the singer is called in, in place of the orator the impresario; libraries are shut tight like tombs, but water organs are manufactured, and lyres as big as wagons and flutes and ponderous instruments for gesticulating performers. See how our standards have been debased: not long ago when foreigners were peremptorily expelled from the city because of an expected shortage of food [A.D. 383] and the few practitioners of the liberal arts were thrust out without respite, the companies belonging to actresses of mimes, genuine or pretending to be such for the occasion, were retained; 3000 dancing girls with their choruses and an equal number of dancing masters remained, with no question being made concerning them.

[1]Ammianus Marcellinus, 14.6.18.

Gratian attempted to improve the moral tone. He strengthened the position of Catholic orthodoxy by measures against the Arians, formulated in a series of rescripts on the Catholic faith:

[1]"It is our will that all peoples under the government of our clemency shall practice that religion which the divine Peter the Apostle transmitted to the Romans . . . that is, according to the apostolic discipline and evangelic doctrine we shall believe in the single deity of the Father, the Son, and the Holy Spirit under concept of equal majesty, and of the Holy Trinity. We command that persons who follow this rule shall embrace the name of Catholic Christians. All others we adjudge demented and insane; they shall bear the infamy of heretical dogmas, their meeting places shall not be called churches, and they shall be smitten first by divine vengeance and secondly by the retribution of our own animosity, which we shall assume in accordance with divine judgment.

"We command that all churches be immediately handed over to the bishops who confess that the Father, the Son, and the Holy Spirit are of one majesty and virtue, of the same glory, and of one splendor. . . . All who dissent from the communion of the faith of those who have been expressly enumerated above shall be expelled from their churches as manifest heretics and in future shall be wholly denied the charge of churches, so that the priesthood of the true Nicene faith may remain pure; after the clear regulations of our law there shall be no opportunity for malicious subtlety. The right of assembly we bestow upon those persons whose belief conforms to the doctrines which were decreed in the days of Constantine of blessed memory as those which should endure forever. . . . Authors of sedition and disturbers of the peace of the church shall pay the

[1]*Theodosian Code,* 16.1.2.

penalty of high treason with their life and blood. Similar punishment shall be visited upon persons who may attempt to supplicate us surreptitiously and secretly contrary to this regulation of ours."

With Gratian disposed of, Maximus was in sole control of Britain, Gaul, and Spain, and Theodosius, who was occupied in the east, could only accord him recognition. In A.D. 387 Maximus invaded Italy, which was held as an independent sphere by Valentinian II, the young brother of Gratian. Valentinian with his clever mother Justina and his beautiful sister Galla appealed to Theodosius, who had come to terms with Persia, and were received by him in Thessalonica. For reasons of policy, or possibly because Valentinian and Justina were Arians whereas Maximus was, like himself, a severe persecutor of Arians, Theodosius could not be persuaded to go to war against Maximus.

[1]But Justina was a woman of practical experience and capable of clever contrivances at need. Being aware of Theodosius' amatory inclinations, she approached the emperor with her singularly beautiful daughter Galla, grasped his knees, and petitioned him not to leave the death of Gratian, who had bestowed the purple upon him, unavenged, nor to allow her family to lie neglected and hopeless. So saying, she pointed to her tearful daughter, who was bewailing her wretched lot. As he listened Theodosius was captivated by the girl's beauty and his glance showed that he was smitten, but he postponed action and only urged them to have better hopes. But as he smoldered with desire for the girl he asked Justina for her hand in marriage, for his former wife Placilla had died. Justina said Galla would marry him only if he made war on Maximus to avenge the death of Gratian and restored Valentinian to his father's

[1]Zosimus, 4.44.

realm. Upon these terms he married the girl, and devoted himself wholly to the war.

Maximus was defeated and executed at Aquileia in 388, and Theodosius' general Arbogast quickly recovered Gaul and the west. When Theodosius returned to the east in 391 he left Valentinian emperor of the west with headquarters at Vienne. But Arbogast resented the young ruler and had him strangled (392). A German could not yet, however, conceive of an emperor who was not a Roman, and so Arbogast set up as his puppet a learned rhetorician named Eugenius, who, though he was nominally a Christian, was sympathetic to the old pagan aristocracy of Rome. In Italy and the west Eugenius' authority was acknowledged, but Theodosius refused him recognition, and in 394 defeated and executed him near Aquileia; Arbogast committed suicide. Four months later (January 395) Theodosius died, and with him, in Gibbon's words, "the genius of Rome expired." He was the last emperor to maintain the integrity of the empire by effective measures against barbarian invaders and usurpers, and the last emperor to strive for decency and sanity within the empire. Imperial panegyrists are not the most trustworthy of witnesses, but the direction of their adulation can be revealing; this is what Pacatus said to Theodosius:

[1]"Such was your generosity that you wished to honor more persons than there were offices to bestow; the possibilities were poorer than your wishes, and the empire, extensive as it is, was not so spacious as your good will. But those you could not advance you solaced with your esteem, and for many, surely, that consolation was sufficient. One was honored by your address, another blessed by your table, a third hallowed by your kiss. All who trusted your administration advanced in dignity or were satisfied by your hu-

[1]Panegyrici Latini (Pacatus), 12.

manity—a quality as illustrious in an emperor as it is rare. For since unreasoning arrogance is a constant attendant upon high prosperity it falls to the lot of very few to abound in fortune and yet remain free of pride. Pride our ancestors so hated that they always regarded contemptuousness as worse than slavery, and were so irked by it that even after warrior Tullius and saintly Numa and founder Romulus they still hated even the name of kingship. Tarquin, whom they execrated and cursed for his headlong lust, his blind avarice, his monstrous cruelty, his unrestrained passion, they called 'the Proud,' and thought that a sufficient reproach. If Nature could make it possible for Brutus, that defender of Roman liberty, that hater of the word 'king,' to be returned temporarily to life and to see your age, filled wholly with zeal for virtue, frugality, and humanity, with every trace of pride, lust, and cruelty banished from the world, and yourself as citizen and ruler living according to the rugged ways of the ancient generals, the purity of the pontiffs, the moderation of the consuls, he would, at long last, change his opinion and declare that Roman dignity and freedom is in better state under your rule than it had been under his consulship, and he would confess that it was Tarquin, not kingship, that needed to be abolished."

The Christians in particular found Theodosius a pillar of strength. When, in a fit of anger of which he soon repented, he allowed his soldiers to massacre a Thessalonian mob which had murdered his general, Ambrose excluded him from the church until he should do public penance; and after eight months of obduracy Theodosius publicly humbled himself and acknowledged his guilt. The Christian view of Theodosius' career is summarized by St. Augustine:

[1]Theodosius not only avenged the death of Gratian, but like a true Christian assumed guardianship over his little

[1]St. Augustine, *City of God*, 5.26.

brother Valentinian, when Maximus had driven him from his state, and cared for him like a father. . . . When Maximus prospered and Theodosius was reviled, he did not seclude himself in his palace with wizards and conjurers but sent to John, who lived in an Egyptian desert and who, as he had heard, possessed the spirit of prophecy by divine grace; and from John he received a true promise of victory. Soon he killed the tyrant Maximus and restored the child Valentinian to the rule from which he had been driven, and showed him respect and affection. Then Valentinian was killed, by treachery or accident, and Eugenius was unlawfully set in his place. Theodosius received another response from John, and deposed Eugenius, rather by prayer than by power. . . . In all these troubles, from the beginning of his reign, he remembered to assist and support the laboring Church, which the Arian heretic had greatly harmed, by all the wholesome laws which he could promulgate against unbelievers. He took greater satisfaction in being a member of the Church than in being emperor. He ordered all gentile idols destroyed, because he knew that not even earthly blessings are in the devil's power, but all in God's. And what could be more memorable than his pious humility? When his courtiers forced him to avenge an injury upon the Thessalonians (at the bishop's entreaties he had promised them pardon), he was excommunicated and showed deep repentance. The people interceded for him; they were sorrier to see His Majesty dejected than afraid to incur his wrath. These good works and countless others he carried with him out of the transitory smoke of all human glory; their reward is eternal felicity, given by the true God only to the good.

Before his death Theodosius had arranged that his sons Honorius and Arcadius, aged ten and sixteen, each of whom had been made an Augustus, should rule the west and east respectively. Each of the young emperors was under the influence of a strong minister, and their rival ambitions resulted in a permanent cleavage between east and west. In the west, moreover, the minister was, as he had to be, in effect a military dictator, and was succeeded by other military dictators, against whom the bureaucracy was powerless. By the end of the fifth century the fiction of civilian rule was abandoned, and the barbarian generals who controlled the armies ruled Italy as well as all the west. In the east the greater solidarity of Hellenic tradition was able to resist the barbarian invasions and the ambitions of its own barbarian generals. The bureaucracy never permitted any single general to dominate the state.

10. The Empire Divided

[1]After the death of Theodosius, Arcadius and Honorius held nominal authority, but in fact the supreme power in the east was in the hands of Rufinus, and in the west in Stilicho's. All decisions were taken at their will, and suitors prevailed according as they were able to purchase or through some influence acquire the favor of the minister. Great wealth, which gave them high general esteem, came to them from persons who bestowed large gifts as a means of avoiding prosecution and from others who hoped to obtain some high office or procure the destruction of some city. And while all manner of wickedness proliferated in the cities, wealth flowed in to Rufinus and Stilicho from all sides. Everywhere houses once wealthy were impoverished. The kings were wholly ignorant of what was afoot, but merely signed whatever Rufinus or Stilicho put before them. When they had accumulated enormous wealth, Rufinus began to dream of acquiring kingship for himself. He designed to approach his goal by betrothing his marriageable daughter to the king.

The inventory of Rufinus' malefactions to which Zosimus proceeds is eulogy compared to the invective showered upon him by the poet Claudian, Stilicho's panegyrist. This is how the Fury Megaera introduces him to her sisters:

[2]"To bring universal destruction upon the world I have a prodigy more monstrous than all the hydras, suppler than the mother tigress, fiercer than Auster's gale, more treach-

[1]Zosimus, 5.1.   [2]Claudian, *Against Rufinus*, 1.86–115.

erous than the tides of Euripus—Rufinus. Directly from the womb I received him in my bosom, where he nestled and reached his arms to my neck and sought the breast with baby tears. My snakes molded his limbs by licking them with their three-forked tongues. At my instruction he learned craft and the art of hurting, how to simulate loyalty, to conceal intended mischief, to disguise treachery with a smile. He is steeped in savagery and seething with lust for gain. . . . He surpasses me, I confess; his quick genius has outstripped his teacher. Not to detain you further, he alone possesses our combined criminality. I shall introduce him, if the plan is agreeable to this company, to the royal court of the emperor of the world. Though he be sager than Numa and juster than Minos he must succumb to the cunning manipulations of my protégé."

But Rufinus was outmanipulated by a bald old eunuch, the lord chamberlain Eutropius, who secured his own precedence by contriving that the emperor marry his own candidate Eudoxia. Eutropius gave Claudian's invective even richer scope:

[1]"Is this the mode of your rule, Fortune? Is this a cruel jest? How far will you indulge your orgies at the cost of humanity? If it was your pleasure to befoul the curule office with the reproach of slavery, let a consul come dragging his broken chains, let the dungeon dress itself in the Quirinal cincture, but at least give us a man! There are degrees among slaves, and each has his own boast; the status of one who has served only one master is not so degraded. But you can number Eutropius' owners only if you can count the waves of the sea or the sands of the desert. How many slave rosters, how many sales lists, how many names can he count! How many times has he stood stripped while the buyer's doctor probed for flaws and diseases! All regretted the pur-

[1]Claudian, *Against Eutropius*, 1.24–44.

chase and sent him back to the market while he was still salable. When he looked like an ugly corpse, all old bags and wrinkles, his owners tried to get rid of him as a present and thrust the loathsome gift on innocent friends."

But there were still thoughtful people, at least in the east, who expected kings actually to rule. Upon festive occasions it was customary for various communities to send ceremonial addresses to the emperor; an extant address to Arcadius by the neoplatonist and poet Synesius of Cyrene, later bishop of Ptolemais, is a relatively outspoken Mirror of Princes, and passages in it throw interesting light on the imperial office at this period:

[1]"Outspokenness should be valued by a ruler. Constant praise is seductive but harmful; it is like the honey-coated drugs offered to men condemned to death. . . . I affirm that nothing has been more harmful to the Romans in the past than the protection and solicitude bestowed on the sovereign, of whom a mystery is made as by priestcraft. . . . The fear that Your Majesty may be reduced to a human level by becoming a familiar sight causes you to be cloistered and isolated from seeing and hearing the things by which practical wisdom is acquired. Your pleasures are corporal, and mainly of touch and taste, so that your life is like that of a sea polyp. If you deem humanity unworthy of you, you cannot attain human perfection. The associates of your daily life, who have easier access to the palace than marshals and generals, the men on whom you bestow your royal approval, have limited and petty intelligence, faultily shaped by nature as dishonest bankers falsify coins. A dullard is a royal gift, and the duller he is the greater the gift. These men are ready to laugh or weep without measure, to act the clown with grimaces and noises and any other means; they consume your leisure and accentuate the mental myopia

[1]Synesius, Migne P. G., 66.1053.

with which an unnatural life infects you. The puerile
thoughts and conversation of these men are more accessible
to you than clear and terse philosophic doctrines. This astonishing inertia pleases you; you distrust the thinking part
of your people and assume solemn airs before them, while
you are intimate with the feather-headed and strip before
them. But you must understand that the same arts which
shape a thing control its growth. . . .

"I do not think that the ancient institutions of the
Romans should be transgressed by their king. It is not the
innovations of yesterday, when the commonwealth had already changed its habits, that must be considered ancestral
institutions, but those by which the Romans won their empire. In the name of the God who presides over kingship
(bear with me: my story bites into the soul), at what period
do you suppose Rome flourished most? Is it from the time
you have been robed in purple, bedecked with gold, adorned
with gems from foreign mountains and seas, wearing them
now on your brow, now on your feet, now round your waist,
now hanging from your bosom, now buckled on your robes,
now used as a seat? You are turned into a particolored peacock, cursed, as Homer said, with a tunic of stone. But not
even this garb is enough: you cannot go into the council to
perform your functions, when magistrates are to be elected
or any other matter considered, unless you have swathed
yourself in a particular robe. And now men who may law-
fully do so see you; they alone of the senators are happy, for
they alone carry the burden of government. . . .

"Once our lives have been corrected and Prudence restored, it must follow that the glories of the past will accompany her and contrary elements be transformed. And do
you, sire, rule over the return of good works, give us back
the king who is a public-spirited servant of his kingdom.
. . . Exclude from magistracies and the privileges of the

council any who are ashamed of what Rome has held sacred from ancient times. . . . Purify the army of barbarian elements, like a heap of wheat from which we separate coarse grain and weeds which are ruinous to the noble and legitimate seed. . . . A king must not exhaust cities by taxation: if he has reduced the items for which imposts are required he needs no surplus. He can become a harmless collector of revenue by eliminating deficits and being satisfied with amounts within the means of the taxpayer; a king who is greedy of money is more shameful than a huckster."

The most significant part of Synesius' advice is that urging that barbarians not be allowed too much power in the army: during all of Arcadius' reign the most powerful single individual in the world was Honorius' general Stilicho. Stilicho's first step was to claim for Honorius the prefecture of Illyricum, including the Balkans, which, until Gratian resigned it in 379, had been subject to the ruler of the west. The Visigoths, who had been settled between the Danube and the Balkans, revolted and (then or later) made Alaric their king. Stilicho marched against them but unaccountably neglected an opportunity for a decisive victory and so permitted them to ravage all Greece. Rufinus ordered Stilicho's troops, but not himself, to come to Constantinople. Having been supplanted by Eutropius, Rufinus intended to win the support of the Goths for his imperial ambition and to use them against an invasion of Huns. Doubtless upon Stilicho's instructions, the Goths murdered Rufinus. From across the Caucasus, meanwhile, hordes of Huns were sweeping through Armenia, Mesopotamia, and Syria. A letter of St. Jerome, who was in Palestine at the time, gives an eyewitness account:

[1]"Suddenly messengers flying in all directions bring the fearful news that from distant Maeotis, the icy Don, the

[1]St. Jerome, Letters, 77.8.

savage Massagetes where Alexander's strong works hold the barbarians back at the Caucasian cliffs, hordes of Huns had swept through and were spreading slaughter and terror in all directions. The Roman army was occupied with civil wars in Italy. . . . These savages were everywhere when they were least expected; their speed outstripped rumors of their coming. They spared neither religion nor dignity nor age. The wails of infants roused no pity; babies who had not yet begun to live were forced to die, and, ignorant of the intended mischief, smiled in the hands of their executioners. There was a general and persistent report that their objective was Jerusalem, to which they were hurrying to satisfy their lust for gold. The walls, neglected in the security of peace, were repaired. Antioch was under siege. Tyre broke off from the mainland and retreated to its ancient island. We too were compelled to provide ships and stay at the seashore as a precaution against the enemy's coming. Though the winds were wild we were less afraid of shipwreck than of the barbarians; it was not so much our own safety as the chastity of our virgins for which we were concerned."

[1]"How many monasteries were seized? How many rivers stained with human blood? All the cities on the Halys, the Cydnus, the Orontes, including Antioch, were besieged. Herds of captives were dragged away; Arabia, Phoenicia, Palestine, Egypt, were led captive by fear."

In Africa there was a serious uprising in 397. When, in 379, the Moor Firmus revolted, Theodosius had been supported by Firmus' brother Gildo and had rewarded him by making him count of Africa and marrying him to the emperor's niece Salvina. The defection of Africa was no slight matter, for it was Rome's granary, and shortages were felt in Italy at once.

[2]When Gildo learned of Theodosius' death he revolted

[1]St. Jerome, Letters, 60.16.   [2]Orosius, 7.36.

with a view to adding Africa to the eastern empire. Some think his motive was envy, others a belief that the young rulers' case was hopeless, for scarcely any who inhert rule young survive to manhood. . . . Gildo's brother Mascezel abhorred Gildo's subversive actions and returned to Italy, leaving his two sons with the troops in Africa. Gildo suspected his brother's intentions, and treacherously seized and killed his two nephews. When it was decided to make war upon Gildo as a public enemy Mascezel was given the command; grief for his own bereavement guaranteed his effectiveness. . . . [Reinforced by prayer and a vision of the recently deceased St. Ambrose, Mascezel confronted the 70,000 troops of Gildo in Africa with 5000.] While he was piously urging those he first encountered to make peace, one of their standard-bearers insolently rejected his entreaties and exhorted his side to begin the battle. A blow upon the arm from Mascezel's sword compelled him to lower his banner to the ground, whereupon the other cohorts, thinking that the front ranks were surrendering, hurriedly reversed their standards and gave themselves up to Mascezel. Deserted by the regular troops, the numerous barbarians whom Gildo had mustered fled in all directions. Gildo himself sought to escape by seizing a ship and putting out to sea, but he was driven back to shore and some days later strangled.

In the same year (398) Stilicho had Mascezel executed, and strengthened his own position by marrying his daughter Maria to Honorius. In 401 Alaric, who was apparently dissatisfied with the command he had received, ravaged Italy and Stilicho, who had been dealing with the heathen Radagaisus across the Alps, was barely in time to relieve Milan where the emperor was being besieged. Stilicho pursued Alaric to Pollentia, where a battle was fought on Easter Sunday, 402. Unaccountably Stilicho again failed to press his victory home and Alaric retired. To celebrate the victory Honorius made a triumphal entry into Rome—the third visit of an emperor to the capital in a hundred years. But Honorius knew the triumph was hollow and that Milan was no longer safe. He retired to Ravenna, where the marshes afforded protection, and devoted himself to keeping chickens.

In 406 a German horde under Radagaisus descended into Italy and was driven off from the siege of Florence by Stilicho. Soon the Rhine was crossed by hordes of Suevi, Vandals, Alans, and Burgundians, who destroyed the romanized cities and settled down in Gaul. Britain was now stripped of its army.

[1]In the year 407 . . . Gratianus Municeps set himself up as dictator in Britain and was killed; then Constantine, a common soldier of no merit, was chosen emperor solely on account of his name. Having obtained power, he crossed into Gaul, where the barbarians deceived him with empty treaties. He caused the state great harm, and upon Honorius' orders Constantius marched into Gaul, besieged him at Arles, and put him to death. His son Constans, a monk whom he had made Caesar, Gerontius killed in Vienne. . . . Roman rule came to an end in Britain almost 470 years after the landing of Julius Caesar. The Romans had held the country south of the earthwork which, as I have pointed out, Severus built across the island; to this day cities, temples, bridges, and paved roads bear witness to the Roman occupation. The Romans also held nominal authority over the remoter parts of Britain and the islands beyond it.

All of the disasters of Honorius' reign Orosius lays to the machinations of Stilicho.

[1]Bede, 1.11.

[1]Sprung from the cowardly, greedy, treacherous, and crafty race of Vandals, Stilicho was not satisfied with his imperial power under a nominal emperor but tried by every means possible to place his own son Eucherius on the throne. It is common knowledge that Eucherius was planning to persecute the Christians from his boyhood on. When Alaric and the Goths begged humbly and honestly for a place to settle, and on very favorable terms, Stilicho secretly supported them but officially left them neither war nor peace, reserving them to wear down and intimidate the state. The numerous and strong Alans, Suevi, Vandals, and Burgundians who are now oppressing Gaul and Spain, Stilicho instigated to war, banishing their fear of Rome. His plan was to weaken the Rhine frontier and afflict both Gauls, so that, in the crisis, he could wrest the imperial title from his son-in-law and give it to his son. He thought it would be as easy to repress the barbarian peoples as to arouse them. When the nature of these crimes was made known to Honorius and the army [by a pious Christian named Olympius] the soldiers properly mutinied and killed Stilicho and Eucherius [408].

However justified the murder of Stilicho may have been, there was now no one to deter Alaric from working his will on Rome. Now Italy was to be barbarized.

[2]It was during Honorius' rule of the west that barbarians took his domains; I shall tell who they were and how they did so. There have been and are many Gothic nations, but the greatest and most important are Goths, Vandals, Visigoths, and Gepaedes. The ancients called them Sauromatae and Black-cloaks, and some called them Getae. Though their names, as we have said, differ, they are the same in other respects. They all have fair skin and yellow hair, are tall and handsome, use the same laws and practice the same

[1]Orosius, 7.38. [2]Procopius, 3.2.

religion. They are all Arians in faith, and their only language is Gothic. I think they derive from a single tribe, and later assumed their several names from their leaders. Of old this people lived above the Ister, but later the Gepaedes acquired the country on both sides the river around Singidunum and Sirmium, and there they have remained until my time.

The Visigoths left the others and entered into alliance with the emperor Arcadius, but later (barbarians are incapable of keeping faith with Romans) under the leadership of Alaric they turned hostile to both emperors and, beginning with Thrace, treated all Europe as enemy country. The emperor Honorius had been sitting in Rome, with nothing further from his mind than war but glad enough, I suppose, to be left quiet in his palace. But when word came that a large army of barbarians was somewhere in Illyricum not far off, he abandoned his palace and fled in disorder to Ravenna, a strong city near the end of the Ionian Gulf. Some say that he himself brought the barbarians in because his subjects were in revolt, but on the basis of the man's character I cannot believe it. When the barbarians met with no opposition they proved the most brutal of mankind. All the cities they took, especially south of the Ionian Gulf, they so destroyed as to leave them unrecognizable, unless a tower or a single gate or some such relic happened to survive. All the people that came their way, young and old, they killed, sparing neither women nor children. That is why Italy is depopulated to this day. They plundered all the money out of all Europe and, most important, in Rome they left nothing of value, public or private, when they moved on to Gaul. Now I shall tell how Alaric captured Rome.

[Alaric besieged Rome in 408 but was bought off by a huge ransom; in 409 he besieged it again, and set up a puppet emperor named Attalus, whom he deposed the following year, when he again besieged the city.] After he had wasted much time in the siege without being able to take the city by force or stratagem he contrived the following plan. He chose out of his army 300 beardless but full-grown youths whom he knew to be of good birth and courage beyond their years and secretly told them that he would present them, in the guise of slaves, to certain patricians in Rome. . . . When the appointed day came Alaric armed his whole force for attack and kept them ready at the Salarian gate, where he had encamped at the beginning of the siege. At the hour agreed all the young men came to this gate and fell upon and killed the guards. Then they opened the gates and received Alaric and the army into the city with no difficulty. The houses nearest the gates they set afire; among them was that of Sallust, who wrote the history of Rome long ago. A good part of it stands half burned to this day. When they had plundered the whole city and destroyed most of the Romans they moved on. They say that in Ravenna one of the eunuchs, probably the poultry keeper, told the emperor Honorius that Rome was lost, whereupon he cried out, "But it has just eaten out of my hands!" He had a very large cock, you see, named Rome. The eunuch understood the situation and explained that the city Rome was lost to Alaric. With great relief the king rejoined, "And I supposed my fine bird Rome was lost." Such is the degree of silliness ascribed to that emperor. Others deny that Rome was taken in this way and say that Proba, a lady of the senatorial class distinguished for wealth and reputation, took pity on the Romans who were perishing of hunger and other suffering; indeed, they were reduced to eating one another. When Proba saw there was no reasonable hope, the river and harbor being in the hands of the enemy, she ordered her slaves to open the gates by night.

From Rome Alaric marched south to Rhegium, taking

Nola and Capua on his way, to take ship for Africa, either to settle there or to control the grain supply. His fleet was wrecked by a storm, and he died (410) before he could procure another. He was succeeded by his brother-in-law Athaulf who, in 412, crossed into Gaul, where barbarian invasions and the neglect of the central government had given rise to a number of usurpers.

[1]In 411, when nothing could be done against the barbarians because of the numerous usurpers, the emperor Honorius ordered that these should first be destroyed, and entrusted the campaign to Constantius [the successor of Stilicho as principal general]. The state finally realized the advantages of having a Roman general and the ruinous oppression to which it had long been subjected by barbarian generals. Constantius marched into Gaul, and at Arles besieged, captured, and killed Constantine. To follow the succession of usurpers as concisely as possible, Constantine's son Constans was killed at Vienne by his count Gerontius, a worthless rather than upright man, who put a certain Maximus in his place. Gerontius was killed by his own soldiers. Maximus was stripped of his purple and abandoned by the Gallic troops, who were transferred to Africa and then recalled to Italy; he is now a penniless exile among the barbarians in Spain. Later the tyranny of Jovinus, a man of position in Gaul, collapsed as soon as it was established. His brother Sebastian chose to die as a usurper; he was killed as he took office. What shall I say of the unlucky Attalus, for whom it was an honor to fall among the usurpers and a blessing to die? Alaric, who made, unmade, remade, and unmade his emperors in almost less time than it takes to tell, laughed at the farcical comedy of emperorship. . . . Attalus' hand was cut off, but he was let live.

[1]Orosius, 7.37–42.

Meanwhile Heraclian, who was made count of Africa while Attalus played at emperor and had vigorously defended Africa for Honorius against Attalus' agents, obtained the consulship and was swollen with pride. . . . After illegally withholding the grain supply for some time Heraclian sailed for Rome with a large fleet of an unheard-of size. He is said to have had 3700 vessels, a number the historians tell us neither Persian Xerxes nor Alexander the Great nor any other ruler possessed. As he marched towards the capital he was terrified in an encounter with Count Marinus and fled. He seized a ship, returned to Carthage alone, and was immediately killed by a band of soldiers. His son-in-law Sabinus fled to Constantinople but was soon brought back and sentenced to exile. This whole series of open usurpers or mutinous generals was overcome by the singular piety and good fortune of the emperor Honorius and the vigor and diligence of Constantius.

In 414 Constantius, with headquarters at Arles, drove the Goths from Narbonne, and by blockading ships and imports forced them into Spain. At this time the Gothic peoples were under the rule of King Athaulf, who had succeeded Alaric and married the emperor's sister Placidia, who had been taken captive in Rome. Athaulf proved to be an earnest seeker after peace and preferred to fight loyally for the emperor Honorius and employ the forces of the Goths for the defense of the Roman state. When I was in Bethlehem in Palestine I myself heard a pious and intelligent Narbonese who had served with distinction under Theodosius tell the most blessed priest Jerome that he had himself been intimate with Athaulf at Narbonne and had often heard his answers to questions when he was in good health and spirits. At first, it seems, he had been set upon blotting out the Roman name and turning Roman territory into a Gothic empire in fact as well as name; Gothia was to supplant Romania as a popular designation, and Athaulf was to become all Caesar Augustus had once been. But long experience had taught him that unrestrained barbarism made the Goths incapable of obeying laws; and since he believed that no state could be a state without laws, he chose to aspire to the glory of restoring and augmenting the renown of Rome by the power of the Goths, and, since he could not transform the Roman empire, to have posterity look upon him as its restorer. That is why Athaulf endeavored to refrain from war and promote peace. His wife Placidia, a singularly intelligent and pious woman, was of special help to him and guided and urged him to measures which would promote sound government. But while he was busied in seeking and offering peace he was killed, in Barcelona in Spain, reportedly by the treachery of his own men [415].

Athaulf's successor Wallia was not so philo-Roman. Wallia planned an invasion of Africa, and upon its failure came to terms with the Romans. He received 600,000 measures of grain for his Goths, and agreed to return Placidia, Honorius' sister and Athaulf's widow, and make war on the barbarians in Spain (416). Constantius married Placidia in 417. Wallia's successes against the Vandals and Alans in Spain alarmed Constantius, and he recalled the Goths and settled them in southern Aquitania (418). Theodoric I, who succeeded Wallia upon the latter's death in 418, forced the Romans to acknowledge his complete sovereignty over Aquitania. The Vandals and Alans retained their hold on southern Spain, and in a few years would invade Africa under Gaiseric. In 421 Honorius co-opted Constantius as Augustus, and the two emperors then made Placidia, who had borne Constantius two children, Augusta. Constantius died within a few months, and Honorius in 423. The eastern emperor had refused to recognize the titles of Constantius and Placidia, possibly because Placidia had married a barbarian, possibly because their children obstructed eastern hopes of reuniting the empire. As a ruler Honorius was negligible, but his reign marks the passing of western Europe from Roman to Teuton. The capital had been captured and sacked, Gaul and Spain were ruined, Britain lost. Italy was so unsafe that in 416 Rutilius Namatianus, the last of the pagan poets, found the sea a safer route to southern France. His poem On His Journey Home is bitter against the Christians, who he felt had subverted the old order, and contains a passionate apostrophe to Rome:

[1]"Listen, queen fairest in all your world, Rome welcomed among the stars of heaven, listen, mother of men and mother of gods, your temples bring us near to heaven. To you we sing praise and ever shall, so long as fates allow. None can be whole, forgetful of you. Sooner shall guilty oblivion overwhelm the sun than reverence for you depart from my heart. Your works spread wide as the rays of the sun, where curving ocean surrounds the world. For you Phoebus himself, who contains all things, revolves; the rising of his chariot and its setting are in your domain. Africa has not retarded you with its scorching sands, the northern Bear has not repulsed you with its cold. As far as living nature has stretched towards the poles, so far has earth proved accessible to your valor. A single fatherland you have made for nations far apart. Even the unjust have found it profitable to be taken under your dominion. By offering the vanquished partnership in your own laws you have made a city of what was once a world."

Pagan inculpation of Christianity for the fall of Rome was refuted by St. Augustine in his City of God, and at St. Augustine's behest by Orosius in his Seven Books to Confute the Pagans. In the On the Governance of God, written between 439 and 451, Salvian, a priest of Marseilles,

[1]Rutilius Namatianus, 47–66.

argues that God had withdrawn His care from Rome because the Christians themselves were grown so corrupt and oppressive that they were morally inferior to the barbarians:

[1]"All the while the poor are despoiled, widows groan, orphans are trodden underfoot, to the degree that many—and these of good birth and liberal education—flee to the enemy to avoid death by official persecution. They seek among barbarians the dignity of the Roman because they cannot bear barbarous indignity among the Romans. Although these Romans differ in religion and language from the barbarians to whom they flee, and differ from them also in personal cleanliness and clothing, nevertheless, as I have said, they prefer to bear among the barbarians a worship unlike their own rather than rampant injustice among the Romans.

"Thus far and wide they migrate either to the Goths or the Bagaudae or to other barbarians wherever they may be in power; yet they do not repent having migrated. They prefer to live as freemen under an outward form of captivity than as captives under a specious appearance of liberty. Therefore the title of Roman citizens, at one time not only greatly valued but dearly bought, is now repudiated and evaded, and it is almost considered not only base but even deserving of abhorrence. What could be clearer proof of Roman wickedness than the fact that many upright and noble men by whom Roman citizenship should be valued as a splendid and dignified state have been driven to such a state of mind by Roman cruelty and wickedness that they no longer wish to be Romans? Hence even those who do not flee to the barbarians are forced to be barbarians. Such is the condition of the greater part of the Spaniards and not the least part of the Gauls, and indeed of all those through-

[1]Salvian, *On the Governance of God*, 5.5.

out the whole Roman world whom Roman wickedness has compelled not to be Romans.

At Arcadius' court in Constantinople the empress Eudoxia was in effective control. It was she who was responsible for the ruin and death of the insubordinate Goth Gainas in 400, and she had the upper hand in the famous quarrel with the eloquent bishop John Chrysostom. When Arcadius died his son Theodosius II (A.D. 408–450) was only seven, and the state was ruled by the capable pretorian prefect Anthemius. But in 414 Theodosius' sister Pulcheria, then fifteen and two years older than himself, was made Augusta, and actually governed for the next forty years.

[1]It was divine providence which set Pulcheria up as guardian over the pious Theodosius and his government. She was only fifteen but possessed prudence and religious devotion beyond her age. First she dedicated her virginity to God and brought her sisters up in the same mode of life, so that no man was introduced into the palace and every occasion of jealousy and plotting was eliminated. In order to confirm this decision by making God Himself, the priests, and all the subjects witnesses of her acts, she dedicated on behalf of her virginity and her brother's rule a sacred table, most admirably fashioned of gold and precious stones, in the church of Constantinople, and on this table she inscribed her decisions, that all might see. When she undertook the charge of the government she administered the Roman world in an excellent and orderly fashion; her counsels were prudent and she gave prompt written instructions for what was to be done. She could speak and write correctly in both Latin and Greek. For all that was done she gave the credit to her brother. She took care that he should be educated in the subjects appropriate to his age

[1]Sozomen, 9.1.

as became a king. He learned the use of horses, arms, and letters from experts. His sister instructed him how to comport himself in his levees as befits a king; he learned how to drape his robes, to sit down, to walk, to restrain his laughter, to show himself mild or stern at need, to give audience to petitioners. But in particular she led him to piety by accustoming him to pray, attend churches, enrich them with offerings and treasures, revere priests and other good men, including such philosophers as observed the Christian rules.

[1][In 421 Eucheria selected a wife for Theodosius.] She was very well educated, being the daughter of the Athenian sophist Leontius, who had taught her all branches. When Theodosius was about to marry her she was baptized a Christian and received the name Eudocia instead of Athenais. Many persons pronounced panegyrics, one to make himself known to the emperor, another out of eagerness to display his oratorical abilities because he wished people to know he possessed the education which had cost him so much labor. I myself have no desire to bring myself to the notice of the emperor, nor do I wish to make a display of my talent; I will give a simple and truthful account of the qualities of our emperor. To bury such a profitable example in silence is to injure posterity. In the first place, though Theodosius was born and bred to the purple, he was not spoiled but so sensible that all who encountered him thought he had practical intelligence. He could abide cold and heat steadfastly, could fast frequently, especially on Wednesdays and Fridays, in his zeal for the observances of Christianity. The discipline of the palace was no different than a monastery's. In the morning he was accustomed to sing antiphonal hymns with his sisters. He could recite Scripture by heart. He discussed theology with the bishops

[1]Socrates, 7.21.

he met like an old priest. He collected books—Scriptures and commentaries—with greater zeal than Ptolemy Philadelphus had shown. He far surpassed all mankind in patience and kindliness.

After the death of Honorius in 423 a court official named John assumed the purple, and Placidia and her two children went to Constantinople. Theodosius espoused the cause of his aunt and her five-year-old son, Valentinian III (A.D. 425–455), whom he betrothed to Eudocia's infant daughter, named Eudoxia for her grandmother. In return for Theodosius' military support Illyricum was to be transferred to the eastern empire. Placidia, as Augusta, became regent for her son.

[1]His mother Placidia brought Valentinian up and educated him most effeminately, so that he was full of wickedness from childhood. Hs associated mostly with sorcerers and astrologers, and wildly pursued affairs with married women though his own wife was extremely handsome. Nor did he recover any part of the empire of which it had been deprived, but he lost Libya also and was himself destroyed. When he died it fell to his wife and children to become captives. The disaster in Libya came about as follows. There were two Roman generals, Aetius and Boniface, of courage and experience in war inferior to none. These two were at odds in politics, but their magnanimity and other virtues were so outstanding that if a man should call either of them "the last of the Romans" he would not go wrong. All the virtues of the Romans were defined in these two men. One of them, Boniface, Placidia appointed general of all Libya. This was contrary to Aetius' desire, but he showed no displeasure. Their hostility had not yet come to light but was concealed in the face of each. When Boniface was out of

[1]Procopius, 3.3.

the way Aetius slandered him to Placidia, saying that he was a usurper and had robbed her and the king of all Libya. He said it was easy to discover the truth: if she should summon Boniface to Rome he would never come. When she heard this Placidia thought Aetius was right and acted accordingly. Then Aetius hastily wrote Boniface in secret, informing him that the king's mother was plotting against him and wished to put him out of the way. He told him that he would shortly have clear proof of the plot: he would be summoned to Rome for no reason whatever.

Boniface's refusal to come to Italy made him an enemy of the state, and an army was sent to subdue him.

[1]When Boniface perceived that he could not himself hold Africa and realized his imminent peril he summoned from Spain the race of Vandals and Alans, which was seething to destroy the state, with their king Gaiseric and introduced them into Africa. There they savagely devastated almost the whole of the country with sword and fire and rapine and moreover subverted the Catholic faith by their Arian impiety. In this turmoil Augustine, bishop of Hippo, that he might not see the ruin of his city, made his way to Christ. This was in the third month of the siege, when he had lived seventy-six years, of which he had spent forty as priest or bishop.

[2]Gaiseric was of medium height, lame from a fall of his horse, had a deep mind, and was sparing of speech. He despised luxury but could not temper his anger or his greed. He was shrewd in inducing foreign peoples to act in his interest and resourceful in planting discord and cultivating hatreds.

After Boniface, Gaiseric defeated Theodosius II's general Aspar, who brought help from the east and Italy, and by 431 Africa was lost to the empire. Aetius resumed direction

[1]Paul the Deacon, 13.10.   [2]Jordanes, 168.

of imperial policy in 433 and continued in it until his death in 454. In 444 the Huns, occupying what is now Hungary, Rumania, and southern Russia, were united under their powerful king Attila.

[1]Attila was born into the world to shake the nations; he was the scourge of all countries and reports concerning him terrified all mankind. He walked arrogantly and rolled his eyes about so that the force of his proud spirit was revealed in the movement of his body. Though he loved war he was yet restrained in action; he was mighty in counsel, gracious to suppliants, and lenient to those he once received under his protection. He was of short stature with a broad chest and large head; his eyes were small, his beard thin and sprinkled with gray; his flat nose and swarthy complexion gave evidence of his origin.

Attila's power spread, and he was receiving large sums of gold annually from both Theodosius and Valentinian III; the emperors were helpless because Attila controlled the peoples from whom the legions now had to be recruited. His ambitions were sharpened by a curious intrigue involving the emperor's sister Honoria, who resented her subordination to her far less competent brother Valentinian. To promote her ambition she entered into a love affair with her lord chamberlain, upon the discovery of which the chamberlain was executed and Honoria married to a senatorial nonentity. She then secretly sent a ring to Attila, who was the most powerful individual in the world, suggesting that he marry her. He then asked Valentinian for her hand, with half the empire for dowry. Upon Valentinian's refusal Attila marched into Gaul, where the kings of the Visigoths and Franks helped Aetius repulse but not defeat him (451). The following year he invaded Italy, but sickness among his troops, the arrival of reinforcements from the eastern em-

[1]Jordanes, 182.

pire, and the appeal of Leo, bishop of Rome, induced him
to withdraw without occupying Rome.

[1]As Attila paused before Rome, Pope Leo approached
him. When he entered the presence of the barbarian king
he obtained all his desires and procured safety not only for
Rome but for all of Italy. Attila was terrified by the sign
of God and was unable to say to the priest anything other
than the priest wished him to. It is said that after the pope's
departure Attila was asked by his own people why, contrary to his custom, he had shown the Roman pope such
reverence and had heeded almost all his demands; the king
replied that it was not the man that had approached him
he revered but that he had seen standing next to him another venerable personage clothed in sacerdotal habit, of
stately figure with hoary head, and that this figure held a
drawn sword and threatened him with a terrible death if he
did not fulfill the pope's requests.

In 453 Attila died and his empire fell apart. In 454
Aetius was murdered by Valentinian at the instigation of
his chamberlain Heraclius, and then Valentinian himself
was murdered as the result of an intrigue.

[2]A Roman senator named Maximus had to wife a chaste
lady who was a celebrated beauty. Valentinian conceived
a passion for her, and since he could not gain access to her
otherwise he devised and carried out an unholy plot. He
summoned Maximus to the palace and sat down with him
to a game of backgammon, the loser to be penalized by a
certain sum. The emperor won and received Maximus' ring
as a pledge; this he sent to Maximus' house with a message
that her husband bade his wife come to the palace at once
to greet the empress Eudoxia. Accepting the evidence of
the ring, she mounted her litter and came to the royal court.
Those assigned to the service conveyed her to a room far

[1]Paul the Deacon, 14.12.   [2]Procopius, 3.4.16.

removed from the women's apartments, and there Valentinian met and forced her. After the outrage she returned to her husband's house, weeping and grieving sorely for her misfortune and calling imprecations down upon Maximus as the cause of what had happened. Maximus was accordingly much aggrieved, and immediately entered into a conspiracy against the emperor.

[1]Later Maximus killed Valentinian with little difficulty, secured the rule, and, his own wife having died shortly before, he married the empress Eudoxia by force. Once, in bed with her, he remarked that it was for love of her he had done all he had done. Eudoxia was already angry with Maximus and eager to requite him for his injury to Valentinian, but at this remark of Maximus, that he had plotted against Valentinian for her sake, she was infuriated. As soon as day broke she sent to Carthage, entreating Gaiseric to avenge Valentinian, who had been destroyed by an unholy man, a disgrace to himself and the empire, and to save her from the indignities she was suffering at the hands of the tyrant. She impressed it upon Gaiseric as a friend and ally that, when so great a calamity had befallen the royal house, it would be a dereliction of duty not to take vengeance. She could expect no help from Byzantium, for Theodosius had now died and Marcian had received the kingship.

Then Gaiseric, whose only motive was the expectation of high profit, sailed to Italy with a large armada. No one obstructed his march to Rome, and he took possession of the palace. Maximus the Romans stoned to death as he attempted to flee; they then dissected his head and body and distributed the members amongst themselves. Gaiseric took Eudoxia, together with Eudocia and Placidia, her children by Valentinian, captive. He loaded his ships with huge

[1]Procopius, 3.4.36.

quantities of gold and imperial treasures [including the spoils brought from the temple at Jerusalem by Titus] and sailed to Carthage.

Maximus was succeeded by Avitus, a follower of Aetius, but Avitus was soon deposed by his general Ricimer, who virtually ruled the western empire from 456 until his death in 472. As a German and an Arian he could not himself be recognized as emperor (the case of Aspar in the east was exactly parallel), and so made and unmade puppets. Majorian lasted from 457 to 461, when he failed in an attempt on the Vandal kingdom in Africa, and Severus from 461 to 465. For the two years following there was no emperor in the west; in such a case the legal position was that the empire continued under the sole authority of the emperor of the east, then Leo. In 467 Leo sent Anthemius, a high dignitary of the eastern court who became Ricimer's father-in-law, to be emperor and procure Ricimer's co-operation for a projected attack on the Vandal kingdom in Africa. The cost of this lavish expedition almost bankrupted the eastern empire, and its failure, largely due to malfeasance on the part of the eastern general, was a severe blow to the pride of the eastern empire. Olybrius, husband of Valentinian III's daughter Placidia, was in Constantinople, and suspect to Leo. Leo sent him to Rome, ostensibly to reconcile Anthemius and Ricimer, but a private letter instructed Anthemius to put Olybrius to death. This letter was intercepted by Ricimer, who promptly made Olybrius emperor. The same year (472) Olybrius and Ricimer both died.

Ricimer's nephew Gundobad assumed his uncle's role and named Glycerius emperor. Leo refused Glycerius recognition and nominated Julius Nepos. Nepos defeated Glycerius, and was in turn defeated by his general Orestes

(475), *who made his son Romulus Augustulus emperor.*

[1]While Zeno ruled in Byzantium the western empire was held by Augustus, whom the Romans called by the diminutive Augustulus because he received the rule while still a lad; his father Orestes, who was a very sensible man, administered it for him. Some time before it happened that the Romans had induced the Sciri, Alans, and certain other Gothic peoples to become their confederates; in consequence they suffered at the hands of Alaric and Attila, as I have related above. In the degree that the barbarian element waxed strong, the prestige of the Roman soldiers declined. Under the specious title of alliance the newcomers tyrannized and lorded it over them. The barbarians ruthlessly forced many measures upon them against their will and finally demanded that they divide all the lands of Italy with them. When they bade Orestes to give them a third part and he would not agree they killed him at once [476].

[2]Seeing his mounting successes, Odovacar [the leader of the insurgents] immediately grasped at royal dignity. When Augustulus, who had assumed the imperial authority, saw that all Italy was subject to Odovacar's power, frightened by inexplicable fear, he miserably cast the purple aside of his own accord, and laid down the imperial majesty, having reigned for scarcely eleven months. And so the imperium of the Romans at Rome, venerated throughout the world, and the sublimity of the Augustus which had taken its origin with Octavian Augustus, perished with this Augustulus, in the 1209th year from the founding of the city, in the 517th from Gaius Caesar's assumption of sole authority, in the 475th of the incarnation of our Lord.

And so when the Augustan dignity was rejected by Augustulus, Odovacar entered the city and obtained the kingship of all Italy. This he held for fourteen years with-

[1]Procopius, 5.1.   [2]Paul the Deacon, 15.10.

out disturbance, and then Theodoric, king of the Goths, came from the east to enter into possession of Italy.

The power long exercised de facto by the commander of the barbarian soldiers was now recognized de jure. The west would no longer have an emperor of equal status with the emperor at Constantinople. The legal position was that the ruler of the east was sole emperor and the barbarian king his regent. But Odovacar's authority did not extend beyond Italy. Not only in Britain and in Africa but in Spain and Gaul the last vestiges of the authority of the central government disappeared. But the eclipse of Rome did not mean that the European unity or civilization which Rome had fostered had vanished. A measure of organizational unity was supplied by the Church, which consciously emulated the centralized organization of the empire. And the provinces which had originally been thoroughly romanized, Gaul in particular, had assimilated their invaders and exhibited a flourishing cultural life, with a lively interest in rhetoric and poetry. Our easiest evidence for this is in literature, and especially in the writings of Sidonius Apollinaris, the son-in-law of Avitus, who, after the disappointment of high political expectations, became bishop of Clermont. Here is Sidonius' description of Theodoric II, whose court was at Toulouse:

[1]Theodoric is a man worth knowing even if one cannot enjoy his personal acquaintance. Providence and nature have conspired to endow him with the perfect gifts of Fortune, and his habits are such that not even the envy which besets kings can deprive him of the praise which is his due. First I shall describe his person. He is of stalwart figure, above average height but no giant. His head is round, and his curly hair recedes somewhat from his brow. His neck is sinewy, but not disfigured by lumps. His eyebrows are bushy

[1]Sidonius Apollinaris, Letters, 1.2.

and arched, and when the lids are down the lashes cover almost half his cheeks. His nose is aquiline, his lips thin, his mouth not distended. Every day the hairs protruding from his nostrils are cropped. . . . The daily routine of his public life is as follows. Before daybreak he attends the service of his [Arian] priests with a small suite. He is assiduous in prayer, but rather, one suspects, out of habit than conviction. The rest of the morning is occupied with official business. About the throne stand armed nobles; the ordinary guards, dressed in furs, are kept within call but remain at the vestibule, between the curtain and the outer wall, for the sake of quiet; only a murmur carries in. Foreign envoys are introduced; the king hears them and says little. If a matter requires consideration he postpones it; he acts at once on matters ready for decision. At the second hour he rises from the throne and inspects the treasury or the stables. If a hunt is in preparation he joins it. . . .

On ordinary days his table is like a private person's. It is not weighed down with massive silver carried by panting footmen; the weight is rather in the conversation, which is always sensible. The draperies are sometimes of purple silk, sometimes of linen; art, not expense, commends the food, as cleanliness rather than bulk the silver. Toasts are few; you will sooner see a thirsty guest impatient than a full one refusing a drink. In a word you will find elegance of Greece, good cheer of Gaul, nimbleness of Italy, the dignity of state banquets combined with the attentive service of a private host. . . . At backgammon he gathers the dice quickly, examines them shrewdly, shakes the box expertly, throws rapidly, addresses the dice humorously, and awaits the issue patiently. He is silent at a good throw but jokes over a bad; he is not annoyed by fortune and always remains the philosopher. . . . I myself am glad to be beaten by him when I have a favor to ask, since the loss of my game may mean the winning of my cause. About the ninth hour the burden of government is resumed. Back come the importunates, back the ushers to remove them. . . . At supper there is no drone of the water organ, no chorus with conductor performing a selection; there are no players on lyre or flute, no musical virtuoso, no girls with zither or tabor. The only music which appeals to the king is that which charms the mind with virtue as well as the ear with melody.

We return to the east and Theodosius. His reign was marked by reasonably successful wars against the Persians and disastrous inroads of Huns, who had to be bought off with large indemnities. For posterity the two most important events in the reign of Theodosius were the foundation of a Christian university in Constantinople, to compete with and eventually supplant the schools of Alexandria and Athens, and the systematization of the law in the Theodosian Code. Here is part of the imperial constitution, dated 438, which introduced the great Code:

[1]"The Emperors Theodosius and Valentinian, Augusti, to Florentius, Pretorian Prefect of the East.

"Our clemency has often been perplexed to understand why it is that, though so many rewards are held out for the maintenance of arts and liberal studies, persons endowed with a full knowledge of the civil law are few and rare; out of the many whose lucubrations have made them pale, hardly one or two have attained sound and complete learning.

"When we consider the countless multitude of books, the diversity and difficulty of legal procedures, and moreover the huge mass of imperial constitutions which a wall of obscurity renders impenetrable to human ingenuity, we

[1]Theodosian Code, Nov. Tit. 1.

feel that we have met a real need of our age; we have dis-
pelled the darkness and have given the laws light by a
short compendium. We selected noble men of approved
faith and acknowledged learning, who are charged with the
responsibilities of civil office, and clearing away interpreta-
tions, we have published the constitutions of previous emperors, so that men may no longer have to await formidable responses from the jurisconsults as from an inner
shrine, since it is now quite plain how a gift may be validly
bestowed, an inheritance claimed, a condition stipulated for
the collection of a debt. These details, unveiled by the
assiduity of our jurists, have been brought into open day
under the radiant splendor of our name.

"Those jurists to whom we have entrusted the divine
secrets of our heart must not imagine that their reward is
slight. If our vision of the future is correct, their names
will descend to posterity linked with ours.

"Wherefore, having swept away the cloud of volumes on
which many have wasted their lives and explained nothing,
we establish a compendious knowledge of the imperial constitutions since the time of the sainted Constantine, and
allow no one after next January first to use any authority in
the practice of the law except those books which bear our
name and are kept in the sacred imperial bureaus. None of
the earlier emperors, however, has been deprived of im-
mortality, the name of no lawgiver has perished; rather do
they enjoy a borrowed light in that their august decrees are
associated with us. The glory of the originators of the laws
remains and will remain forever; to our name no light except that of brevity has passed."

[1]So then Theodosius died [A.D. 450]. Before the death
of the emperor was made public Pulcheria summoned
[1]Zonaras, 13.24.

Marcian, already quite old, an upright and prudent man, and told him of the king's death. "I have chosen you before all others to be emperor," she said, "if you will give me your promise to preserve untouched the virginity which I have dedicated to God." Upon his consent she convoked the patriarch and the senate, proclaimed Marcian emperor, and crowned him with the diadem. Previously Marcian had not been distinguished by office or family, but had been a simple soldier.

Marcian (450–457) was a frugal and conscientious ruler. He cut off the large indemnities to Attila, which he was able to do because of Attila's preoccupation in the west, and alleviated the pressure of taxes. He permitted the Ostrogoths to settle as foederati in Pannonia. In church history Marcian is remembered for having convoked the Fourth Ecumenical Council at Chalcedon. Pulcheria died in 453 and Marcian in 457. With their deaths the Theodosian dynasty ended in Constantinople.

Again there was no designated successor. The most powerful man in the army was Aspar, who could not himself aspire to the throne because he was a barbarian and an Arian. Aspar's choice was Leo (A.D. 457–474), an uneducated but competent officer. It happens that the elaborate ceremonial of Leo's coronation has been preserved; after he had been robed and crowned and had received ceremonial addresses, he responded, through his state secretary, as follows:

[1]Emperor Caesar Leo, Victorious, Ever August (says): "Almighty God and your choice, most valiant fellow soldiers, elected me emperor of the Roman state." All: "Leo Augustus, you are victorious. We who chose you will keep you; God will protect his choice." Leo: "As master and ruler you shall have me who as your fellow soldier learned

[1]Constantine Porphyrogenitus, On Ceremonies, 1.423.

to endure labor with you." All: "Our good fortune! The army accepted you as emperor, victorious one. We all desire you." Leo: "I have decided what donations I shall give the soldiers." All: "Pious and powerful and prudent!" Leo: "To inaugurate my sacred and fortunate reign I will give five gold pieces and a pound of silver to each soldier." All: "Pious, generous, author of honor, author of riches! May your reign be blessed, a golden age!" Leo: "God be with us."

To neutralize Aspar's power, which was based on the Gothic mercenaries and foederati, Leo recruited into his service the hardy Isaurians of southern Anatolia who were virtually untouched by Hellenism and had defied the empire under Arcadius and Theodosius. Leo married his eldest daughter Ariadne to the Isaurian Zeno, but in 470 Aspar was still strong enough to force Leo to marry his younger daughter Leontia to his own son Patricius and to make him Caesar. In 471 Aspar and his sons were assassinated. In 473 Leo made his grandson and namesake, son of Zeno, his colleague. Leo I died in 474, and Leo II made his father Zeno co-emperor; Leo II died the same year, and Zeno became sole ruler (474–491).

Would-be usurpers and revolting Gothic foederati made Zeno's reign difficult. Leo I's widow Verina had her own ambitions and was supported by her brother Basiliscus and Zeno's chief officer Illus. They so frightened Zeno that he fled to his native Isauria and Basiliscus overreached his sister and made himself emperor. Basiliscus' adherence to heretical monophytism made him unpopular, and Zeno returned, executed Basiliscus, and relegated Verina to a nunnery. Next Marcian, son-in-law of Leo I, headed an insurrection in protest against the predominance of Isaurians in the government, but was quickly subdued. Then Illus induced Verina to crown Leontius emperor; the leaders of this re-

volt *were all put to death* (488). *Theodoric* (the Amal),
*who had first supported Zeno, then became hostile, but later
came to terms with him, received a grant of lands in Dacia
and lower Moesia and a warrant for the conquest of Italy.
When he led his Goths westward the eastern empire was
relieved of the danger of German domination.*

[1]The emperor Zeno understood how to exploit the situation, and so advised Theodoric to march to Italy, attack
Odovacar, and acquire the rule of the west for himself and
the Goths. . . . The forces of Odovacar were defeated in a
number of battles and then shut themselves up with their
leader in Ravenna. . . . After Theodoric had spent three
years on the siege of Ravenna, the Goths, who were weary
of the siege, and Odovacar's party, which was hard pressed
by shortages, reached an understanding through the media-
tion of the priest of Ravenna by which both Theodoric and
Odovacar should reside in Ravenna on terms of equality.
For some time they observed this agreement, but presently
Theodoric caught Odovacar plotting against him, as they
say, and so he craftily invited him to a feast and killed him.
Theodoric won over such of the hostile barbarians as survived and secured the rule over both Goths and Italians. He
did not claim the right to assume either the dress or title
of emperor but was called "king," as the barbarians are
accustomed to call their leaders. But in governing his subjects he exercised all the qualities of one who is an emperor
by birth. He was particularly careful to observe justice, he
preserved the laws stoutly, he protected the country and
kept it safe from surrounding barbarians, and he attained
the highest degree of prudence and courage. He perpetrated
scarcely one injustice against his subjects, and did not tolerate such conduct on the part of others, except that the
Goths distributed among themselves the land which Odova-

[1]Procopius, 5.1.

car had given his own people. Though he was in name a usurper, in fact Theodoric was as truly an emperor as any who distinguished themselves in this office from the beginning. Among both Goths and Italians he came to be greatly loved. . . . He reigned for thirty-seven years [until 526] and he died a terror to his enemies and deeply regretted by his subjects. The manner of his death was as follows.

Symmachus [a descendant of St. Ambrose's opponent] and his son-in-law Boethius [author of the *Consolation of Philosophy*] were nobles of ancient family and had been consuls and leaders of the senate. They practiced philosophy and cultivated justice in the highest degree; they relieved the needs of citizens and strangers with generous largesse. This brought them high reputation but aroused the envy of wicked men. Theodoric credited the slanders of these envious men, killed Symmachus and Boethius on the ground that they were attempting subversion, and confiscated their property. When he was at dinner a few days later the waiters served the head of a big fish. To Theodoric this seemed to be the head of Symmachus newly killed. The teeth set in the lower jaw and the grim, insensible stare did give the impression of someone threatening. Theodoric was terrified at the prodigy and scurried to his bed quaking in panic, and ordered many coverlets to be piled upon him as he lay. Subsequently he told his physician Elpidius what had happened and wept for his sin against Symmachus and Boethius. When he had lamented and grieved over the disaster he died shortly afterwards. This was the first and last injustice he committed upon his subjects, and the reason was that he had not followed his usual practice of making a thorough investigation before passing judgment.

[1]After Zeno's pitiful death [491] Ariadne raised Anas-

[1]Zonaras, 14.2.

tasius, who was a lowly silentiary, to the imperial office, with the approval of senate and army; the eunuch Urbicius, who was very influential at the time, urged this appointment. Anastasius was called Dikoros ("of double pupils") because the pupils of his eyes did not match: the right was dark, and the left hazel. Before he was crowned the patriarch Euphemius demanded that he submit in writing a confession of his faith and an engagement not to disturb the established dogmas of the Church. . . . When Euphemius received the agreement in Anastasius' own hand that he would preserve all the dogmas of the Church and the definitions of the Synod of Chalcedon he crowned him. Anastasius was betrothed to Ariadne at once and canceled the obligations of certain debtors to the state. Forty days after the burial of Zeno the marriage was consummated. He abolished the tax called chrysargyron, which had been very oppressive to his subjects. Every pauper and beggar, every prostitute, every freedman living in country or city had been compelled to pay this tax annually. This impost had also been collected for horses, mules, cows, asses, and dogs. For each person the impost was a silver piece, and the same for horse, mule, or cow; for each ass six follis, and the same for a dog. This was very oppressive and widely resented. The emperor Anastasius abolished the tax and publicly burned all documents referring to it in the Hippodrome. This made him popular, and indeed his management of political matters was excellent: appointments which had previously been acquired by purchase he bestowed without price. But in respect to religion he was not a good emperor.

This last remark, like the patriarch's insistence upon a written engagement to preserve orthodoxy, is explained by Anastasius' persistent inclination towards monophysitism. When he appointed a monophysite bishop in Constantinople in 512 he almost lost his throne. His heterodoxy encouraged Vitalian, the commander of the Bulgarian foederati, to revolt, and Vitalian had to be bought off with 5000 pounds of gold and a promotion; when Vitalian marched on Constantinople a second time (515) he was crushed. Now the Balkan peninsula was being overrun by Slavic invaders, and to protect the capital Anastasius built a wall, forty miles long, across the peninsula on which Constantinople stands. In 502 the Persians under King Kawad invaded Roman territory but were repulsed, though not subdued, after four years of fighting. At the start of Anastasius' reign the Isaurians in southern Asia Minor, annoyed by his expulsion of Zeno's Isaurian officials and troops from the capital, revolted. Their subjugation required seven years of fighting, but their power was permanently broken. In 518 Anastasius died and was succeeded by Justin (518–527).

11. Justinian

[1]In Leo's reign three young Illyrian farmers, Zimarchus,
Dityvistus, and Justin, who had had a hard struggle with
poverty, set out from Vederiana [near Sofia] to improve their
condition by joining the army. They walked to Byzantium
with their cloaks on their shoulders, carrying nothing but
hard tack from home. When they enlisted, the emperor
assigned them to the palace guard, for they had fine figures.
Later Anastasius became emperor and made war on the
Isaurians who had revolted. He sent a considerable army
against them, under the command of John called the
Hunchback. John jailed Justin for some offense and was
going to execute him the following day, but was prevented
by a dream. . . . So it happened that Justin was saved, and
as time went on he attained high authority. Anastasius
made him commander of the palace guards, and this
office enabled him to succeed to the throne upon the death
of Anastasius. He was already ripe for the grave and completely illiterate—a thing which was unexampled among
Roman rulers. . . . In order that documents might bear
the witness of the emperor's hand the appropriate officials
contrived the following device. They cut the four Latin
letters which mean "I have read" in a block of dressed
wood, and then they would dip the pen in the imperial
ink, put it into the emperor's hand, place the document
over the block, guide the emperor's pen over the tracing of
the letters, and thus obtain the royal autograph. This was
[1]Procopius, Secret History, 6.2.

the sort of Roman emperor Justin was. His wife's name was Lupicina; she was a slave and a barbarian, and had been her previous owner's concubine. She and Justin came to the throne in the decline of life. Justin did his subjects no harm, nor, indeed, any good. He was quite naïve, inarticulate, and a yokel. The business of government was managed by his nephew Justinian, who was still young.

Justinian [527–565] was responsible for greater disasters than had ever been heard of in all antecedent Roman history. He would proceed to murder innocent men and seize other men's goods without a qualm; to him it was nothing that many myraids should be destroyed though they had given no offense. He was completely indifferent to the preservation of established institutions, but was bent on subverting everything. In a word, this man was the great destroyer of all tradition.

This is how Procopius begins his sketch of Justinian in his Secret History, and from Justinian he proceeds to the empress Theodora. If Procopius' Justinian suggests a Tamerlane, nowhere in literature is a woman painted as black as his Theodora. It seems incredible, then, that the same Procopius also described the same Justinian in language like the following:

[1]Our own age has seen the birth of the emperor Justinian. He received the state when it was distressed and tottering, and has not only enlarged its extent but enhanced its glory. . . . He has added to the empire domains which belonged to others in his own time and has created countless cities which never before existed. When he found religious belief straying and forced into many deviations, he destroyed all paths to error and established religion on a single firm foundation. Finding the laws obscure because they had proliferated into confusion and inconsistency, he

[1]Procopius, *Buildings*, 1.

preserved them by purging them of discrepancies and trickery and by firmly harmonizing their differences. Of his own accord he dismissed the charges against those who plotted against him. The needy he surfeited with wealth, and he overpowered their malignant fortune. He gave prosperity permanent residence in the state. The Roman realm, exposed to barbarians on all sides, he strengthened by a host of soldiers; all its frontiers he fortified by building strongholds.

Procopius' adulation is doubtless as exaggerated as his denigration, but each stroke in either picture has a basis in the career of Justinian as it can be gathered from more temperate sources. Here is what might be called the authorized version of Justinian's career:

[1]When the state was being assailed by waves and gusts of disaster Fortune opposed the diligence of Justinian to the sloth of his predecessors, setting up as an overseer of the common welfare the most viligant of emperors. He regarded it as a dereliction on his own part if all others did not show a similar vigilance, and fight on behalf of the state not only to recover Roman possessions which the lassitude of his predecessors had lost, but to add to them the possessions of the enemy. Impulsive Chosroes and the Persians he restrained at first with gold, and then, when Chosroes again took up arms, with steel. He made a swift attack upon the Vandals, a Germanic people who had devoured Libya, and conquered them in barely two months. His war captives he exhibited to the imperial city— Gelimer, the nobles of his race whom the barbarians call *astingi*, his wife and children, and his great treasures—and he bestowed their persons upon the Romans like the vilest of slaves. And as if this were a slight matter, he attacked the Getae, who had long desecrated the sacred name of

[1]John Lydus, 3.55.

Rome and all that appertained to it and had insulted Rome's ancient nobility; he ravaged them root and branch and brought them to Rome along with their tyrant Vitigis, and restored her own to Rome.

And here is the summary of a Latin writer which shaped the medieval conception of Justinian:

[1]At the time when the imperium of the Romans had ceased among the Italians and many nations invaded them down to the sea, Justinian Augustus happily was Roman emperor. He waged wars with success and was outstanding in civil law. Through the patrician Belisarius he vigorously subdued the Persians: through this same Belisarius he annihilated the race of the Vandals and captured their king Gelimer, and after an interval of ninety-six years restored Africa to the Roman empire. Again, by the forces of Belisarius he defeated the race of Goths in Italy and captured their king Vitigis. The Moors also, who subsequently infested Africa, and their king Atalas he subdued with marvelous energy through the ex-consul, John. Similarly he suppressed other nations by the right of war. Because of all these victories he well deserves the titles Alamannicus, Gothicus, Francicus, Germanicus, Anticus, Alanicus, Vandalicus, and Africanus.

The laws of the Romans also, which were very diffuse and impracticably discrepant, he corrected with admirable brevity. All the imperial constitutions which had reposed in numerous volumes he concentrated into twelve books. He enjoined that this work be called the Justinian Code. Again the laws or decisions of individual magistrates or judges, which extended over almost two thousand books, he reduced to fifty, and that Code he called by the name of Digests or Pandects. He composed anew four books of Institutes, in which the text of all laws is presented in brief

[1]Paul the Deacon, 17.1.

form. The new laws which he established he ordained to be edited in one volume and called the Novella.

This same emperor also constructed within the city of Constantinople to Christ our Lord, who is the wisdom of God the Father, a temple which he named Hagia Sophia in Greek, that is, Blessed Wisdom. So far did this edifice surpass other structures that its like cannot be found in the whole wide world. This emperor was a Catholic in faith, upright in works, just in judgment, and therefore in him all qualities united for good.

For Justinian's wars we have an ample and excellent account in the history of Procopius, who was an aide to Justinian's famous general Belisarius. In 530 Gelimer, a great-grandson of Gaiseric, seized the Vandal kingdom of Africa from his cousin Hilderic, and Justinian grasped the opportunity to send an expeditionary force against Gelimer. Belisarius' skill and the psychology of a Nordic king in Africa may be illustrated by the circumstances surrounding the surrender of Gelimer. When he was besieged on Mount Papua Belisarius' lieutenant Pharas wrote urging him to yield honorably. In reply Gelimer thanked him cordially, said that he could not, and requested the gift of a lyre, a loaf of bread, and a sponge.

[1]Pharas was unable to understand the concluding words of this letter until the messenger explained that Gelimer wanted the bread because he had not seen a loaf since he had gone up on Papua. A sponge he needed because one eye was swollen for lack of washing. And because he was a good musician he wanted a lyre to accompany an ode he had composed on his present misfortune so that he could weep his fill. . . . Gelimer endured his affliction with surprising fortitude until a certain spectacle moved him. A Moorish woman had managed to scrape up a little corn,

[1]Procopius, 4.6.

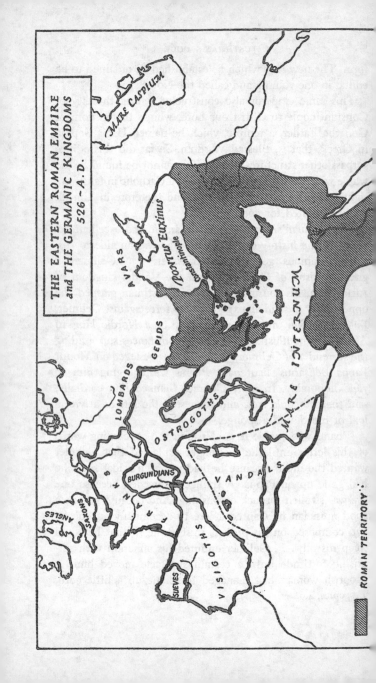

THE EASTERN ROMAN EMPIRE
and THE GERMANIC KINGDOMS
526 - A.D.

MARE CASPIUM

Pontus Euxinus

Constantinople

MARE INTERNUM

AVARS

GEPIDS

LOMBARDS

OSTROGOTHS

BURGUNDIANS

VANDALS

F R A N K S

SAXONS

ANGLES

SUEVES

VISIGOTHS

ROMAN TERRITORY:

which she made into a tiny cake and put in the hot ashes on the hearth—that is the way the Moors bake bread. Beside the hearth were sitting two starving children, one the son of the woman and the other the nephew of Gelimer, eager to seize the cake as soon as it should seem done. The Vandal got ahead and snatched the cake; though it was hot and covered with ashes his hunger made him throw it into his mouth. The other beat him over the head and pummeled him and forced him to disgorge the cake, which was down his throat. This Gelimer could not endure. . . . When he came before Belisarius to surrender he laughed so hard that he could not conceal his laughter. Some of the spectators suspected that his extreme affliction had deranged his reason and that his laughter had no significance. But his friends insisted that he was in his right mind . . . and that he laughed because he was convinced that man's lot was a ridiculous thing.

But after the Vandals were defeated the Moors revolted and were not crushed until 539. Libya was depopulated and ruined, but it remained part of the empire until the Saracen invasions in the seventh century. Italy afforded Justinian a similar occasion for intervention. Upon the death of Theodoric's grandson and successor Athalaric, his mother Amalasuntha became regent and married Theodahad, who put her to death. To avenge his ally Justinian sent Belisarius to invade Italy. Belisarius was besieged in Rome for a year (537–538; it was on this occasion that the aqueducts were ruined and the Castel San Angelo stripped) and relieved by new forces under Narses. In 540 the Gothic king was captured in the siege of Ravenna, and Italy was declared a Roman province. In 541 the energetic Totila led a revolt and drove the Roman garrisons out of Italy. Preoccupation with the Persian War prevented Justinian from taking vigorous measures until 552, when Narses defeated and killed Totila, and then an invading horde of Alamanni and Franks who had been nominal allies of the Goths. By 554 Roman dominion was re-established in Italy, but the country was now totally impoverished. Now an opportunity to intervene in Spain presented itself, but the Roman forces were unable to advance beyond the coastal cities. Justinian had succeeded in destroying the Vandal and Ostrogoth kingdoms and in recovering Africa, Italy, and the Mediterranean islands, and a strip of the Spanish coast.

To free himself for his western campaigns Justinian had agreed (532) to pay Chosroes I of Persia an annual indemnity. But in 539 Justinian's successes in the west roused Chosroes to action. He overran Syria and carried the population of Antioch into captivity. In 562, after some twenty years of desultory fighting, a fifty-year peace was concluded. The negotiations leading to this treaty and its terms are preserved in a fragment of the historian Menander. Here are some excerpts:

[1]"Persons who during the war deserted from the Romans to the Persians or from the Persians to the Romans shall not be prevented or hindered from returning home if they so desire. But those who desert or escape from one side to the other in time of peace must not be received; every means must be used to hand them over, even against their will, to those from whom they escaped.

"Nationals of one state who complain of injuries by nationals of the other shall settle their dispute by arbitration, the plaintiffs acting for themselves or through agents meeting on the frontier at the officials' quarters of either state. He who is at fault must make the loss good.

"Neither state shall henceforth fortify against the other nor strengthen the walls of frontier positions, in order that

[1]Menander "Protector," in *Historici Graeci Minores*, 2.22–24.

there shall be no occasion for friction and the infringement of the truce. . . .

"When decisions had been reached and adopted separate consideration was given to the position of Christians in Persia. It was agreed that they could build churches and worship freely . . . and that they should not be compelled to attend Magian rites or invoke, against their will, the gods in whom the Medes believe. The Christians on their part agreed they would not attempt to convert Magians to our faith. It was further enacted, in regard to the dead, that Christians would be permitted to bury them in graves as is our custom.

"When agreement had been reached and reduced to proper order, designated officials received the drafts and sharpened their precision by finding words of equal force and significance. Additional copies were made, and the originals rolled up and secured with wax and Persian seals and with signets of the envoys and of the twelve interpreters, six Roman and six Persian. Then they interchanged the documents bearing the terms of the peace."

The empire had always been an open autocracy, but the imperial bureaucracy was so elaborate and rigid that it retained a kind of independent momentum under indifferent emperors. Justinian was the perfect autocrat because he made the bureaucracy his own instrument. We can see into the structure through his Code as well as through other contemporary records. Here is an enactment against evasion of state service, under date of 535:

[1]"Justinian to John, the most glorious pretorian prefect of the east: Those who of old established our form of government thought right that, following the precedent of the

[1]*Corpus Iuris Civilis*, Nov. 38 (trans. C. H. Munro).

263

capital city, they should form in each city an assembly of the wellborn and give it a senate through which public business should be conducted and everything done in its proper order. The scheme so prospered and gained such reputation that the greatest and most numerous families had members in the senates, the senators forming a large body, and what were regarded as the burdens of the service being by no means unsupportable to any of them. For through being distributed amongst a large number the burden was almost imperceptible to those who shouldered it. But when gradually certain individuals began to get their names removed from the senatorial lists and to discover pretexts why they should be exempt, then little by little the senates shrank. . . . The state system has become a sink of all iniquity. This condition of things we have been constantly investigating and we have decided that we must apply a remedy. But the more we labored at this problem the more the senators devised every trick to thwart our right and just enactments and the public interest. . . . Most impious of all, they abstain from lawful marriage and choose rather to die legally childless than to prove themselves useful to their race and to their senate."

The ritualism of the bureaucracy is illustrated by the ready-made formulae for admission to various offices of state. Cassiodorus, the friend of Boethius, composed two books of such formulae; here is the commission for the quaestorship:

[1]"We embrace the quaestorship with our whole heart, for we regard it as the voice of our own tongue. Its holder must be privy to our own thoughts, that he may say rightly that which he knows we feel. If in aught we hesitate, we seek aid from the quaestor, who is the treasury of the state's fair fame and the armory of its laws. Other officials

[1]Cassiodorus, *Variae*, 6 (trans. E. S. Duckett).

may seek the comfort of collaborators; your dignity, O Quaestor, ministers counsel to the sovereign. Persuaded, therefore, by the repute of your prudence and eloquence, we hereby confer on you the quaestorship: the glory of letters, the shrine of civilized living, the mother of all honors, the home of temperance, the seat of all virtues."

Justinian's autocracy extended to religion, and he constantly strove to realize what has been called Caesaropapism. In such a system religious heresy is a political crime. The principle involved in his numerous enactments on heresy is stated in a measure entitled "Edict to the People of Constantinople concerning the Truth":

[1]"We hold that the first and greatest blessing for all mankind is the true and irreproachable confession of the Christian faith to the end that all holy priests the world over may be joined in unity and with one voice proclaim and profess the orthodox Christian faith, and that every plea devised by heretics be rendered null and void. Previous edicts and declarations clarify this policy. But inasmuch as heretics without sense or fear of God or thought of the severe penalties the law imposes on their kind persist in carrying on the devil's work; they deceive the naïve, secretly hold illicit gatherings contrary to God's holy and apostolic Church, and perform unlawful baptisms. We therefore deem it our sacred duty to admonish such offenders by our present edict that they may desist from heretical madness and not corrupt the souls of others, but rather rally to God's holy Church where true dogmas are respected and heresies and their champions anathematized. Know all men that we shall not tolerate the convening of unlawful assemblies or foregathering with such as do convene them. Buildings in which such offenses are committed will be transferred to the possession of the holy

[1]*Corpus Iuris Civilis,* Nov. 132.

Church. Our orders are that those who convene such assemblies or join with them shall be punished to the full extent of the law."

These penalties were not mild. Despite the strictness of the administration, or perhaps because of it, popular riots did break out. The best known is called the Nika, brought on by the partisans of the circus factions called Blues and Greens.

[1]Law and orderly government were confounded by the disturbances of these partisans. First they adopted a peculiar style of cutting their hair, unlike the ordinary Roman fashion. Their mustaches and beards they never touched, but wished to have them long, like Persians. But on their heads they shaved their hair as far as the temples and let it grow long behind in an absurd way, like Huns; that is why they called it a "Hun-cut." Next, in the matter of dress, they all wanted to wear fine clothes and dressed too elegantly for their position. . . . Their sleeves were tight at the wrist, and billowed out up to the shoulders. When they waved their arms in theaters and hippodromes, shouting and cheering as their habit was, this part of their dress would soar aloft.

[2]At this time [532] an unexpected riot broke out among the populace of Byzantium and caused great harm to people and senate. In every city the population has long been divided into Blue and Green factions. . . . Victory in their rivalries they put beyond all other considerations human or divine. They pay no attention to any sacrilege to God or lawbreaking by friend or foe, they are indifferent to lack of necessaries or to unjust abuse of their country if their side can derive any advantage. They call their side Fellow-factioneers. Even women join in this strife; they not only follow their men but offer resistance upon

[1]Procopius, *Secret History*, 7.7.   [2]Procopius, 1.24.

occasion, though they themselves never go to the theater nor have any similar motive. . . . Now it happened that the city officials of Byzantium were taking some of the factioneers to execution. But the two parties made a truce and conspired together to snatch the culprits away. They entered the jail and released all felons condemned for sedition or other crime. All the city employees they killed indiscriminately; all the sensible people were taking refuge on the opposite shore, and the city was set afire as if some enemy had conquered it. The church of Sophia, the baths of Zeuxippus, and the palace from the entry to the so-called house of Ares were burned down. So were the great colonnades which extended to the market place called Constantine's, many houses belonging to rich people, and much treasure. The emperor and his consort with a few senators shut themselves up in the palace and remained quiet there. The watchword which the populace passed to one another was Nika ("Conquer!") and so that riot has been called Nika down to the present.

Justinian's reconstruction of the church of St. Sophia still stands as an impressive monument. We have a number of descriptions and appreciations of this building by contemporaries, in prose and verse. Here is a selection (omitting all details of the actual structure) from the poem of Paul the Silentiary:

[1]Nurturing Rome, crown your life-giving emperor with unfeigned hymns, heaped up and abiding, not because he has imposed your yoke upon the peoples of the earth, not because he has extended the measureless bounds of your seat to the remotest shores of ocean, but because in thine angle he has raised an enormous temple and has made thee more illustrious than the Tiber which gave thee birth. Make way, you glories of the Capitol at Rome, make way:

[1]Paul the Silentiary, St. Sophia, 145ff.

so far has my king surpassed that marvel as Great God surpasses an idol. . . .

Who can worthily sing his calling that temple into new life of magnificent beauty? Who can characterize the fertile sagacity of our all-powerful monarch? The ingenuity of your architectural skill, scepter-bearer, I shall leave aside, and proceed to the end of your well-bestowed labors, looking to the miracle newly accomplished over which divine love has thrilled the sight of all beholders. A mortal who raises his eyes to the radiance of heaven cannot long bear to gaze upon the arched and star-studded mead with neck craned but must turn his sight to look upon the green hills. . . . But he who steps into that divine temple is unwilling to leave it. His eyes are enchanted, and he turns his head hither and thither. Satiety is repulsed afar from that edifice. So faultless a structure has our lord, guarded over by the clairvoyant counsel of immortal God, erected. By your labors, great chief, you have procured that all-glorious Christ is forever gracious.

But a far more enduring and effective monument is Justinian's codification of the law, known as the Corpus Iuris Civilis. In point of fact only a very small proportion of the Corpus comprises enactments of Justinian's own period; what the learned Tribonian and his associates did was to collect, systematize, and harmonize. But it is from the Code that western Europe learned law. The Corpus includes three parts: the Code, in twelve books, which sets down the law under its various "titles" or subjects; the Digest, in fifty books, which contains thousands of pronouncements, under the appropriate "titles," dating from Hadrian onwards; and the Institutes, a short handbook or learner's textbook, expounding the law on subjects of greatest current interest. The preface to the Institutes explains the nature of the whole Corpus:

[1]"In the name of Our Lord Jesus Christ . . . to the youth desirous of studying the law. . . . Having removed every inconsistency from the sacred constitutions hitherto inharmonious and confused, we extended our care to the immense volumes of the older jurisprudence, and, like sailors crossing the mid-ocean, by the favor of Heaven, have now completed a work of which we once despaired. When this, with God's blessing, had been done, we called together Tribonian, master and ex-quaestor of our sacred palace, and the illustrious Theophilus and Dorotheus, professors of law . . . and specially commissioned them to compose by our authority and advice a book of Institutes, whereby you may be enabled to learn your first lesson in law no longer from ancient fables, but grasp them by the brilliant light of imperial learning. . . . After the completion therefore of the fifty books of the Digest or Pandects, in which all the earlier law has been collected by the aid of the said distinguished Tribonian and other illustrious and most able men, we directed the division of these same Institutes into four books, comprising the first elements of the whole science of law. . . .

"Receive then these laws with your best powers and with the eagerness of study, and show yourselves so learned as to be encouraged to hope that when you have compassed the whole field of law you may have ability to govern such portions of the state as may be entrusted to you.

"Given at Constantinople, the twenty-first day of November in the third consulate of the emperor Justinian, ever August [A.D. 533]."

A fourth part of the Corpus are the Novels, which are 160 new laws issued in Justinian's reign subsequent to the publication of the Code. They deal with administrative and ecclesiastical matters and with private law. It is from

[1]Trans. of J. B. Moyle.

269

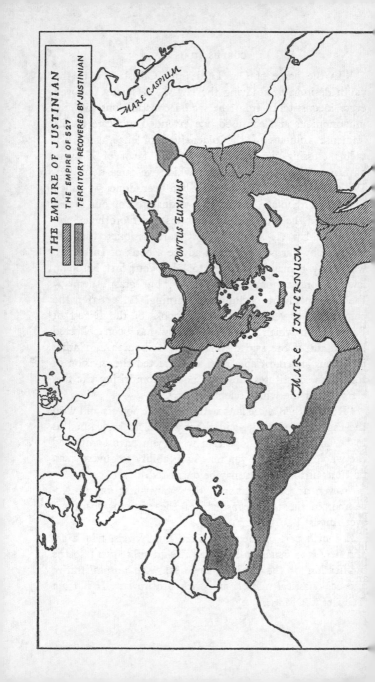

the Novels that we get our most intimate view of the public and private life in Justinian's reign. One of the matters which concerned Justinian was what we should call the "white-slave" traffic. Here is the Novel on the subject:

[1]Ancient laws and earlier emperors have regarded the name and trade of brothel-keeper with extreme abhorrence and have enacted many laws on the subject. We have increased the penalties and enacted additional laws to supply the omissions of our predecessors. But lately we have been informed of iniquities of this kind flourishing in this great city and have given the matter our attention. Some persons, we discover, maintain themselves outrageously by making accursed profit by abominable means. They travel about the country far and wide and decoy poor young girls by promising them shoes and clothing, and when they have enticed them bring them to this rich city where they keep them shut up in dens with a pitiful allowance of food and clothing. They hire their bodies out to the public and keep the miserable fees themselves. . . . We have resolved to free the city of such pollution.

Justinian not only legislated to protect these unfortunates but provided for their rehabilitation.

[2]From ancient times a numerous company of brothel-keepers exploited licentiousness in the city, selling others' youth in the public market and forcing virtue into slavery. The emperor Justinian and the empress Theodora (who shared in the piety of good works) devised the following plan. They purged the state of the pollution of brothels and banished the very name of whoremonger, and they liberated women oppressed by poverty from enslavement to licentiousness by providing them independent sustenance and emancipating virtue. This is how they managed this.

[1]*Corpus Iuris*, Nov. 39.   [2]Procopius, *Buildings*, 1.9.

On the right of the strait as you sail towards the Euxine they converted a palace into a magnificent convent for women who repented of their former life. By occupying themselves with piety and religion they would be able to cleanse the sins of their sojourn in the brothels. They named this refuge Repentance, in keeping with its object. Their Majesties endowed it with a generous income, and have built strikingly handsome and elegant houses for the women's comfort, so that none should be compelled to chafe at the practice of virtue in any particular.

An instructive gauge of Procopius' bias is offered by the parallel passage in his Secret History:

[1]Theodora collected more than five hundred prostitutes who worked in the market place at a fee of three obols—scarcely enough to maintain life—sent them to the opposite shore, and pent them up in a convent called Repentance to compel them to change their way of life. Some threw themselves down from a height at night to be rid of the change they did not wish.

But of all Justinian's measures the one which most significantly marks his reign as the end of antiquity and the beginning of a different order is his closing of the philosophical schools of Athens which for a thousand years had been the hearth of free investigation. There is a special poignancy, and a special timeliness, in the story of the displaced scholars who went to an alien land to find a philosopher-king, discovered that human nature is the same everywhere, and returned to the directed orderliness from which they had fled.

[2]The outstanding philosophers of our age were dissatisfied with the conceptions of authority prevalent among the Romans and thought that the Persian polity was far

[1]Procopius, Secret History, 17.5.   [2]Agathias, 2.30.

superior. They were persuaded by notions which had been spread broadcast to the effect that the Persian rule was most just, that, as Plato would have it, philosophy and kingship were united in a single person, that discipline was prudent and seemly in the highest degree, that there were found among them no thieves or brigands or other malefactors, so that if a thing of value were left unguarded in any deserted place no passer-by would appropriate it but it would remain safe until he that left it returned. Aroused by these reports, which they believed true, and moreover being prevented by law from remaining in these parts if they would not accommodate themselves to our established institution, they departed and betook themselves to a foreign land and alien people with the intention of remaining for the rest of their lives. First they found that the officials were arrogant and swollen with pride, and so they despised and disapproved of them. Then they observed that there were many burglars and footpads, some of whom were apprehended while others escaped, and that every species of wickedness flourished. The powerful oppressed the weak, and men dealt cruelly and inhumanly with one another. What was most absurd, though they were permitted to marry many wives and did in fact marry many, they nevertheless indulged in adultery. All of these things distressed the philosophers, and they reproached themselves for having changed their residence.

Though Christianity and Hellenism had achieved a complete symbiosis, so long as the philosophic schools maintained their independence there remained a certain tension between secular learning and orthodoxy. Its very loss of independence, paradoxically, liberated literary scholarship and fostered a particular pride in what its latest representatives regarded as an uninterrupted tradition from classical antiquity. Constantinople cultivated the classics as assiduously as ancient Alexandria had done, and so preserved them for transmission to the west when the Byzantine empire fell.

So in the west, after Symmachus' attempt to restore Victoria proved abortive, pagan learning was no longer dangerous, and a renewed consciousness of continuity with the remote past enhanced the Italian sense of responsible superiority. As the Byzantines harked back to their classical period and tended to overlook the centuries intervening, so the Italians harked back to their own Golden Age under the first Augustus. It was Augustan Vergil whom Dante would look to as philosopher and guide, and from the Augustan reign that he would argue, in the De Monarchia, that Rome was a divinely ordained preparation for the evangel of Christianity and the divinely ordained model for Italian polity. Vergil's writings Italian Christendom regarded virtually as hagiographa, and a passage such as his famous praise of Italy must therefore have exerted very great influence in fostering a renewed pride in Italy:

> [1]But neither flowering groves
> Of Media's realm, nor Ganges proud,
> Nor Lydian fountains flowing thick with gold,
> Can match their glories with Italia;
> Not Bactria nor Ind, nor all the wealth
> Of wide Arabia's incense-bearing sands.
> This land by Jason's bulls with breath of flame
> Never was plowed, nor planted with the teeth
> Of monstrous dragon, nor that harvest grew
> Of helmed warrior heads and myriad spears.
> But full-eared corn and goodly Massic wine
> Inhabit here, with olives and fat herds.

[1]Vergil, Georgics, 2.136–74 (trans. T. C. Williams).

The war horse here with forehead high in air
Strides o'er the plain; here roam thy spotless flocks,
Clitumnus; and for noblest sacrifice,
The snow-white bull, bathed oft in sacred stream,
Leads Roman triumphs to the house of Jove.
Here spring is endless and the summer glows
In months not half her own. Twice in the year
The herds drop young, and twice the orchard bears
The labor of its fruit. But tigers fell
And the fierce lion's brood are absent here.
No deadly aconite deceives the hand
That gathers herbs; nor in enormous folds
Or lengthened twine the scaly snake upcoils.
Behold the famous cities!—what vast toil
Upreared them!—and the host of strongholds piled
By hand of man on out-hewn precipice,
While swift streams under ancient bulwarks flow.
Why tell of two salt seas that wash her shore
Above, below; her multitude of lakes—
Thee, Larius, chiefest, and Benacus, where
Are swelling floods and billows like the sea?
Why name that haven where the lofty mole
Locks in the Lucrine lake, while with loud rage
The baffled waters roar, and Julian waves
Echo from far the sea's retreating tide,
And through the channels of Avernus pours
Th' invading Tuscan main? In this rich land
Deep veins of silver show, and ores for brass,
With lavish gold. Hence sprang the warlike breed
Of Marsi, hence the proud Sabellian clans,
Ligurians to hardship seasoned well,
And Volscian spearmen; hence the Decii,
Camilli, Marii, immortal names,
The Scipios, in wars implacable,

And Caesar, thou, the last, the prince of all,
Who now victorious on far Asia's end,
Art holding back from Roman citadels
The Indian weakling. Hail, O Saturn's land,
Mother of all good fruits and harvests fair,
Mother of men!

And Christian Italy could exult in the glorification of its
pagan past without misgivings, because the grandeur of
pagan Rome, men now knew, was part of a divine plan to
bring peace and brotherhood, under Roman guidance, to
all the world.

[1]Over all countries within the bounds of the western
ocean, over all lighted by Aurora's rosy dawning, raging
Bellona had confounded all things human and had armed
savage hands to inflict wounds one upon another. To
bridle this madness God taught the nations everywhere
to bow their heads under the same laws: all whom Rhine
and Danube water, or gold-bearing Tagus, or great Ebro,
all that Hesperian Tiber flows through or Ganges nourishes
or the seven mouths of the warm Nile sustains—all these
did God teach to become Romans. A shared law made
them peers, intertwined them under a single name, brought
the vanquished into bonds of brotherhood. In regions
most diverse life proceeds as if fellow citizens of the
same breed dwelt within the walls of a single ancestral
city, as if all were at peace under their grandfathers' roof.
Areas geographically remote, shores divided by the sea,
now merge in allegiance to a single jurisdiction, now
their trade and their handicrafts bring them to a single
thronged market, now dwellers in disparate regions unite
in solemn wedlock, and a single progeny is the issue of
the mingled blood of diverse races. Such was the achieve-

[1]Prudentius, Against Symmachus, 2.598–635.

ment of the enormous successes and triumphs of Roman power. It was for Christ, who was even then on his way, that the path was prepared; the general amity of our peace had long since paved it, under the direction of Rome. What room could there have been for God in a world that was savage, in human hearts at discord with one another, each proffering its own claims and asserting its own rights? Such was the situation of old, and when the passions of the human heart are disordered and the parts of the soul dissevered by confused partisanship, neither limpid wisdom can find access nor God enter in. But if high intelligence gains rightful sovereignty and bridles the impulses of the pugnacious temper and the rebellious flesh and constrains all passions under a single rationale, the poise of life is made stable and firm conviction draws God into the heart and yields authority to a single Lord. Now the earth is in concord: infuse it, Almighty, with thy presence; now, Christ, a world receives thee which peace and Rome hold together in a bond of union.

The Growth of the Roman Empire

Chronology

Literary figures are shown in italics; emperors in capitals. Dates are sometimes only approximate.

B.C.

1184	Legendary arrival of Aeneas in Italy
753	Founding of Rome; regal period until—
510	Ejection of Tarquins, establishment of republic
494	First secession of plebeians
445	Canuleian law, permitting marriage of patricians and plebeians
390	Battle of Allia; Rome sacked by Gauls
343–290	Wars with Samnites and Latins
287	Last plebeian secession
281–272	Tarentine (Pyrrhic) Wars
284–204	*Livius Andronicus*, first Latin poet
270–266	War with Umbrians and Etruscans; Rome supreme in Italy
270–201	*Naevius*, Roman playwright and epic poet
239–169	*Ennius*, "father of Latin poetry"
264–241	First Punic War
251–184	*Plautus*, comic playwright
?–168	*Caecilius Statius*, comic playwright
224–222	Conquest of Cisalpine Gaul
220–219	Second Illyrian War
220–130	*Pacuvius*, Latin dramatist
218–201	Second Punic (Hannibalic) War
215	First Macedonian War
201	Carthaginian Spain annexed

201–118	*Polybius*, Greek historian of Rome
200–196	Second Macedonian War
195–159	*Terence*, comic playwright
191–189	Syrian War; battle of Magnesia
184	Censorship of Cato
180–102	*Lucilius*, pioneer satirist
171–167	Third Macedonian War
170–85	*Accius*, Latin tragic poet
155	Carneades and colleagues lecture at Rome
149–146	Third Punic War; Carthage and Corinth destroyed
143–133	Numantine (Spanish) War
133	Pergamum willed to Rome; tribunate of T. Gracchus
122	Tribunate of G. Gracchus
116–27	*Varro*, Latin polymath
111–105	Jugurthine (African) war
106–43	*Cicero*
102–101	Defeat of Cimbri and Teutones by Marius
94–55	*Lucretius*, Latin Epicurean poet (*On the Nature of Things*)
90–88	Social (Italic) War
88–85	First Mithradatic War
86–34	*Sallust*, Latin historian
84–54	*Catullus*, Latin lyric poet
82–79	Sulla dictator
74–63	Second Mithradatic War (Lucullus, Pompey)
73–71	Slave revolt under Spartacus
70–19	*Vergil*, Latin poet
65–8	*Horace*, Latin poet
63	Cicero consul; Catilinarian conspiracy
60	Coalition of Caesar, Pompey, and Crassus
59	Caesar's first consulship; beginning of Gallic conquest
59–A.D. 17	*Livy*, Roman historian
53	Death of Crassus at Carrhae
50–10	*Propertius*, Latin elegiac poet

49–46	Civil war: Caesar vs. Pompey and senatorial party
48	Battle of Pharsalus; death of Pompey
48–19	*Tibullus*, Latin elegiac poet
44	Assassination of Caesar
43	Triumvirate of Octavian, Antony, Lepidus
43–A.D. 17	*Ovid*, Latin poet
42	Battle of Philippi; Octavian and Antony defeat republican leaders Brutus and Cassius
31	Battle of Actium; Octavian defeats Antony and Cleopatra
27–A.D. 14	AUGUSTUS
19–A.D. 32	*Velleius Paterculus*, Roman historian
15–A.D. 50	*Phaedrus*, Roman fabulist
4–A.D. 65	*Seneca*, Latin philosopher and dramatist

A.D.

14–37	TIBERIUS
23–79	*Elder Pliny*, Latin encyclopedist
34–62	*Persius*, Roman satirist
37–41	CALIGULA
38–100	*Quintilian*, Latin educator
39–65	*Lucan*, author of *Civil War* (*Pharsalia*)
40–104	*Martial*, Latin epigrammatist
40–120	*Dio Chrysostom*, Greek orator and essayist
41–54	CLAUDIUS
45–96	*Statius*, Latin poet
50–130	*Juvenal*, Roman satirist
50–120	*Plutarch*, Greek biographer and essayist
50–120	*Epictetus*, Stoic philosopher (Greek)
54–68	NERO
55–120	*Tacitus*, Roman historian
61–112	*Pliny the Younger*, letter writer
64	Burning of Rome, persecution of Christians
?–65	*Petronius*, Roman satirist
68–69	GALBA, OTHO, VITELLIUS
69–79	VESPASIAN

69–140	*Suetonius*, Roman biographer
70	Destruction of Jerusalem by Titus
79	Destruction of Pompeii and Herculaneum by Vesuvius
79–81	TITUS
81–96	DOMITIAN
96–98	NERVA
98–117	TRAJAN
100–175	*Appian*, Greek historian of Rome
101–106	Dacian Wars
114–117	Parthian War
117–189	*Aelius Aristides*, Greek panegyrist of Rome
117–138	HADRIAN
120–185	*Lucian*, Greek satirist
123–165	*Aulus Gellius*, Latin antiquarian
123–175	*Apuleius*, Latin novelist
138–161	ANTONINUS PIUS
150–212	*Clement of Alexandria*, Greek Christian apologist
155–235	*Dio Cassius*, Greek historian of Rome
160–225	*Tertullian*, Latin Christian apologist
161–180	MARCUS AURELIUS
161–169	LUCIUS VERUS
161–175	War with Marcomanni, Quadi, Iazyges
180–192	COMMODUS
193	PERTINAX, DIDIUS JULIANUS
193–211	SEPTIMIUS SEVERUS
200–250	*Arnobius*, Christian apologist
211–217	CARACALLA
211–212	GETA
217–218	MACRINUS
218–222	ELAGABALUS
222–235	SEVERUS ALEXANDER
230–233	Persian War
235–285	"Thirty Tyrants"
235–238	MAXIMINUS
238–244	GORDIAN I, II, III

244–249	PHILIP THE ARAB
249–251	DECIUS; persecution of Christians
250–317	*Lactantius, Latin Christian apologist*
253–260	VALERIAN
253–268	GALLIENUS
260	Gallic "empire" established
260–340	*Eusebius, Greek church historian*
268–270	CLAUDIUS GOTHICUS
270–275	AURELIAN. Dacia abandoned; walls built around Rome
275–284	TACITUS, FLORIANUS, PROBUS, CARUS, CARINUS, NUMERIANUS
285–305	DIOCLETIAN
286–305	MAXIMIAN
301	Edict on prices
305	Diocletian and Maximian abdicate; wars of succession
307–324	CONSTANTINE and LICINIUS
310–395	*Ausonius, Latin (Gallic) poet*
313	Edict of Milan
324–337	CONSTANTINE sole emperor
325	Council of Nicaea
330–400	*Ammianus Marcellinus, Latin historian*
330	Constantinople founded
337–360	CONSTANTIUS
337–397	*Ambrose, Latin Church Father*
340–402	*Symmachus, Latin orator*
340–420	*Jerome, Latin Church Father*
344–407	*John Chrysostom, Greek homilist*
348–405	*Prudentius, Christian Latin poet*
?–408	*Claudian, Latin epic poet*
354–430	*Augustine, Latin Church Father*
360–363	JULIAN THE APOSTATE
364–375	VALENTINIAN I
364–378	VALENS
378	Battle of Adrianople
378–395	THEODOSIUS I

395	Empire divided
395–423	HONORIUS (West)
395–408	ARCADIUS (East)
402	Stilicho defeats Alaric and Visigoths
408–450	THEODOSIUS II (E)
410	Alaric sacks Rome
412–418	Visigoths settle in Gaul and Spain
425–455	VALENTINIAN III (W)
429	Vandals invade Africa
431–482	*Sidonius Apollinaris*, Latin poet and letter writer
438	Theodosian Code
450–457	MARCIAN (E)
453	Death of Attila
455	Vandals sack Rome. PETRONIUS MAXIMUS (W)
455–456	AVITUS (W)
456–472	Ricimer master of soldiers in west
457–474	LEO I (E)
457–461	MAJORIAN (W)
461–465	SEVERUS (W)
467–474	ANTHEMIUS, OLYBRIUS, GLYCERIUS (W)
474–491	ZENO (E)
474–476	JULIUS NEPOS, ROMULUS AUGUSTULUS (W), last to be recognized as colleague of eastern emperor
476–493	Odovacar king in Italy
480–524	*Boethius*, Roman philosopher
480–575	*Cassiodorus*, Latin antiquary
491–518	ANASTASIUS (E)
493–526	Theodoric the Great
500–565	*Procopius*, Greek historian
518–527	JUSTIN (E)
527–565	JUSTINIAN (E)
536–582	*Agathias*, Greek poet and historian
528	*Corpus Iuris Civilis*

529	Schools of Athens closed
532	St. Sophia first completed; Nika riots
533	Africa reconquered by Belisarius
535-555	Italy and Spain reconquered
565	Death of Justinian

Sources

Unless otherwise noted the dates of the authors here listed are A.D. and their language Latin

AELIUS ARISTIDES (117–189), Greek orator. Fifty-five of his ceremonial speeches are extant; the *Roman Oration* was delivered at Rome in 156.

AGATHIAS (536–582), Byzantine lawyer, best known as anthologist of epigrams. His laudatory *Reign of Justinian* (Greek prose) covers the years 552–558.

AMBROSE (337–397), bishop of Milan.

AMMIANUS MARCELLINUS (330–ca. 400), Antiochene Greek soldier, pagan. His sound history (in Latin) covered the years 96–378, in 31 bks.; bks. 14–31, covering 353–378, are extant.

APPIAN (100–175), loyal Roman civil servant, of Egyptian origin. Appian wrote 24 bks. of Roman history in ethnographic divisions (Samnite Wars, African Wars, Civil Wars, etc.) in Greek; 10 bks. and fragments are extant.

AUGUSTINE (354–430), bishop of Hippo (Africa).

AUGUSTUS (63 B.C.–A.D. 14), first emperor of Rome. His *Acts*, extant on a temple at Angora (hence called *Monumentum Ancyranum*) and elsewhere, were written to be inscribed on his tomb.

AULUS GELLIUS (123–165), Roman grammarian and antiquary. His *Attic Nights* in 20 bks. is a literary miscellany.

AURELIUS VICTOR (late 4th century), Roman official. His *Caesares* (from Augustus to Constantine) show an interest in moralizing and in prodigies; pagan.

BEDE (673-735), ecclesiastical historian of England.

CAESAR (102-44 B.C.), Roman dictator. Wrote *Commentaries* on his own *Gallic War* (7 bks. with supplement) and *Civil War* (3 bks.).

CARACALLA (188-217), Roman emperor.

CASSIODORUS (487-583), Roman noble. Wrote (among other things) *Historia Gothica* in 12 bks., known from excerpts in Jordanes, and 12 bks. of *Variae*, specimens of official correspondence and formulae.

CICERO (106-43 B.C.), celebrated orator and senatorial leader.

CLAUDIAN (?-408), Roman poet of Egyptian origin. His long narrative poems celebrate Honorius and Stilicho and denigrate their enemies.

CLAUDIUS (10 B.C.-A.D. 54), Roman emperor.

CONSTANTINE PORPHYROGENITUS (905-959), Byzantine emperor and antiquarian. Wrote on provinces, administration, and ceremonials of the eastern empire.

CORPUS IURIS CIVILIS, definitive legal work compiled under Justinian.

DIO CASSIUS (155-235), Roman senator. Wrote Roman history (in Greek) from beginnings to A.D. 229 in 80 bks., of which 36-54 are preserved complete and much of the remainder in excerpts; based on good sources, excellent on own period.

EUSEBIUS (ca. 260-340), Greek church historian, from Palestine. Wrote, among other things, *Ecclesiastical History*, *Evangelical Preparation*, *Life of Constantine*, all naturally with strong anti-pagan bias.

EUTROPIUS (4th century), served under Julian (363). Wrote *Epitome* of Roman history in 10 short bks., based on standard sources, and at the end on personal experience.

GREGORY (538–594), bishop of Tours. His *History of the Franks* is a prime source for his own period.

HERODIAN (early 3d century), Roman official. Wrote (in Greek) 8 bks. of superficial but agreeable history on the period 180–238.

HISTORIA AUGUSTA (probably 4th century), a collection of the lives of emperors (including Caesars and usurpers) from Hadrian to Numerian (117–284), with some omissions. These are attributed to six named authors, but modern scholars doubt the attributions.

HORACE (65–8 B.C.), virtually poet laureate under Augustus.

JEROME (340–420), Latin Church Father.

JORDANES (6th century), pupil of Cassiodorus; his excerpts of Cassiodorus' Gothic history, perhaps with patriotic additions of his own, are extant.

JOSEPHUS (37–ca. 100), pro-Roman Jewish historian. Wrote (in Greek) *Jewish Antiquities* (mainly biblical history) in 20 bks.; *Jewish War* (against Rome) in 8 bks.; *Against Apion* (Jewish apologetics); and *Life* (autobiography).

JULIAN (332–363), emperor. Wrote, in Greek and with strong pagan bias, satires, encomia, letters, etc.

LACTANTIUS (ca. 250–317), Christian apologist. His *On the Deaths of the Persecutors* is useful historically.

LIVY (59 B.C.–A.D. 17), Roman historian of the Augustan circle. Wrote 142 bks. from the beginning of the city to his own day, of which 1–10, 21–45, and epitomes of the remainder are extant. Livy's purpose is patriotic rather than scientific.

LYDUS, JOHN (6th century), Byzantine antiquarian and panegyrist of Justinian.

MACROBIUS (early 5th century), Roman official and antiquarian. Wrote, among other things, a literary miscellany called *Saturnalia*.

MENANDER "PROTECTOR" (6th century), Byzantine lawyer. Wrote a continuation of the history of Agathias, covering the period 558–582.

OROSIUS (early 5th century), Spanish ecclesiastic. Wrote *Seven Books to Confute the Pagans* at Augustine's suggestion to prove from Roman history that Christians were not responsible for the fall of Rome.

PANEGYRICI LATINI (mostly 4th century), a series of 12 laudatory addresses, by various hands, to reigning emperors.

PAUL THE DEACON (720–800), Lombard nobleman. Wrote *History of the Lombard People*.

PAUL THE SILENTIARY (6th century), Byzantine official. Wrote Greek poems celebrating Justinian's buildings.

PLINY (61–112), Roman lawyer and administrator, nephew of Pliny the Elder. Wrote ten bks. of letters, the last as governor of Bithynia addressed chiefly to Trajan.

PLUTARCH (ca. 50–120), Greek biographer and essayist. His biographical interest is chiefly ethical, but he uses sound sources.

POLYBIUS (ca. 201–218 B.C.), displaced Greek statesman and historian of Rome. Of his 40 bks., 1–5 are extant complete and the remainder in excerpts. Polybius is concerned with political theory; his bias is aristocratic.

PROCOPIUS (6th century), aide to Justinian's general Belisarius. His *History* in 8 bks. (in Greek) is divided, after the model of Appian, into 2 bks. on the Persian, 2 on the

Vandal, and 3 on the Ostrogothic wars, with a final book on the period 551–554; it is based on critical firsthand knowledge. His *Secret History*, not published till after his death, is a vitriolic attack on Justinian and Theodora. His adulatory *On the Buildings* (of Justinian) is valuable for the history of art and Byzantine administration.

PRUDENTIUS (4th century), Spanish Christian poet.

QUINTILIAN (ca. 38–100), Roman professor of rhetoric; his *Education of an Orator* is in 12 bks.

RUTILIUS NAMATIANUS (early 5th century), probably of Toulouse; strongly anti-Christian poet.

SALLUST (86–34 B.C.), lieutenant of Caesar and historian. His *History* in 5 bks. is lost except for fragments; his extant monographs on the *Catilinarian War* and the *Jugurthine War* show an anti-aristocratic bias.

SALVIAN (5th century), priest at Marseilles. His 8 bks. *On the Governance of God* blame the fall of Rome on current immorality.

SIDONIUS APOLLINARIS (431–482), Gallo-Roman noble, son-in-law of emperor Avitus, eventually bishop of Auvergne. His poems and letters provide some historical data.

SOCRATES (5th century), Byzantine (Greek) church historian. His 7 bks. cover the period 307–439.

SOZOMEN (5th century), Byzantine (Greek) church historian. His 9 bks. cover the period 323–423.

SUETONIUS (ca. 69–140), secretary to Hadrian, biographer. His extant *Caesars* cover the emperors through Domitian; his other biographical works are fragmentary. Suetonius had access to official sources but his main interest is in gossip.

SYMMACHUS (ca. 340–402), Roman noble and orator. Defended the traditional order against Christian innovations.

SYNESIUS (ca. 370–412), litterateur and bishop in Cyrene.

TACITUS (ca. 55–120), Roman consular and historian. The *Annals* and *Histories* together covered the period from 14 to 96 in 30 bks.; a little more than 14 are extant. Their outlook is aristocratic and conservative. In addition Tacitus wrote *Agricola*, a biography of his father-in-law; *Germania*, on the geography and manners of the Germans; and a *Dialogue on Oratory*.

THEODOSIAN CODE (438), first comprehensive codification of Roman law, supplanted by Justinian's *Corpus Iuris Civilis*.

VELLEIUS PATERCULUS (ca. 19 B.C.–A.D. 32), Roman officer under Tiberius. His 2-bk. summary of history shows an interest in literature and is fulsome in praise of Tiberius.

VERGIL (70–19 B.C.), Roman poet, protected by Augustus.

ZONARAS (12th century), Byzantine chronicler. His 18 bks. cover the period from the creation to 1118.

ZOSIMUS (5th century), Byzantine official. The 6 bks. of his history cover the period from Augustus to 410 and show a strong pagan bias.

Index

Data on authors will be found under Sources (287ff.), and on emperors under Chronology (280ff.). Modern equivalents of place names or tribal areas are given in parentheses.

Issus, victory of Septimius Severus, 149

Italian relations with Rome, 23, 55

Jerome, St., 232; cited, 224f.

Jerusalem, 106, 119ff., 133, 225, 243

Jewish War, 119ff.

Jews, 106, 108, 133

John, successor of Honorius, 238

Jordanes, cited, 159, 209, 239ff.

Josephus, cited, 121

Jovian, emperor, 202

Juba, African king, 79

Judaea, 65, 116, 133

Jugurthine War, 51ff.

Julia, daughter of Julius Caesar, 68, 72

Julia, daughter of Augustus, 102

Julia Domna, wife of Septimius Severus, 149f., 154

Julian, emperor, 192ff., 198ff., 211; cited, 194, 200

Julianus Didius, emperor, 140ff., 146

Juno, advent in Rome, 20

Justin, emperor, 254ff.

Justina, mother of Valentinian III, 215

Justinian, emperor, 256ff., 271f.

Justinian Code, 258

Kawad, Persian king, 254

Labarum, Constantine's cross, 184f.

Lactantius, cited, 167, 180, 185

laesa majestas, 103

Lambaessis (Lambese), 129

Larentia, foster mother of Romulus and Remus, 2

Lars Porsinna, Etruscan hero, 14ff.

Latin League, 23, 55

Lavinium (Pratica di Mare), 1, 5

law, see codification

Lentulus, Catilinarian conspirator, 67

Leo, emperor, 243, 249f.

Leo, Pope, 241

Leontius, usurper under Zeno, 250

Lepidus, opponent of Sulla, 61

Lepidus, triumvir, 82

Libanius, Greek orator, 201

Libya, 28, 238

Licinian laws, 367 B.C., 50f.

Licinius, emperor, 183f., 187f.

literature, 63, 96f., 158, 273f.

Livia, wife of Augustus, 102

Livius Drusus, instigated Italian liberation, 55

Livy, cited, 2, 6ff., 13, 15, 17f., 21, 23f., 31ff., 35, 37, 40f.

London, 116

Luca (Lucca), 71

Lucania, 25

Lucretia, victim of Tarquins, 13f.

Lucullus, general in Mithradatic war, 58, 62f., 65

Lugdunum (Lyons), 149

Lupercalia, festival, 3, 81